Ways of Following

Immediations
Series Editor: SenseLab

> "Philosophy begins in wonder. And, at the end, when philosophic thought has done its best, the wonder remains"
> – A.N. Whitehead

The aim of the Immediations book series is to prolong the wonder sustaining philosophic thought into transdisciplinary encounters. Its premise is that concepts are for the enacting: they must be experienced. Thought is lived, else it expires. It is most intensely lived at the crossroads of practices, and in the in-between of individuals and their singular endeavors: enlivened in the weave of a relational fabric. Co-composition.

> "The smile spreads over the face, as the face fits itself onto the smile"
> – A. N. Whitehead

Which practices enter into co-composition will be left an open question, to be answered by the Series authors. Art practice, aesthetic theory, political theory, movement practice, media theory, maker culture, science studies, architecture, philosophy ... the range is free. We invite you to roam it.

Ways of Following
Art, Materiality, Collaboration

Katve-Kaisa Kontturi

◯
OPEN HUMANITIES PRESS
London 2018

First edition published by Open Humanities Press 2018
Copyright © Katve-Kaisa Kontturi 2018

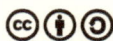

This is an open access book, licensed under Creative Commons By Attribution Share Alike license. Under this license, authors allow anyone to download, reuse, reprint, modify, distribute, and/or copy their work so long as the authors and source are cited and resulting derivative works are licensed under the same or similar license. No permission is required from the authors or the publisher. Statutory fair use and other rights are in no way affected by the above. Read more about the license at creativecommons.org/licenses/by-sa/4.0

Cover Art, figures, text, and other media included with this book may be under different copyright restrictions.

Cover Illustration © 2018 Leslie Plumb
Cover Design by Leslie Plumb

Typeset in Open Sans, an open font.

Print ISBN 978-1-78542-059-7
PDF ISBN 978-1-78542-060-3

Freely available online at:
http://openhumanitiespress.org/books/titles/ways-of-following/

OPEN HUMANITIES PRESS

Open Humanities Press is an international, scholar-led open access publishing collective whose mission is to make leading works of contemporary critical thought freely available worldwide. More at http://openhumanitiespress.org

Contents

Introduction: ... With ...	7

Encounters

1.	Breathing and Dancing	26
2.	Work of Painting	47

Co-workings

3.	Impersonal Connections	70
4.	Autonomy of Process	82
5.	Manual Labour	97
6.	Zigzagging Art and Life	117

Sensations

Prelude: An Oral Triptych		130
7.	The Grimacing Mouth	136
8.	The Preaching Mouth	154
9.	The Screaming Mouth	176
A Follow-Up: Three Propositions		191
Notes		203
Acknowledgements		234
References		238
Index		259

Introduction: ... With ...

To follow this book's ethos and focus, let us begin ... with art. There are two women at an unidentified urban train station. They wait, and discuss a work of art in the making. They are both involved; a collaboration is in process. One is in front of the camera, the other out of its scope. The voice outside the frame suggests that this is not an ordinary documentary: 'There is no storyboard ... it is not planned' – instead, the project is open to elements of surprise. The woman on camera agrees: yes, it is 'a lot more organic' – implying that this video is true to the event as it unfolds.

This excerpt is from the video *Following Amie: The Artist at Work* (2015) that documents the daily life of Amie Anderson, an art-worker who, among her other jobs, co-directs the artist-run initiative 'Food Court' in Melbourne's Docklands. The video follows Amie through her diverse engagements, starting in a wintery dawn in her bedroom, where she packs her bags for the day. The collaborator shooting the video and following Amie is artist-researcher Maria Miranda [Figure 0.1].

As attested by the conversation at the train station, the video follows Amie's day as it evolves. Capturing the sense of unrolling – the non-scripted unfolding of Amie's day – requires reciprocity from the participants. Maria is not a director-follower in control of the situation, nor is Amie accounting for her day as she knows it. She is on the cusp of experience, facing what is to come. Here, following is not about tracing an already-happened

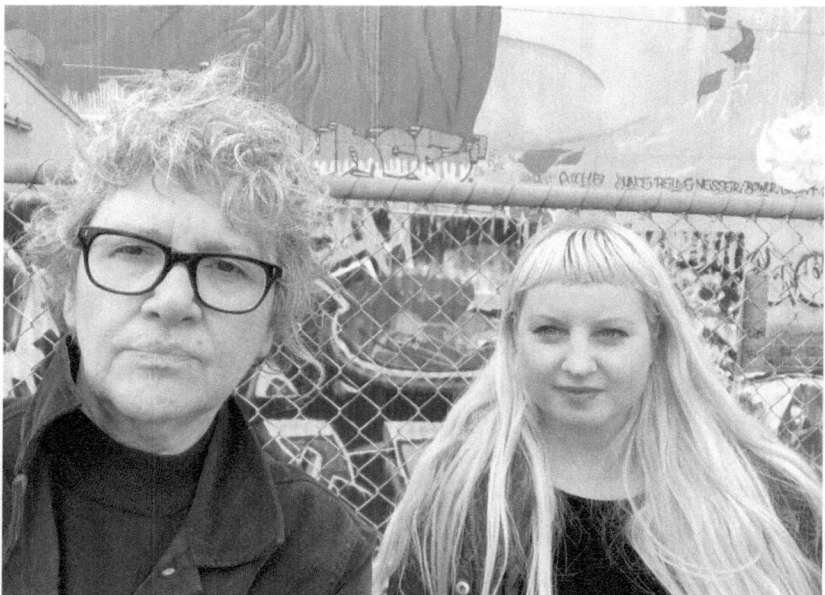

Figure 0.1. Maria Miranda (left) and Amie Anderson (right) in *Following Amie: The Artist at Work* (2015) by Maria Miranda and Amie Anderson – a video filmed with a smartphone on a selfie stick.

story or experience. It is about entering a wave of life unfurling; about being taken up in its motion, moving *with* it – '"getting into something" instead of being the origin of the effort', as philosopher Gilles Deleuze (1995, 121) puts it.[1]

In the video, this sense of following is created through images and sounds recorded by the mobile phone on a selfie stick. 'Being taken up' in the wave of Amie's day is actualised in videographic movement that is 'parallel to' rather than 'a step behind': the two women often walk side by side. This parallel movement is enabled by the selfie stick; the camera is a step ahead of the women walking – it is, then, less a point of leverage between the follower and the followee than an 'intercessor' in attunement.[2] An intercessor, according to Deleuze (1995, 125), is more than a mediator: it has creative powers as it enters into what is happening and opens up be(com)ings to a new mutual movement – making the event more than it was.

In the video, the selfie stick's mobile point of view loosens the positionalities of the follower and the followee, engaging them in a movement where their roles are not fixed, and the story is still in the making. This is evident, for example, in Miranda adapting her actions according to the conditions of the day, even moving outside her director's role to become Amie's driver when public transport fails them. This way of following is not about shadowing a few steps behind, but about opening oneself up to a movement that exceeds the position one holds, the experiences one has had, or the knowledge one possesses. In the video, we see Amie listening attentively to her art students, being inspired by them; we hear her laughing with them, and note the encouraging hand gestures that also enter into her own art-making. We also sense the time it takes her to travel to earn extra money from cleaning. In short, we experience art in the making as it unfolds in its multiple relations.

This book is about following art in movement, about being attentive to art in the making. It approaches a set of contemporary paintings, photographs, and installations as lively and shifting. The book shows that although paintings and photographs are often approached in their still finality, they are nevertheless imbued with perpetual movement: brushstrokes have their rhythm, paint cracks quietly, photographic stills wave gently in the air, and a model's body tries to stay still by moving minutely. It is crucial to acknowledge art's perpetual movement because it is in this movement and in the connections it fosters that, as this book claims, the singularity of any work of art persists: its potential to make a difference, to challenge habitual ways of being, thinking, and feeling.

Grasping this often-subtle movement necessitates multiple ways of following. First, the book steps into the processes by which art emerges in studios and exhibitions. It follows artists working and audiences encountering art. Looking, listening, discussing, modelling, and dancing are some of the modalities of following with which the book engages. The motivation for approaching art in this way is to value the intricate processes of making and sensing – their capacity to open even the stiffest of materials and figures beyond their seeming stillness. To follow, then, is to embrace the 'work' of art, its material, affective, and relational doings that push it beyond the representational function, offering something new instead of what is already known. Following Barbara Bolt's practice-based, materialist-phenomenological postulation in *Art Beyond Representation: The Performative Power of the Image* (2004a; see also 2004b; 2014), the emphasis here is on the intensities of the 'work' of art, on what art can do rather than on what art means or refers to. Erin Manning's process philosophical practice is equally insightful in attending not to the artwork as such but to 'how the work works', how it opens, troubles, complicates, nuances, and emboldens (new) fields of experience (2013, 102; 2016, 84–85).

Second, the foregrounding of art's processual emergence through following is inseparable from the practice of writing. As noted above, this book argues that art's ability to suggest new ways of living and being is embodied in its processual movement. This is the domain of intensities and flows that trickle up in the cracks of signification and representation. Writing is the practice through which these intensities can be harnessed and passed on. In a way, writing, too, is an intercessor in attuning to the unfolding event that is art. At its best, it can enhance the intensity of the event and relay its potential to the reader. At its worst, it can block the intensity of unfolding and impede the work from moving onwards. This book, then, is an experiment in writing as interceding *with* art, where language is used to enter into the swell of art in the making.

Writing with ...

... processes and flows

The aim of following is to overcome the kind of analysis that detaches art from its processes of production. This is an incentive central to creative practice research, which branches out in various directions and with different philosophical and epistemological emphases – from artistic to practice-led research and research-creation (see, for example, Barrett and Bolt 2007, 2013; Arlander 2016). How to write about art, *with* art, in a way that simultaneously appreciates and demystifies the creative process is one of the key concerns of creative practice research. In the book *Material Thinking: The Theory and Practice of Artistic Research* (2004), Paul Carter suggests that this way of writing values the material practice of art as a modality of thinking, and thus embraces the critical potential of materiality and matter. In describing the impetus of research-creation, Erin Manning (2016, 27) proposes that research-creation creates extra-linguistic forms of knowledge. In so doing, research-creation turns toward how knowledge is crafted in the processes of art in the making. Similarly, the kind of art writing that this book pursues aims at providing access to the intensive processuality that is often ignored in academic criticism and media reviews of art that, respectively, tend to 'over-interpret' and 'under-interpret' the meaning of art (Carter 2004, xi) and separate it from the material event in which it emerges. Consequently, *Ways of Following* not only addresses issues relevant to creative practice research, but also claims writing itself as an act of (collaborative) research-creation.

In this book, art processes are followed by way of writing, by trying words and inventing terms with the aim of describing what seems otherwise ungraspable: the singular subtleties of an intensive process.[3] Writing as following, however, is not a retrospective or separate add-on to the art events attended

(Manning 2009, 11; Manning and Massumi 2014, ix). Terms tried and/or invented germinate from the art events experienced; they have been written with, co-created. As both Marsha Meskimmon and Tim Ingold emphasise, 'writing-with' concerns ethics. In her book *Women Making Art,* Meskimmon (2003, 4–6) notes that writing with is an ethical practice that appreciates and attends to the intricacies of the 'work' of art, to the new knowledge it potentially creates, knowledge that is easily curtailed if art is approached with predetermined theories, methods and definitions (see also Meskimmon and Sawdon 2016; Barrett and Bolt 2014). Tim Ingold (2013, 1–7) stresses that the creativity of a productive process gets swallowed up if only completed objects are addressed, and therefore encourages us to be open to processes we can learn *with*, and be moved by – but only if we follow, go along.[4]

What is implied in the practice of writing with is a newly charged position of the follower. In *A Thousand Plateaus: Capitalism and Schizophrenia*, philosophers Gilles Deleuze and Félix Guattari (1987, 372–74, 405–15) challenge the fixed viewpoint of an observer through the notion of following. They argue that a fixed viewpoint reproduces the observed phenomenon from its own, limited perspective. Watching the flow from the bank prevents moving with the flow. Following offers a different position, one that grasps the singularities of matter and is attentive to its connections and movement: following takes place when one 'engages in continuous variation of variables, instead of extracting constants of them' (Deleuze and Guattari 1987, 374). Relatedly, following always takes the follower somewhere else; instead of confirming the already known, finding constants, following affirms what is still unfolding. Its nature is itinerant, replete with curiosity. Water flow, for example, might appear dead calm, allowing the follower to be relatively in control of their body, to dwell in, to sense the caressing milkiness of water-skin.[5] But there might be strong invisible currents too, rips pulling one away from the shore, violently, even fatally. It is difficult to know what a flow can do, where it can take you, without entering into it. To write the felt materiality without mastering its flow, whether of water, the world, or art for that matter, following is your chance. Following aims at being confluent with the present always on the verge of opening into the future. To follow is to become with. The ethos for following: Do not freeze-frame art; instead, follow its flows, and see where it can take you.

Moving with ...

... vital matters

Deleuze and Guattari (1987, 405–13) introduce artisans as exemplary followers – ambulant scientists, as they call them. Metallurgists and woodworkers, joiners, follow their materials. That is their *way* of doing. Whether the grain of wood or liquid metal substance, rather than forging the material with bodily force and technical power, they follow it, and by following they work with it. Again, collaboration is at issue. Following is not only a way of approaching art, with respect to its movement and doings, it is also a relation that artists have with their materials. Artists do not make art *of* materials, but *with* them (see especially Chapters 2–6) – with layers of acrylic paint, lace and underwear, with canvas, magazines, and with their bodies. Instead of moulding matter they co-work with these vital materialities.

By claiming that the quality and density of wood grain actively contributes to joinery, Deleuze and Guattari link following to a material vitalism, where matter is 'neither a thing nor an organism' (1987, 411). This materiality, natural and artificial, often simultaneously, is of the moving, doing kind – it is expressive (see also Coole and Frost 2010a, 8–9; Grosz 2010, 150–51). Its activity undermines the logic of form and matter, wherein form gives integrity and expression to 'mute' matter.[6] To emphasise the moving, flowing character of matter, Deleuze and Guattari introduce the term 'molecularity'. For them, molecularity is a force that traverses, challenges molar structures such as the binary gender system or habitual patterns of writing.[7] In this book, following molecular flows of air and haze inhaled into one's body opens up a light installation beyond its symbolic interpretation (Chapter 1), and the chemical-physical reactions of layers of paper, paint and lacquer bring a new figuration into being (Chapter 2). Deleuze and Guattari maintain that these matter-flows can *only* be followed (1987, 409). Otherwise, it is impossible to understand or participate in what they do – how they challenge and contest conventional ideas and solidified structures. Following, then, is not only an approach applicable to moving matters, it is an approach that welcomes change.

One strand of recent scholarship that works with vital matters, often in conjunction with Deleuze and Guattari's philosophy, is new materialism.[8] This is explicit, for example, in Jane Bennett's *Vibrant Matter: A Political Ecology of Things* (2010b), which concerns vital materialities and materialist philosophy with short experimental excursions into matters such as the obesity of contemporary Americans and the agency of potato chips. According to Bennett (2010b, 38–41), eating potato chips is not just the volitional choice of an 'I', but is about entering, or being in relation with multiple materialities – some of which have solidified into structures of consumerism, others, such as the body's metabolism or sensations of that lovely crunchy crispiness, being more volatile processes. This is to say that new materialisms approach the world by focusing on becomings of both organic and inorganic materialities not as such, but *in relations*. Crucial here is the understanding that materialities constantly reactivate their potentials for being and thus extend from the already-known towards the future (Tiainen, Kontturi and Hongisto 2015c, 5). This gives new materialism its (contested) emphasis on the new.[9] This 'new' is not 'a novelty ... concerned with the capitalist sense of the newest new, but novelty as the creation of mixtures that produce new openings, new vistas, new complexions for experience in the making' (Manning 2016, 58).

To embrace newness, or the vitality of the world, means that readymade concepts or methodologies are not directly applicable, rather, they should be re-singularised in each new relation: we never know how materialities move and affect and therefore should not approach them as being one and the same. As the emphasis is on (co-)emergences, broad modalities of attention to what is occurring are proposed instead of clearly defined methodologies. Following is one such attention or relation 'orientator'.[10] It encourages sensitivity to and appreciation of the movement of the followee and, importantly, incites the motility that underpins *moving with*.

Moving, as Erin Manning (2009; 2013) writes in the context of dance and philosophy, is a relational activity per se. In dance, we might follow our dance partner's movements, but that does not mean that the one doing the leading controls the dance completely (Manning 2007, 88; 2009, 30). This is because relations are not reducible to two or more solid entities with predetermined identities. When following a dance partner, or simply when walking with someone, as Maria Miranda and Amie Anderson do in *Following Amie*, one relates to a moving body, one relates to what is to come, to incipient movement before it is actualised (Manning 2009, 7, 17–18). The artwork followed might already be out of the studio, out of the hands of its maker(s), but that does not solidify its movement altogether – in every encounter, it becomes something more. To emphasise that materiality is not singular, is never just there, but becomes-with, is perpetually moving, *Ways of Following* frequently points out how materialities and materials are relational. When the whirling, colour-changing beams of a light installation hit the body, disintegrate it, as they do in the installation encountered in Chapter 1, this co-becoming is not only material but material-relational. Throughout the book, it is not just materials that give a certain work of art its singularity, but how the work of art *works* materially-relationally: how it reaches beyond its object quality, how it affects.

To attend to the flows of the material-relational, to move with them, to be affected by them, is not a self-evidently forward-going process, nor is that the character of the flows themselves. As Brian Massumi (2017, 79) notes, it is a common misconception that event or process orientated philosophy focuses only on smoothly continuing, 'pure' flows. Movements can and will be cut, disrupted, or as often happens in the pages of this book, they can get stuck: the movement and volume of brushstrokes can solidify into all too recognisable figures (Chapter 2, Chapter 5), the researcher can get stuck in her thinking (Chapter 4), and the expression of anxiety can get stuck in the throat (Chapter 9). But this is not the end. Often the solution to finding movement again is to follow more attentively, patiently. There is a pulsating feel to stuckness, it is stuck stuck stuck stuck … irritatingly so. But the movement never disappears altogether, and eventually stuckness will take the process somewhere else – it is part of the process of making.

Working with …

… art in the making

When this book attends to the 'work' of art, follows how the work works, senses the pulsations of being stuck, it explores *ways* of approaching art in the making. Compared to 'method' as a concept and practice, 'way' has a very different ring. While the words have similar etymologies – their Greek (via Latin) and Germanic origins referring to a journey, to movement – in the contemporary vocabulary of the humanities, and in fact at the latest from the 1600s onwards, 'method' has been mobilised as an approach that predetermines, that limits our attention and the scope of the work, that is, as a regulated, systematic set of practices. 'Way' has more dynamic connotations: 'To speak of a "way" is to dwell on the process itself, on the manner of its becoming' (Manning 2016, 47). To multiply 'way' into ways, as

John Berger (1972) did in his ground-breaking *Ways of Seeing*, is to emphasise the ever-varying options of engaging with the world, and with art in process.

In fields as varied as process philosophy, anthropology, creative arts research, art history and visual culture, this processual approach to making has begun to receive more and more critical attention. In introducing Erin Manning's *Always More Than One: Individuation's Dance*, Brian Massumi (in Manning 2013, xi) reminds that 'making is always bigger than the made'. The process of making involves more than is visible or perceivable in the 'made' object. Making contains all those virtual possibilities that did not quite actualise, but still contributed to the process of becoming – as we will learn when studying a painting with a peculiar double navel (Chapter 2). In short, there are no simple, straightforward processes that *simply* produce clearly defined end results. The material world of moving, ever-elaborating relations, connections and disjunctions is more complex than that. Processes are not orderly but messy; their threads are not (yet) neatly tied off. However, in their non-descriptive neutrality, the verb 'produce' and the result of the process of production, the 'product', seem to imply just that: a solid, predetermined process. Because of this, *Ways of Following* works hard to use more specified terms that, instead of taming, erasing the singularities of process, aim at embracing them. In *Making: Anthropology, Art, and Architecture*, Tim Ingold (2013, 20) calls this sort of making 'making as process' and distinguishes it from 'making as project', which simply follows the production plan to make a desired product. Making as process is open-ended; it is not about making some *thing*, but about letting the process of making do its own work.

Elsewhere, contemporary art scholars have motivated their studies of processes of making by referring to the legacy of Karl Marx in 'older' materialist approaches. This is what Glenn Adamson and Julia Bryan-Wilson (2016, 16–19), authors of

Art in the Making: Artists and their Materials from the Studio to Crowdsourcing, suggest when they explain their focus on the specificity of making, often hidden in the pages of art (historical) writing. They remind us that it was Karl Marx who turned attention to how capitalist products came into being and how this consumed the body and time of the worker. This Marxist materialist legacy is also present in *Ways of Following*, in the sense that I pay careful attention to the processes of making, how they are executed. This is not only to appreciate the art-workers' long hours, months or even years spent creating art – and bodies involved in the making – but also to discuss experiments, successful, abandoned, or failed. In sum, it is to value the work of art-workers by focusing on the singularities of their doings, executed 'just this way' (Manning 2016, 19).[11] While the Marxist materialist approach looks at the systematic structures controlling the process and the body,[12] the vitalist, material-relational mode of this book follows the inconsistencies and peculiarities of process that make it singular and creative, that free the process from its structural and habitual constraints, and so generate something new.

Collaborations with ...

... the artists and the more-than

As vital materialities gain their energetic, transformative movement – and get stuck – always in relation, following them necessarily entails following co-becomings, co-workings. At times, this means recognising the presence and contribution of other people, artist-colleagues, friends and family members, which calls for re-articulation of 'artistic' influences (Chapter 3, Chapter 6). Mostly, however, the emphasis is on artistic actions that are more-than-human, meaning that the materialities involved have their own active role in the process; they are not mastered by the artist alone. In *Ways of Following*, the expressive and agential potentialities of matter are taken seriously, and because of this emphasis, the concept of collaboration is extended to include co-workings with vital materialities of art, of paint, light, canvas, and bodily movement, for example.

Access to these more-than-human collaborations was made possible by following the practice of three artists over several years; through working with them. To appreciate their input in this book, I speak of 'collaborations'. *Ways of Following* could not have been written without them, without the collaborations that emerged. This is not to claim authorship in these artists' work, but to acknowledge my theoretical and methodological indebtedness to them.

From 2003 to 2005, I regularly visited painter Susana Nevado's studio to follow her works of art emerging, and to photograph and discuss the works in process.[13] Altogether, I was involved in seven exhibition processes, both private and group, mostly as a discussant, but Nevado also invited me to model as María Madre de Misericordia for her installation *Honest Fortune Teller* (2005), which reworked Catholic imageries of Saints. These processes, that made use of recycled materials, opened painting into installation art and critically addressed such issues as motherhood, bodily materiality, multiculturalism, family albums, and Catholic practices of religion. My collaborations with sculptor Helena Hietanen are markedly fewer in number. Yet the two projects, both connected to her personal experiences of breast cancer and religiosity, have an important role in this book: the light installation *Heaven Machine* (2005–2006) opens my study into the moving materialities of art, and the second project, a series of photographic self-portraits titled *Sketches* (1999–), concludes it. My engagement in these projects extends from encountering an artwork in a museum space to discussions, emails, and articles where *Sketches*, which was never actually exhibited, continued to live on in a written, conversational mode.[14] With photographer and visual art therapist Marjukka

Irni, I engaged in a project that continued over several years: *Sappho Wants to Save You* (2006–2010) started as a performative community art project and developed into an installation that includes a video and a series of photographic portraits, which I (and others) posed for. This work is infused with theories of gender, and creatively overcomes the art–theory divide as it material-relationally suggests new understandings of gender – with my body enmeshed in the process.[15] My involvement in this collaboration also included conversations and curatorial work through which one of the versions of the installation was actualised.

In this book, I am attracted to the double 'l' in the middle of the term 'co*ll*aboration', that binds it into an expression where the whole becomes more than its parts: to the stretched middle of co*ll*aboration that signals the 'more-than'. This focus troubles conventional understandings of an authoritative, mastering agency, and especially the rigid relations of the knower and the known, the subject and the object of research. William James's (1912) radical empiricism offers a material-relational approach and philosophy that embraces the middle and orientates attention towards it. Radical empiricism 'begins in the midst, in the mess of relation not yet organised into terms such as subject and the object' (Manning 2016, 29). Following is a way to attend to that middle where the world and art are in process in a radical manner. Here, process is not led or directed from someone's point of view, as in poststructuralist positionality, but is dwelling, co-becoming in its relations. Although in the three collaborations described above there is always an artist and a researcher, it is not these entities themselves, as preformed individuals, or even *what* we did together that interests me. I am interested in transversal connections, where art is in the making and where experiences emerge (Barrett, Bolt and Kontturi 2017). This highlights onto-epistemologies of doing research, where what can be known is inseparable from material-relational becomings of the world (Barad 2007). In other words, both 'the world' and 'us' are generated in a co-constitutive relation – 'collaborated' (Tiainen, Kontturi, Hongisto 2015a, 35–36; Bennett 2001, 4). In *Ways of Following*, my aim is to attend to this midst of collaboration, where intensities of process and material-relational becomings count more than individuals or other clearly defined material entities.

In contemporary art writing, 'participation' is an oft-used expression, employed to grasp the experience of being involved in an art process. In this sort of thinking, participation often becomes an added extra to a project already happening (Manning 2016, 54–56). Participatory art is also commonly understood as a genre of its own. In *Artificial Hells: Participatory Art and the Politics of Spectatorship* (2012), Claire Bishop defines participatory art practice as implying the involvement of many people; participatory art employs people as its principal artistic material. What I hope to attain by focusing on collaborations is a more complex ecology of participation. In the pages of this book, the focus is on the more-than-human materialities that participate in any process of encountering or making art; that stretch, contest, and potentially break, for example, the patterns of human intention (see also Springgay and Truman 2018). This is also what Erin Manning suggests of participation – it is essential to any art event to begin with. An event, as it is understood here, is never something that could be reduced to its material structures, contexts, or symbolic message; instead, an event co-emerges as an unpredictable complex of materialities on the move. This connects with the premise of process philosophy: 'a process is by its very nature collective' (Manning 2016, 53).

✷✷✷

What was co-created in my collaborations with the artists and artworks in process has been structured in three parts; the book offers three ways of following, that in their respective manners cherish art in material-relational movement that always occurs in collaboration … with …

The first part, *Encounters*, attends to the lively materialities of art. Here, encountering is an orientation that, instead of mastering art by means of interpretation and tracing intention, allows art to do its work, to affect, to suggest new ways of thinking and being, palpably. This is not to render art alive (Ingold 2013, 20), because art is readily considered to be lively. Art does not need an interpretative intervention to open an 'object' into a relational process, it is a (collective) process to begin with. *Encounters* offers a vocabulary and research modalities sensitive to art's material-relational doings, arising from two intensive art-encounters. The first of these encounters lasted only a matter of hours, while the second encounter lasted more than six months.

In 'Breathing and Dancing' (Chapter 1), the whirling, colour-changing beams of light and the ubiquitous haze of the light installation *Heaven Machine* (2005) invite and entangle the audience into their movement. They challenge critical interpretative distance in favour of embodied and relational approaches. In 'Work of Painting' (Chapter 2), a peculiar double navel, that has surprisingly emerged in the middle of a painting, questions the patterns of intention and the mastery of the artist over an art process.[16] Through a focus on painting practice, the chapter suggests conceptualisations that pinpoint the generative connections between the material and the semiotic. Theoretically, *Encounters* works with and elaborates on such pivotal contributions as Bolt's *Art Beyond Representation* (2004a), Simon O'Sullivan's *Art Encounters Deleuze and Guattari: Thinking Beyond Representation* (2006a), and Elizabeth Grosz's *Chaos, Territory, Art: Deleuze and the Framing of the Earth* (2008), all of which address 'a further turn from the linguistic, a turn towards matter and to the expressive potentialities of the latter' (O'Sullivan 2006a, 4).[17]

The second part of the book, *Co-workings*, focuses on the work of painting as it unfolds in Susana Nevado's studio. The four chapters of this part offer a material-relational take on studio practices, replacing prior emphasis on sociality, that disregarded the fact that painters mostly work alone (Elkins 2000, 194).[18] *Co-workings* contests the loneliness of art-making by elaborating on the active role of materials in art-making: how they collaborate with the artist and each other, relationally. The overarching theme of these chapters is the emergence of artworks through a set of heterogeneous collaborations, energy-flows of bodies, technical capabilities, and physico-chemical compositions of paint, canvas, and paper scraps, among other things. Through attending to art in the making, following art processes in Nevado's studio, the four chapters readdress and complicate issues such as artistic influences (Chapter 3), the autonomy of art (Chapter 4), the physicality of art-making (Chapter 5), and art–life connections (Chapter 6). When attentively attended to, these concerns, once deemed old-fashioned, become central concerns for material-relational art-making. *Co-workings* is transversally motivated by feminist studies on women's art-making (see, for example, Meskimmon 2003; Betterton 2004b)[19] and by Gilles Deleuze's writings on art, including *Francis Bacon: The Logic of Sensation*, where he boldly claims that we should pay more attention to what artists have to say (2003, 99).

The third part, *Sensations,* explores affective relations between art and its viewer-participants, taking into account relational materialities involved in making and encountering art. It aims to harness intensities of art into felt sensations by means of attentive writing. *Sensations* starts with a prelude, titled 'An Oral Triptych', that introduces the idea of direct, immanent relations and the art processes that are followed in this part's three chapters. In 'The Grimacing Mouth' (Chapter 7), Susana Nevado's *D2I* installation makes use of Catholic tradition of relics in affirming the changes involved in shedding milk teeth and growing up. In 'The Preaching Mouth' (Chapter 8), Marjukka Irni's project *Sappho Wants to Save You* (2006–2010) contests the unitary understandings of gender by transforming preaching and religious conversion into vibrating, imperceptible politics of the queer. In 'The Screaming Mouth' (Chapter 9), *Sketches* (1999–), a series of photographic auto-portraits of artist Helena Hietanen, proffers sensations of breast cancer and reconfigures the concept of transfiguration. In their diverse ways, and in conversation with the feminist materialisms of Rosi Braidotti (2006a; 2006b) and Elizabeth Grosz (2004; 2005) as well as the relational philosophies of Manning and Massumi, the three art processes invoke the grand question, 'What can art do?', which is central to Deleuze and Guattari's (1987; 1994) thought.[20]

The book concludes in 'A Follow-Up', where the material-relational approach to art is summed up in three propositions by revisiting the chapters, synthesising conceptions, again ... with art. The first proposition centres on the ontogenetic claim that art is always already moving, and suggests ways to relate to this movement through attentive participation *with* that relinquishes the hold of positionality in favour of openness and change. The second proposition moves on to emphasise the *ethics* of attending to the *work* of artists and the art, so that art's singular subtleties, that have potential to change thinking-feeling, will not be left unprobed. The third and final proposition builds on the previous ones and suggests that the *politics* of art is not only inseparable from but synonymous with each work of art's unique material-relational movement, through which art suggests new ways of thinking and being. All three propositions approach art as a future-orientated process, as material-relational becoming that always already possesses the germinating seeds of change. In what follows, this book hopes to sustain and cherish art's potential for change that lies not only in the flows of process but in the stammering stucknesses too.

Encounters

1

Breathing and Dancing

On a gloomy, late January afternoon in the Northern hemisphere, where the greyness of the air and the sky was one with the greyness of the shrinking, melting snow, I visited the *Light Treatment* exhibition at Wäinö Aaltonen Museum of Art. The exhibition showcased a kind of light art created as a remedy for seasonal affective disorder caused by the reduced daylight in the region between late October and early February. Inside the darkened white cube of the modern museum, twirling beams of light and all-pervading haze filled the space. This suffusing, colour-changing materiality was molecular – hardly graspable, yet pervasive like the grim weather conditions of that day; it was what *Heaven Machine*, a large-scale light installation by Helena Hietanen and Jaakko Niemelä, was mostly made of [Figure 1.1].

An artist's talk event was taking place in the museum and my sensuous encounter was immediately filtered through verbal accounts that located the creation and composition of the installation in several cultural contexts. The artist, Helena Hietanen, described how the themes and structure of *Heaven Machine* related to her experiences of breast cancer (Hietanen, 27 January 2006). First hesitatingly, then growing bolder, she said: 'I am going to talk about my personal situation pretty openly. Eight years ago I had cancer, breast cancer, for the first time, then I healed ... and then it came back ... and now I have fallen

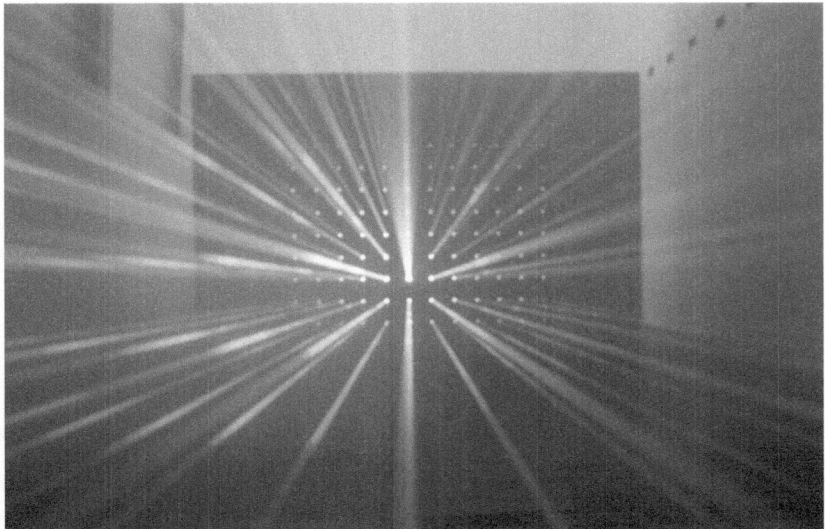

Figure 1.1. Helena Hietanen and Jaakko Niemelä, *Heaven Machine*, 2005. Light installation, size variable, Light Treatment exhibition at Wäinö Aaltonen Museum of Art (Turku City Art Museum), 27 November 2005 – 30 January 2006. Photograph by Raakkel Närhi, WAM, The Museum Centre of Turku.

ill for the third time'. The illness initiated the collaboration with her sculptor husband Jaakko Niemelä, as Hietanen was too frail to work on her own. The key elements of the installation, its light beams and black holes, originated in the powerful visions Hietanen had when she was very sick:

> I was in the middle of very black darkness, as we are here too, but it was even darker, pitch black ... I was in the eye of a storm, alone, but then, suddenly ... from the Heavens descended a light pillar that surrounded me ... An incredibly bright light that came upon me ... For me, light symbolises God. (Hietanen, 27 January 2006)

Hietanen explained how the light spaciousness of the high-ceilinged sculpture room of the museum reminded her of sacred spaces and how it inspired her to express her faith. In *Heaven Machine*, the godly light burst through the black holes of the wall structure that divided the room into the mundane 'here and now' and the celestial 'hereafter', a space closed off from the audience. Hietanen had encountered black holes throughout her sickness. When she was too ill to do anything but stare for hours at the floor, a wood grain pattern transformed into a black hole piercing her hand: 'The hole was death' (Hietanen, 27 January 2006). Then the hole appeared in an X-ray image of her cancerous breast.

Throughout the artist's talk, the thematic and structural opposition between light and darkness, the celestial and the mundane – life and death – was present, enabling an *identification* with religious art. The artist also indicated an *analogy* between the exhibition room and sacred spaces such as churches.[21] Finally, an audience member suggested *resemblance*, asking if *Heaven Machine*'s beams of light refer to radiotherapy. According to Gilles Deleuze, opposition, identification, analogy, and resemblance form the quadripartite logic of representation that he criticises in his book *Difference and Repetition* (1994a). Barbara Bolt suggests that this logic still dominates writing and thinking about art. She explains that representation 'fixes the world as an object and resource for human subjects. As a mode of thought that prescribes all that is known, it orders the world and predetermines what can be thought' (Bolt 2004a, 12–13). When dealt with solely within the frame of representation, the unpredictable, creative materiality of art so essential to its existence may not receive proper attention. The movement of art threatens to be reduced to meanings alone – and often to meanings that are already constituted, already known.[22]

In contemporary art and culture criticism, the production of meaning is often understood as a way of enlivening and keeping artistic and other cultural objects in motion. Every act of reading, framing, and interpretation enlivens the object of study, making the thing 'a living creature embedded in all the questions and considerations' posed, as Mieke Bal suggests (1996, 26, 40; 2007, 2). What is problematic in the process of meaning-making is that the radical potential of art seems to be the result of retrospectively fabricated meanings rather than a productive quality of the (art-)event itself. In other words, while the (representational) practice of meaning-making moves the work, it hardly allows the work to move on its own.

Meaning-making becomes a restrictive, molar power. 'Molar' is a term that Deleuze and Guattari (1983; 1987) borrow from molecular biology and extend to a variety of aspects of cultural life, from the binary construction of sex to institutionalised politics and habits.[23] Importantly, molarities only appear in relation to the molecular, which has a long genealogy in the materialist-vitalist philosophies of Gilbert Simondon, Alfred Whitehead, Henri Bergson, Friedrich Nietzsche, and Baruch Spinoza.[24] If molar powers express the stabilised structures of the world – its institutions and standardised practices – molecular forces unravel stability and conventions; they are a thousand tiny, almost imperceptible movements, sensations, that shatter, stutter, and undermine as they trickle through seemingly stable molar matter.

The task of this chapter is to find modalities and conceptions attentive to this molecular movement, to *Heaven Machine*'s twirling, hazy motion. To start this work, let us enter the installation again, and let *Heaven Machine* embrace us within its movement so that nothing remains settled, 'solved'. Engaging with *Heaven Machine*'s material-relational liveliness in this way, 'encounter' becomes a productive way of moving-with.

Dismantling divisions, breathing sensations

Of course, *Heaven Machine* did not just suddenly appear before my eyes; rather, it opened to me as a series of sensuous experiences. First, there were a few solid but textured stone steps to be climbed. Then to enter the space, to access the work, a heavy, dark, light-blocking velvet curtain had to be touched, pushed, moved. Once inside the installation, I could not see much for a moment as the combination of shadowy darkness, rotating light and pervasive haze infused my senses and confused me – literally fusing into my system. In concert with the words that interpreted the installation as a representation, the work was in material-relational motion, indisputably so. The data projector pushed the whirling beams of light, with their varying shades of yellow, blue, purple, pink and white, through the wall that was pierced with more than a hundred holes, and threw them across the room. The haze machine that filled the sculpture room with minute molecules of oxygen, nitrogen and hydrogen, water as haze, made the projected light more visible. The movement of light came from a simple computer-animation that was hidden behind the wall, in the 'hereafter'. The mechanical humming of the data projector and the haze generator filtered into the human voices of the artist's talk event and guaranteed that the installation was not mute even for a second [Figures 1.2 and 1.3].

To be able to encounter, to sense, *Heaven Machine* as a moving, material-relational constellation necessitates an approach that distances itself from the hold of positionality elemental to representational thinking. While this turn of focus does not equal an abandonment of cultural meanings – we cannot simply step into an aesthetic vacuum – it facilitates sensing what is happening around you, *with* you, without your having to make sense *of* it. What material-relational, molecular encounters necessitate is giving up a positionality that predetermines what can be thought and felt. Despite the well-intended political impetus of positionality, it ends up boxing the liveliness of the process in a cultural freeze-frame, 'subtracting movement from the picture'; in other words, 'thinking away its dynamic unity, the continuity of its movements' (Massumi 2002b, 2–3, 6).

What if, then, *Heaven Machine* was thought of, emphatically, as its title suggests, as a machine, as a dynamic constellation that,

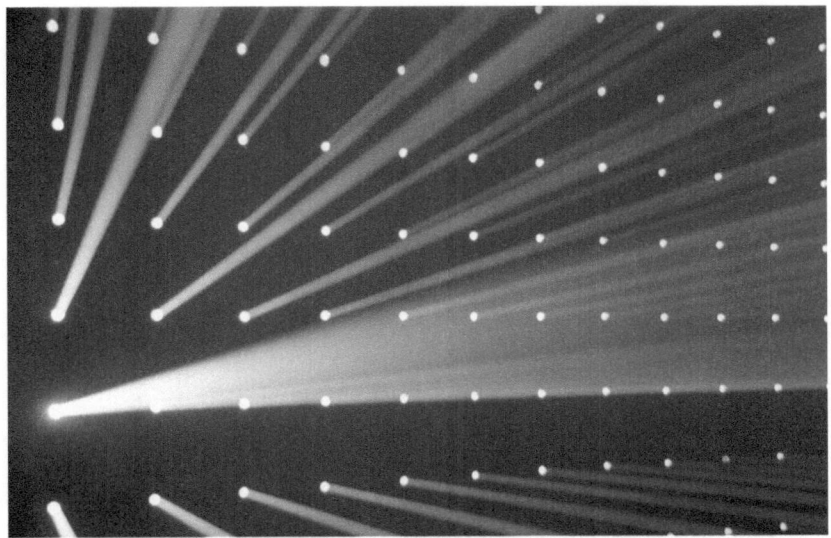

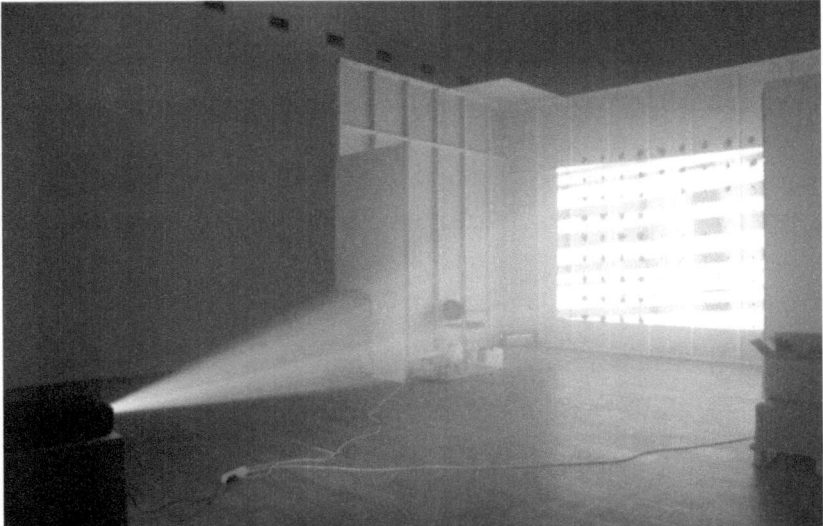

Figures 1.2 and 1.3. *Heaven Machine* and its technical machine. Photographs by Raakkel Närhi, WAM, The Museum Centre of Turku. For videos of *Heaven Machine* go to http://www.jaakkoniemela.com/ > Heavenmachine 2005 > videos 1–2.

by way of its working, brings something new into this world? How would that change the relation between an artwork and the subject experiencing it? In the writings of Deleuze and

Guattari (1983; 1986; 1987), we are asked to abandon a common sense understanding of what a machine is: the machinic is not to be confused with the mechanical or technical. If in mechanics a technological apparatus is defined by a structural interrelationship between discrete parts that work together to perform a task, in Deleuze and Guattari's take, machines are not instrumental, not just means to an end or to completing a task, but are defined by what they do – how they connect and transform.[25]

This is what I am after in what follows; machinic materialities or technicalities are not interesting in themselves but in how they do things – relationally. Relational openness and inclusion are the characteristic qualities of a machine: '[t]o enter or leave the machine, to be in the machine, to walk around it, to approach it – these are still components of the machine' (Deleuze and Guattari 1986, 7). So when I entered the exhibition space, the work, I had already become a participant in its work, moving with and as part of its material-relational constellation. Although I eventually left the actual proximity of its elements in the museum space, the sensation of the subtle haze and moving, radiating beams of light stayed with me, to be actualised again and again, in writing and rewriting our encounter.

Machine, then, is a convenient concept here, first and foremost, as it never refers to a fully closed system, but to an open dynamism that 'has to work in order to live, to processualise itself with the singularities which strike it' (Guattari 1995, 94). It is also a worthwhile concept as it begs for attention to be paid to how the machine works, and so tries 'to break down the ontological iron curtain between being and things' (O'Sullivan 2006a, 26). In other words, it helps to reconfigure our relationship with the world by loosening the hold of positionality.[26] To emphasise the multiple varying elements co-involved, interconnected, Deleuze and Guattari speak of machinic assemblages, or simply of assemblages.[27] As a concept, assemblage does not repudiate more stable structures; it is not only about connective flows. Deleuze and Guattari (1987, 332–37) insist that an assemblage always has two sides, one territorialising and one deterritorialising. Here, territorialisation refers to the creation of a territory, a zone of comfort, a sort of home in the middle of chaos (1987, 311–12). Constructing *Heaven Machine* as a multi-layered network of signification is the work of territorialisation – creating a homey feeling by putting up walls of contexts and a roof of discourses, so to speak. Territorialisation is at work also in relation to Hietanen's personal history. In the midst of sickness and fear of death, *Heaven Machine* constructed a safe haven of life, a shelter of hope where life goes on beyond the limitations of an organic body.

But an assemblage always has its deterritorialising, unpredictable side that dismantles conventional ways of being and disrupts learned habits. I was not untouched by this deterritorialising action, this agentic capacity of the assemblage, or 'agencement', as highlighted by the original French term revived by Erin Manning (2016, 123). I was taken into it, as *Heaven Machine* connected to me – as the rapid change of rhythm and the movement of light made me momentarily lose my sight, weakened my sense of balance, and as the haze drifted to my lungs, and further into my blood circulation when I inhaled. What I felt was 'a kind of collapse of visual coordinates, of orientation, of the separate positioning of the subject at a distance from the object' (Grosz 2008, 84). According to Elizabeth Grosz, this is what happens when 'sensation' is at work. In her work, Grosz retrieves the concept of sensation, which has a long history in the field of aesthetics of the sublime, especially of the Kantian sort. Inspired by Deleuze's materialism and Darwin's philosophy of becoming, she suggests that sensation is an event of direct connection; a connective principle indispensable for art to work.[28]

> Sensation is the zone of indeterminacy between subject and object, the block that erupts from the

> encounter of the one with the other. Sensation
> impacts the body, not through the brain, not through
> representations, signs, images or fantasies, but
> directly, on the body's own internal forces, on cells,
> organs, the nervous system. Sensation requires no
> mediation or translation. It is not representation,
> sign, symbol, but force, energy, rhythm, resonance.
> (Grosz 2008, 73)[29]

Working, connecting by sensation, artworks 'do not signify or represent, they assemble, they make, they do, they produce' (Grosz 2008, 75). In this understanding, artworks are not so much to be read, interpreted, deciphered, but responded to, engaged with. And to be frank, the deterritorialising movement of *Heaven Machine*, 'the zone of indeterminacy' it created, did not easily allow the distance necessary for reading or interpretation. It was not only that the ubiquitous haze landed on our faces, hair, hands, and clothed bodies. Its moving molecular materiality was more pervasive than that. No one in the space could *not* breathe the haze, inhale its molecules. As the haze seeped its way into the human bodies, *Heaven Machine* connected with the participating audience in a most fundamental, direct manner. Verbally presented cultural contexts, stories and suggestions were not separate from this movement; rather, they intermingled with the body, inhaled, absorbed in the light haze. This was not a position from which to fix meanings, to master the work. It is relevant to ask, with Brian Massumi, how would it even be possible to 'master what forms us? And reforms us at each instant, before we know it?' (2009a, 10). Every breath I took drew us closer, made us more intertwined, making me more-than-human, molecule by molecule.

The contemporary philosopher who has most vigorously brought breathing back to theoretical attention is Luce Irigaray (2002). She claims that we have forgotten the fundamental role that breathing has in our lives. Air as a shared medium and as a necessity for life is central to her proposition that Western cultures should revive their relation to the basic ontological premise of all life – breathing.[30] Irigaray reminds us that living equates with breathing; it is our first and most fundamental need, preceding other elementary needs such as eating and drinking (2002, 75). She writes that 'often we confuse cultivation with the learning of words, of knowledges, of competences, of abilities. We live without breath, without remembering that being cultivated amounts to being able to breathe' (Irigaray 2002, 76).[31] For Irigaray, shared air is the key to intersubjectivity, to a more communal becoming; those who do not breathe do not respect their lives and end up taking air from others: 'Breathing is thus a duty toward my life, that of others, and that of the entire living world' (2002, 50). Rosi Braidotti (2006b, 178), for her part, connects breathing to ethical thinking: thinkers must remember to be open to their outside, to connect with the forces of sensation, perception and imagination. In her opinion, this way of thinking is closer to mindful breathing than to the institutionalised reasoning that representational analysis stands for. In this sense, would not breathing be a fitting proposition for an ethical encounter with art that, against distant observation, connects rather than divides?

Dancing vibrations

To further consider the conceptual possibilities of participation that the movement of *Heaven Machine* suggests, let us turn to techno dance events, where the rhythmic and immersive combination of flashing, changing lights, and pervasive, thick, moist haze work as forces of deterritorialisation [Figures 1.4 and 1.5]. Techno-raves, however, are not just another cultural context for *Heaven Machine*; rather, they are a bodily practice that relates to *Heaven Machine* by way of sensation and vibration. For Stamatia Portanova (2005), with their vibrating rhythm of light, sound and dance, techno-raves are a de-individualising

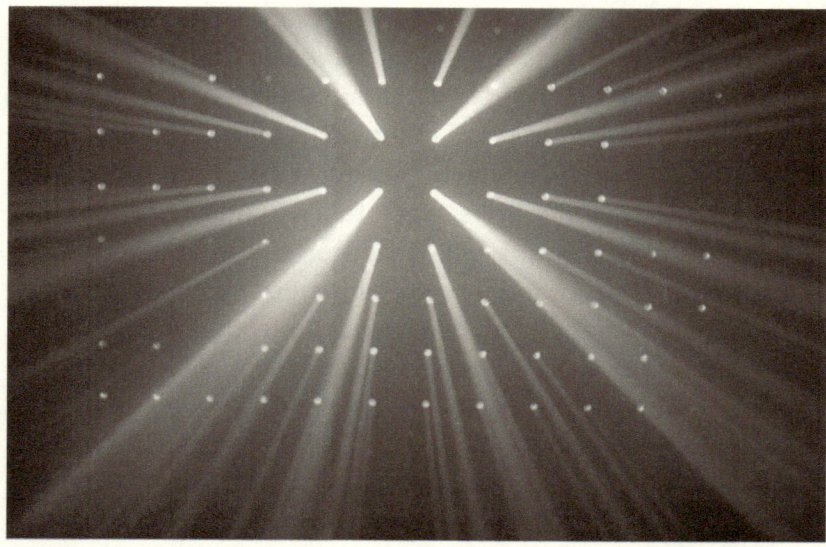

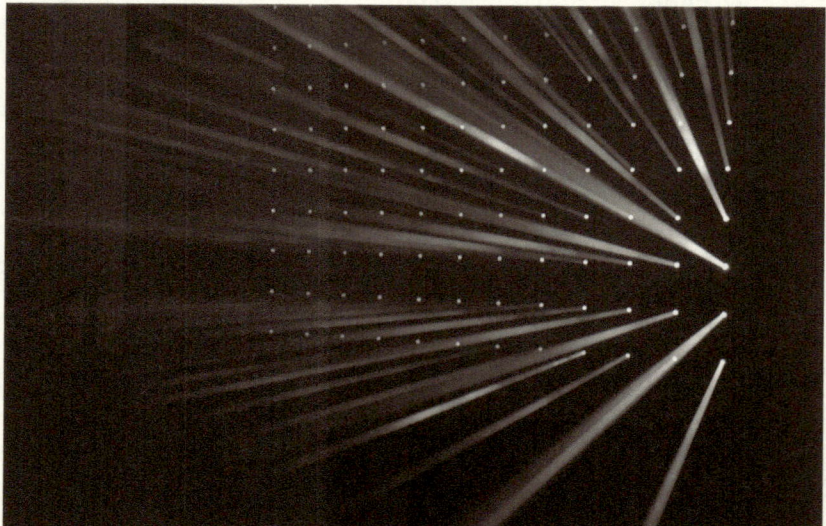

Figures 1.4 and 1.5. *Heaven Machine*'s moving beams of light with their changing colours. Photographs by Raakkel Närhi, WAM, The Museum Centre of Turku.

experience, a social nomadic practice, in which the boundaries between the self and others, the self and the world lose their consistency. Rather than enabling a total overcoming of the body, the techno experience 'allows the body to escape the structures and boundaries that keep it organised' (2005, 12). For Portanova, techno music works like a virus – it intervenes in bodies, connects them, transforms them as the rhythm disrupts habitual bodily movements and modes of being, as well as obscuring clear perceptions, re-organising them after its own order.[32]

Portanova's virological analysis of de-individualising techno culture comes close to Tamsin Lorraine's (2000) (feminist) mode of self-presentation, which is about becoming imperceptible and impersonal – by no means transcendental, but thoroughly connected with the world, with life. She suggests: 'all life processes have molecular elements mostly imperceptible to us, whose configurations into larger aggregates are constantly changing. Human existence is but a part of this larger process' (Lorraine 2000, 184). The scene Lorraine offers not only relates to Portanova's analysis of techno dance but also with my participation in *Heaven Machine*, where human bodies moved, connected and opened outward with the rhythms of light, haze, and mechanical humming. It is the constant, often imperceptible movement of the world – of techno dance and subjectivity – that Portanova and Lorraine stress. Both show a delicate understanding of complex cultural processes that often break out of, and escape from the binary divisions of the human–nonhuman, subject–object, and organic–inorganic in which they are conceptualised. There is always something that flows or flees, that escapes binary organisations: the molecular (Deleuze and Guattari 1987, 216).

In the vocabulary of process philosophy, the term 'dance' is frequently used to express this kind of dismantling effect – a molecular escape from the commonplace.[33] It is, for example, present throughout the work of Deleuze and Guattari, where it moves from the figure of moving life itself (Colebrook 2005, 12) to events that have potential to transform our thinking about life. For instance, in *Difference and Repetition*, Deleuze (1994a, 8) proposes replacing the logic of representation by 'inventing vibrations, rotations, whirlings, gravitations, dances or leaps': dancing enables deterritorialisation. In the intensity of dance, conventional boundaries are broken and new connections suggested as the human body flows, becomes more-than-human in and through a variety of rhythms, speeds, movements, rests, relations not ordinary or habitual. This is what Erin Manning's *Always More Than One: Individuation's Dance* (2013) accomplishes; when it follows the practice of contemporary dance to create the term 'dance of attention' (indicating an open, relational approach to the world) dance emerges to escape the commonplace and perform its dismantling effect. Dance is also central to Simon O'Sullivan's conception of encounter as 'participation with':

> [W]e as participants with art ... are involved in a dance with art, a dance in which ... the molecular is opened up, the aesthetic is activated, and art does what is its chief modus operandi. It transforms, if only for a moment, our sense of our 'selves' and our experience of our world. (O'Sullivan 2006a, 50)

To avoid understanding 'dancing' as a theoretical figure of speech only, let me return to my encounter, my participation with *Heaven Machine*. When the whirling beams of light, with their repetitive rhythms and continually changing colours, connected to my body, 'cut' the body, and when my body was suffused, through breathing, by the haze surrounding it, I was dancing – subtly moving my own body in relation to the moving, humming body of *Heaven Machine*. In both *Heaven Machine* and the practice of techno dance, bodies vibrate, lose their linearity, borders, as the monotonic music-humming and beams of light, with their varying, up-tempo rhythms and changing colours connect to them.

Portanova (2005) applies the term 'bio-physical' to the re-organisation of matter that occurs when rhythm enters the body's bio-cellular system. In this process, 'matter loses its static appearance and becomes an ensemble of dancing molecules' (Portanova 2005, 3).[34] Following Portanova and Lorraine, to move, think and transform along *with Heaven Machine* is to abandon one's body as a closed and strictly organised entity and open it up to molecular flows, enabled and enhanced by rotating beams of light and the diffusing haze that do not heed borders between inside and outside.

Deleuze and Guattari (1987, 149–66) call a disorganised, opened body, that has escaped its function as a composition of organs, a 'Body without Organs'.[35] This concept captures a body which is beyond the confines of representation; a body emerging in and through molecular flows. To fabricate a body without organs, experimentation needs to be substituted for interpretation: this 'is a question of life and death, youth and old age, sadness and joy. It is where everything is played out' (Deleuze and Guattari 1987, 151). When experimenting, it is intensities that count: flowing, intense matter; matter equalling energy, relational matter in movement, in transformation. Matter as intensity is not a calculable quantity, but a quality that can only be experienced – and experimented with. Through its intensive matter, *Heaven Machine* offers the participating human bodies potential for intensification that is experienced in and through multiple, multisensory connections – as beams of light hit, pierce, cut the body and as the haze gently caresses the skin, suffuses the body, is inhaled into the body's system; in other words, intensification experienced in and through rhythmic actions that make the body vibrate.[36]

> What seems to be transmitted, transformed, located and relocated in this dance of forces ... is nothing but vibration, resonance, the mutual condition both of material forces at their most elementary levels, and music at its most refined and complex. ... Vibration is the common thread or rhythm running through the universe from its chaotic inorganic interminability to

> its most intimate forces of inscription on living bodies of all kinds and back again. (Grosz 2008, 54)

Grosz (2006; 2008, 53) suggests that this kind of rhythm and intensity of life is best appreciated in the arts – not so much in science, which creates functions to order chaos, and not even in philosophy, which works with concepts – and of all the arts, it is finest in music.[37] *Heaven Machine*'s music emerges through its mechanical humming, inseparable from the intensive multisensory rhythm of constantly twirling, colour-changing beams of light that co-create vibration – vibration that is a central quality in Grosz's definition of music.

For Grosz, vibration links with a future: '[l]iving beings are vibratory beings: vibration is their mode of differentiation; the way they enhance and enjoy the forces …' (Grosz 2008, 33). Thus, vibration is as fundamental to life as breathing. Introducing vibration into contemporary discussions of art and feminism is part of Grosz's (2005; 2006; 2011) materialist project that re-evaluates the work of evolutionary biologist Charles Darwin.[38] According to Grosz, studies of culture might benefit from a dynamised, uncontainable and unpredictable conception of natural life, as is assigned by evolutionary biology, and especially from the detailed attention that Darwin has given to these qualities of nature.[39] This is because his work offers a peculiarly subtle and complex critique of essentialism and teleology, which are both long-held concerns of feminist criticism.[40] Above all comes his antihumanist understanding of life as productive dynamism and endless becoming that is open to otherness and subject to unpredictability and surprise.

Vibration connects to molecularity; it is the pulsing rhythm of the molecular, or, as Grosz puts it, the common thread of both organic and inorganic life. In other words, vibration opens up the lived body to nonhuman forces of the universe. 'Vibrations are oscillations, differences, movements of back and forth, contraction and dilation: they are a becoming-temporal of spatial movements and spatial process, the promise of a future' (Grosz 2008, 55).[41] Grosz's vitalist suggestion that art can offer us a new world, a new body, makes sense here (Grosz in Kontturi and Tiainen 2007, 256). Following Grosz, *Heaven Machine* can offer an experience of a body that we do not yet have – within the limits of our everyday experience. It proposes an intensive body that vibrates, oscillates towards a future.

In her artist's talk, Hietanen gave a short explanation for the intense vibratory rhythm of the work (Hietanen, 27 January 2006). When making the installation she was living through a very intense period in her life; she had fallen ill with cancer again, and wanted to live life to the full, with all the intensity possible, for she did not know if she would soon die. In this sense, *Heaven Machine* gave her *a* new body – a body that was not limited to the 'here and now', a body no longer organic or human; a body vibrating towards a future that was not sealed or determined, but open. A body, with its indefinite article, is not yours or mine, yet it does not lack anything; rather, it 'expresses the pure determination of intensity, intensive difference' (Deleuze and Guattari 1987, 164), it is the opening of the body. By transmitting its vibratory resonance to bodies that participate with it, *Heaven Machine* opens new futures far beyond the body of its (co-)maker.

Following lines of (f)light

If we let *Heaven Machine* connect with our bodies, if we let the beams of light and the haze transpierce the body, make the body vibrate, we are experimenting – if not instead of, then parallel to the act of interpreting. It is this parallel activity, instead of erasure of the other, that Deleuze and Guattari encourage:

> Lodge yourself on a stratum, experiment with the opportunities it offers, find an advantageous place on it, find potential movements of deterritorialization,

> possible lines of flight, experience them, produce
> flow conjunctions here and there, try out continuums
> of intensities segment by segment, have a small
> plot of new land at all times. ... It is through ... [this]
> meticulous relation that one succeeds in freeing lines
> of flight. ... Connect, conjugate, continue. (Deleuze and
> Guattari 1987, 161)

While Deleuze and Guattari encourage us to experiment beyond the limits of recognition, the already known, they do not advise us to surrender to unknown forces altogether. Instead, their lesson is one of dosage: gently deterritorialise your territory, 'have a small plot of new land at all times'. This is also what Rosi Braidotti argues when she warns against a total immersion in the flows of intensities. Thinking in a nomadic mode always requires composition, selection and dosage – 'the careful layout of empowering conditions that allow for the actualisations of affirmative force' (Braidotti 2006b, 168). Do not get stuck in the habitual or with the common: search, experiment, try out, but only 'segment by segment'. This is the way to leave one's territory – to free lines of flight. Only by taking or creating lines of flight can we say that we truly continue. This is passive, material-relational vitalism; vitalism that does not force becomings but follows them.

Yet this is not to say that those clues or connections that were offered in the artist's talk and that can be elaborated to research contexts should not be counted as important. These elements, such as the conception of light as a symbol of God or of the black hole as a symbol of death, could be understood as molar moments that stop the molecular movement of the world for a while but in no way congeal it altogether (Bolt 2004a, 45–47). The 'do's and don'ts' of an art gallery could be conceived as molar moments too. In fact, according to Hietanen, and also to her disappointment, most of the exhibition guests tried carefully not to disturb the movement of light, and not to connect with it. People stepped back, trying to find a secure place at the outskirts of the exhibition room, a place where their bodies would not interact with the work in too profound, too intense a manner. This concerned predominantly adults. Children were more daring; they playfully hunted the beams of light and some even opened their mouths as if trying to eat them. Indeed, eating could offer us another conception of transformative encounter, because eating so clearly connects us, opens us to other bodies, both human and nonhuman: 'as we ingest, we mutate, we expand and contract, we change – sometimes subtly, sometimes violently' (Probyn 2000, 12–14, 18). But adults know that a gallery space is no place to eat and perhaps it is this knowledge of rules and the willingness to hold on to them that sometimes prevents adults from digesting art in a transformative way.

The regulatory power of the molar is not something inherently bad. To claim so would be just another molar judgment. Molarities might, however, get too tight, too overpowering. One might, for example, stick within one's comfort zone, the territory of confirmed meanings, too tightly to be able to grasp the beams of light as anything but signs of something else. Still, according to Deleuze and Guattari, this is only habitual blindness, not a state of affairs as such. Molecular flows traverse the molar at every level.

> Molar aggregates ... are perpetually being undermined by a molecular segmentation causing a zigzag crack, making it difficult for them to keep their own segments in line. It is as if a line of flight, perhaps only a tiny trickle to begin with, leaked their segments, escaping their centralization, eluding their totalization. (Deleuze and Guattari 1987, 216)

The powerful conceptualisation that Deleuze and Guattari (1987, 3–4, 9) draw from molecular movement cracking the molar organisation is a 'line of flight' or line of escape [*ligne de fuite*].[42]

In *Heaven Machine*, lines of flight can be found in the movement of the light beams that confuse the senses and disturb the interpretative event of association, inviting members of the audience to join the movement. Finding such transformative lines is not a given; it is meant for those who trust that something may come out, though they are not sure what (Rajchman 2000). Thus, finding lines of flight requires trust in change: a willingness to reject what is common sense and the courage to throw oneself into a state of insecurity. In the end, is that not what all critical thinking should be about? Not just about tracing and tracking down (oppressive) meanings, but about trust in change?

To take *Heaven Machine*'s beams of light as lines of flight offers an escape from the restricting oppositions that can easily govern analytical work. Following them, one might arrive at new ways of being, instead of being stuck with what was already known, like the artist's sickness or the confirmed Christian references of the work. Yet, it is important to repeat, this does not equate to the abandonment of cultural meanings. Rather, it complicates the perception of art as an event. Conceived as lines of flight, *Heaven Machine*'s beams of light do not index the god of a certain religion. They become vibration and the movement of life itself – an affirmation of a life, an impersonal life beyond any single (human) being, as expressed in Deleuze's (2001) essay 'Immanence: A Life', first published just before his death.[43]

In this way, in the way of following, the beams of light do not affirm a certain life, not the life of Hietanen, nor more generally a Christian way of life, but an indefinite life not restricted by the juxtaposition of 'here and now' and 'hereafter'. Relatedly, the direction of light in *Heaven Machine* differs from that commonly found in Christian iconography: the direction of God's light is usually vertical or diagonal, from the top down, but rarely horizontal. Remember that in Hietanen's vision, also, a pillar of light descended from the Heavens to save her. In *Heaven Machine*, on the other hand, the participant encounters the dismantling beams of light horizontally. In this sense, *Heaven Machine*'s movement of light (or life!) disrupts the original Christian reference as it vitally streams out of the black holes of the wall and connects with the bodies attending the installation, making them vibrate and lose their commonsensical confines.[44]

Importantly, Deleuze and Guattari insist that it is no use finding lines of flight or taking molecular escapes if one is not capable of converting them to re-arranged molar structures: '[m]olecular escapes and movements would be nothing if they did not return to the molar organizations to reshuffle their segments, their binary distributions' (Deleuze and Guattari 1987, 216–17). It is not enough, then, to be able to dismantle binary oppositions or to be content with getting past the wall separating the subject from the object in just one encounter. So let us get back to the questions central to this chapter. What the encounter with *Heaven Machine* suggests is that when works of art are seen merely as passive 'battlefields' for representation and interpretation, their potential lines of flight, their material-relational capacity to change and move thinking is easily missed. Therefore, it is important to pay attention to what is singular in artworks, their modus operandi, the material-relational movements of art, and not to override material and corporeal intensities with textual and discursive powers. This requires giving up at least a bit of the comforting mastering agency that is geared to fixing meanings and sealing interpretations (if not permanently, then at least temporarily). Only then can it become possible to acknowledge and encounter artworks as something other than objects; as complex material-relational processes, agencements, that not only move without the practice of interpretation but also engage, co-involve the audience in their dance.

It is crucial to emphasise that the reference to molecular movement does not propose to relocate writing with art to the realm of natural sciences; molecularity is not offered to achieve a microscopic gaze (Deleuze and Guattari 1987, 227–28).[45] Instead, the persistent and perpetual (evolutionary) becoming of nature, with its material-relational agencements – often denied and disavowed by cultural theories – might 'provide [us even] more complex and accurate models for the cultural', as Grosz (2005, 48–49) suggests. Surely, the complexities of movement, for example, of such an art event as *Heaven Machine*, are flattened by the con-textual models of representation and meaning-making that have long dominated the ways in which we understand the cultural. However, when encountered by breathing and dancing rather than by reading and explaining, art writing joins in what Grosz (2004, 189–214) calls 'the philosophy of life'[46] – a project that affirms change and movement of all life on the nature–culture continuum.

2

Work of Painting

There, right in the middle of the abdomen of a girl painted, portrayed in her black underwear, is a curious detail: not a navel, but two navels – a double navel. And then, an older woman in her white underwear – again with two navels, not aligned, not in perfect harmony, marking her painted belly. In yet another painting, a middle-aged woman has an ascending series of navels, four or five of them, climbing up towards her ribs.

Having regularly visited artist Susana Nevado's studio while she was in the process of making the installation to which these paintings belong, I am well aware that these multiple navels were not something that the artist was aiming for in the project. The navels are not mentioned in any of the discussions concerning the piece that I had with Nevado during the six-month period of its most intensive making. Nor does this theme figure prominently in the photographs I took to document the process. The obscure navels feature only in the very last pictures. Also, Nevado extensively studies her subject in the making both visually and through literature, as she did this time too – only her subject was not navels. Rather, the installation, that the artist later named *Honest Fortune Teller*, was to bring together the imageries of Catholic holy cards and contemporary female bodies.[47] The project was a response to a Turku Biennale 2005 call, themed *Holy and Unholy*. The rich materiality of Catholic art and architecture, that in comparison with the more severe Protestant aesthetics might seem unholy even, inspired Nevado, whose plan was to create a lavish shrine of contemporary embodiments.

Through making the installation, Nevado wanted to study Catholic imagery and the attitudes inherent in it towards women's bodies. In particular, she was interested in the glaring contradiction between the lived, corporeal experience of (contemporary) women and the disembodied, virgin-like appearance of saintly women on the holy cards. To tackle this, she asked her friends and colleagues, me among them, to model for her: at the photo shoot we were shown a pocket-sized holy card of María Madre de Misericordia [Mother of Mercy] and asked to pose like her, arms wide open, in a blessing, protecting stance [Figures 2.1 and 2.2]. Later, other materials entered the project, such as a found pile of 1950s women's magazines, and books, including sadomasochist and tattoo imageries from Nevado's then partner. It was across and among these materials that the female figures with multiple navels emerged – among the thirty-five paintings and small sculptures that the installation consisted of. While Nevado indisputably had her hands in the process and even some tentative intentions, these did not rule the project; the navels were a surprise to the artist too! This brings us to the main questions of this chapter: How did the navels emerge? How do we conceptualise the matters of art moving the work, making the painting – those multiple navels?

In visual media, navels are not an uncommon subject and indeed have an extensive history as hotspots of theological dispute and popular culture alike. Adam's navel was a burning subject of biblical debates for centuries, and when Adam and Eve are depicted with navels in Christian imagery, original sin, separation from Paradise is stressed (Botting 1999, 3–4). Then, there is the more contemporaneous sexualisation and eroticisation of the navel, for which the pop icon Madonna was famous in the 1980s

Work of Painting   49

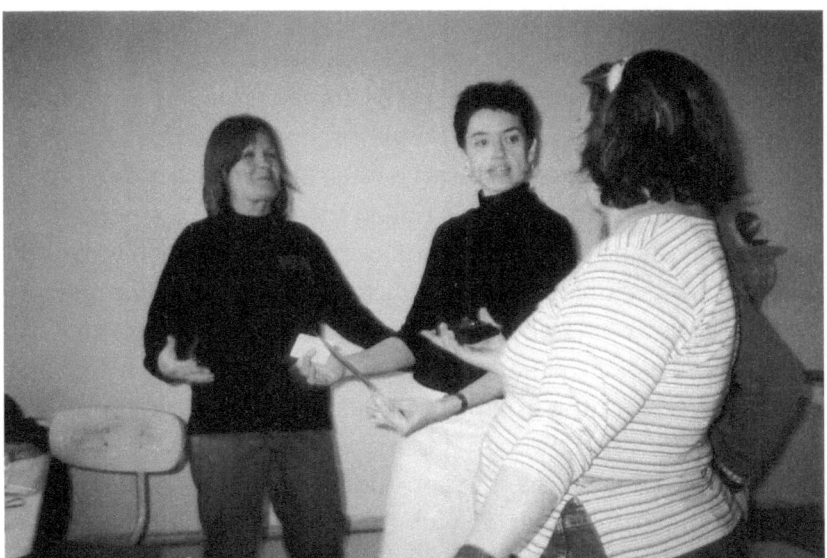

Figure 2.1. Striking poses for *Honest Fortune Teller* at Susana Nevado's studio, October 2004. Photograph by Katve-Kaisa Kontturi.

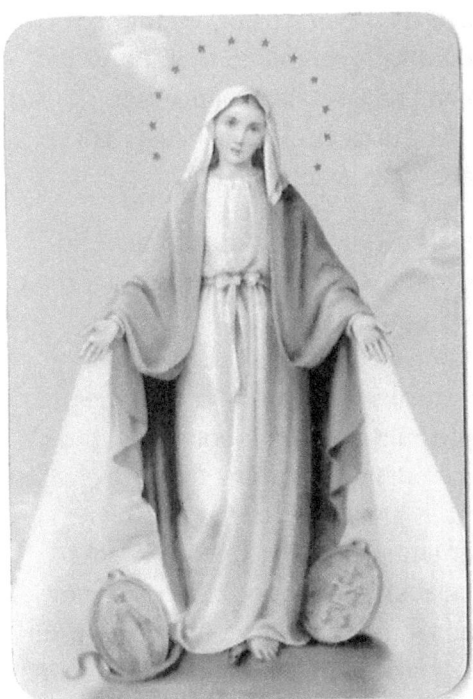

Figure 2.2. The original holy card of María Madre de Misericordia. Photograph by Katve-Kaisa Kontturi.

when navels hit the catwalks and street fashion (Botting 1999, 10). Earlier in the twentieth century, navels were censored. The Hays code, that applied ethical restrictions on movies produced in America from the 1930s to 1960s, insisted on women's navels being covered, for example, with jewels. Elisabeth Bronfen (1998, 4) finds an explanation for this rule in the fact that the navel echoes the vagina, therefore transforming the stomach into an erotically exciting place and a cultural taboo zone. For her, navels have incontestable cultural significance: 'in the cultural repertory of western imagery, the navel is the firmly privileged representative for the origin of human existence' (Bronfen 1998, 3). Tracing the navel through the stories of the Bible and through Freudian psychoanalysis, she concludes that the navel signifies lack, and the lost connection with the mother, and consequently also with the immanent pre-symbolical world of the womb. In addition to the visual debates, there are theoretical discussions that revolve around the navel. For instance, Mieke Bal (1991, 21–24) has introduced the navel as a 'democratic' metaphor of difference that is at once loaded with gender connotations, yet cannot be reduced to one sex alone (see also Palin 2004b, 47–49). In sum, there is no denying that the (single) navel has a rich discursive history, both visual and written.

However, there is no semiotic history for the double navel, let alone for a series of them; no signifying network or iconographic record which would travel through various domains from painting to literature and further. Of course, all sorts of wild associations could be drawn, stories fabricated: for instance, if the single navel signifies lack, would not the double navel then suggest a double lack? This is actually something that Félix Guattari (1995, 39) has discussed in relation to the Lacanian signifier that he finds simultaneously too abstract, as it lacks ontological becoming, and not abstract enough, as it does not understand specificities of the larger aggregates it is part of. Yet, as Barbara Bolt wisely claims: 'in the satisfaction of explanations, something else gets elided' (2006, 59). This 'something else' is the process that made the interpreted sign emerge, the 'work' of art, as Bolt (2004a; 2004b; 2014) calls it elsewhere. Bolt (2004a, 5) contrasts the concept of 'work' of art to that of 'artwork'. Whereas artwork is clearly a noun, 'work' of art is, rather, a verb. In her account, 'artwork' refers to the object quality of art and 'work' of art to its processual nature.

Work of art

The concept 'work' of art stresses the *work-being* of art that stands against the instrumental-being of art – art as a carrier for the artist's or the interpreter's ideas (Bolt 2004a, 87–122).[48] To draw attention to how an art process *works* actively in itself, and not just as a vehicle for already existing representations or identities, is to engage with the work-being of the work of art.[49] To emphasise the *work* of art is not to deny the importance of symbolic meaning, nor to undervalue the work of the artist. While the artist might not master the art process, she still works meticulously with the materials, making them work on their own. The focus on the work of art, then, appreciates the intensive, and often long-term work put into process, valuing the material-relational complexities involved.

Let us return to Nevado's studio and engage with the paintings in more detail, to follow the work of art. The smallest of the paintings, a little oval one, presents a girl who has just given birth – the baby was with her when we posed as saintly women [Figure 2.3]. In the painting, the girl's belly appears round, swollen but oddly empty, that is, post-natal. The lead white-yellowish acrylic paint with which most of the surface of the piece is covered appears to be thin and rather fragile: it seems that there is too much underneath it for it to fully cover. It is clearly evident that the girl was not painted on a blank surface. The painting seems as pregnant as the girl was just a few weeks earlier. In other words, both the double navel and the girl emerge through the material layers the painting is pregnant with. In an almost life-sized portrait, a woman in white underwear, with two navels in her fleshy belly, emerges amongst colourful covers of 1950s fashion magazines and the figure of a solemn María Madre de Misericordia [Figure 2.4]. Careful scrutiny reveals yet another layer beneath the surface of the painting: delicate lines of hips and knickers reveal that there is not only a second navel but another whole figure (see also Chapter 5 Manual Labour). But when it comes to navels, the third painting goes beyond the other two [Figure 2.5]. In it, surrounded by a solid arch, in an archetypical South European cityscape, the middle-aged woman's whole body seems to tremble in layers. There are multiple, almost transparent layers on top of each other, giving her not only three or so pairs of legs and arms, but also a series of navels. What the women with their multiple navels suggest is how intrinsically the formal matters of art, such as layers, contribute to the 'content' or meaning of art. This also confirms that it might be a dead end to try to trace these multiple navels anywhere *outside* the painting process.

In the book *What Painting Is*, James Elkins turns his attention to painting as a material process. He reminds us, for example, that a sky in a painting is never just a sky:

> It is a world of paint, where the airiest clouds are resinous smears, the most verdant field is a compound of rock and oil. The streaming air is not air at all, but tracks left by the brush, and their tufts are no cloudy castles but tiny serrations and crescents where the sticky medium clung to the bristles.
> (Elkins 2000, 195)

What Elkins describes above as a world of painting, as a concentration of paint, energy and material thought, is what Bolt calls the 'work' of art. To access, to experience the smears, tracks, serrations and crescents of paint, and to appreciate the

Work of Painting 53

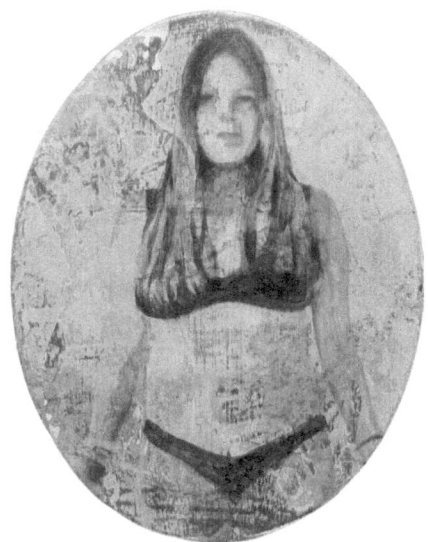

Figures 2.3, 2.4 and 2.5. Paintings with multiple navels (not in scale). Details of *Honest Fortune Teller*, mixed media, 30 x 21 cm, 130 x 70 cm and 150 x 81 cm, Spring 2005. Photographs by Katve-Kaisa Kontturi.

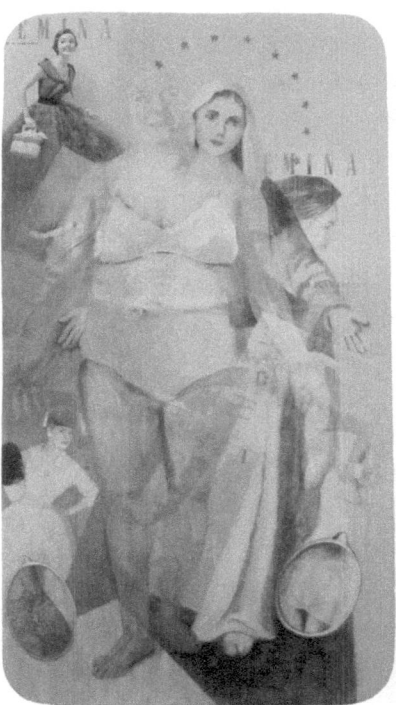
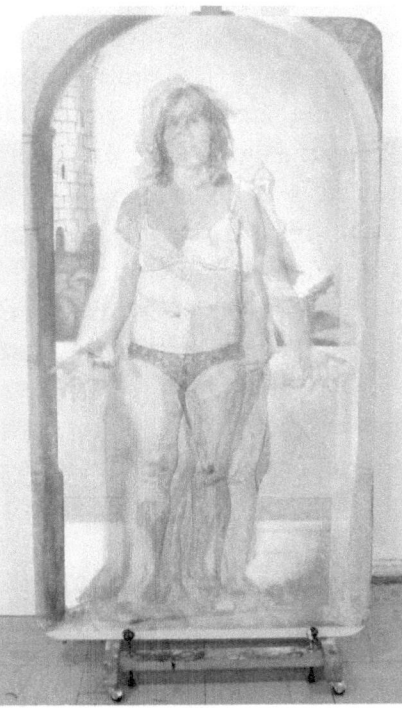

energy, thought, and hours put into work – in other words, the work of painting – it is useful, again, to move from interpretation to encounter. As a way of approaching, interpretation maintains the matter/content divide that the rest of this chapter seeks to surpass. As Gregg Lambert suggests (2007, 14), in interpretation, the work does not speak itself, it is something or someone else that speaks through it. Thus, what is spoken through does not have a say; it merely appears as a neutral medium. Content is understood as being independent of matters that made it (co)emerge. For Simon O'Sullivan (2006a, 1), interpretation is a non-encounter. It does not allow the work of art to work, but diminishes it to an 'object of recognition', to what we already know (for example, about the navels), thereby missing the opportunity to be truly affected by the work of art, by what it can do.

In the Biennale exhibition at the Ars Nova Museum the paintings with multiple navels were displayed (along with over thirty other pieces in Nevado's installation) on the cool white surface of a ceramic tiled wall specifically designed for the pieces. There, the figure and gesture of María Madre de Misericordia was easily recognisable, repeated, as it was, in the paintings, sculptures, figurines: bodies, solemnly standing, their arms wide open – whether in the form of a headless doll with white fluffy angel wings, a work with multiple coats of various pastel shades, flowery wallpapers, or the painted, layered women with which we are already acquainted. This recognisable figure sort of settles the work, renders its materiality less important, and so turns the paintings with multiple navels into objects of recognition. Careful attention to the material-relational becoming of these pieces – for example, in the case of the double navel painting, with its cracking surface hiding multiple, almost swarming, layers of paint – produces uncertainty, perplexity even, antithetical to recognition. This turn of attention allows the work to emerge as something that Deleuze (1994a, 139) calls an 'object of fundamental encounter'. For Deleuze, an object of fundamental encounter forces us to think; it is something that challenges our habitual being in the world (O'Sullivan 2006a, 1). The object of fundamental encounter unsettles one's understandings, bearings. To begin with, the double navel contests the habitual understandings of what is essential to the processes of art-making. As will be discussed in more detail below, it challenges nothing less than the hegemony of semiotic systems and the causal logic of intention.

If Nevado's paintings are conceived of as *works* of art, rather than as artworks, then how they work – that is, how they co-emerge, and how in their co-emergence they bring about something new – must be the focus of the analytical encounter. Whilst the work of art provides a basic conceptual possibility for approaching art in material-relational terms, it also inspires a search for further conceptions. To suggest conceptions sensitive to complexities of the work of art, in which the semiotic and the material do not inhabit separate realms, the rest of the chapter will focus on one painting in its emergence which included both painstakingly long-term phases and intensive spurts. This small oval painting, which among other paintings brought us to the issue of the work of art, provides access to the material-relational action of art-making in which the artist is only *one* actor.

As we have learned above, the emergence of the double navel cannot be attributed to the intentional workings of the artist alone, nor is it a mere sign mediated by means of painting. The focus of what follows is the co-emergence of the double navel, where matter acquires expressive qualities; where it emerges as an active and indispensable participant that scrambles and goes beyond the conventional binaries of painting. In what follows, no image, no sign stands self-sufficient, independent of 'actual textures' of painting that are 'always stamped with the mark of singularity' (Guattari 1995, 38). Thus, beyond unifying and generalising tendencies that uproot signs from their emergence in and through materials, this chapter hopes to attain the intricacies of an art process in which juxtapositions of form and matter, content and expression, and human and non-human continuously collapse. Instead of overpowering or mastering singularities of a material-relational process with socially and institutionally established discourses or approved images of the semiotic canon, I aim to attend to their transformative co-emergence.

Powers of stratification

> Strata are Layers, Belts.
> *Deleuze and Guattari*

To tackle the emergence of the double navel and of the whole painting in and through the layers – that is, the *work* of layers – I will turn to the concept of 'strata', and the practice of 'stratoanalysis' as introduced in Deleuze and Guattari's *A Thousand Plateaus* (1987, 39–74). Whilst 'strata' is nowadays widely employed in social sciences to analyse, for example, the sediments of class, it has its origins in geology, where it refers to rock formations taking shape in layers.[50] The eclectic array of disciplines, including geology and cellular biology, that Deleuze and Guattari draw from in stratoanalysis enables thinking the impersonal and pre-individual singularities out of which human and non-human worlds are constituted (Lorraine 1999, 113–14).[51] The geological term 'strata' is one of the concepts they have deterritorialised to give voice to the non-human in humanity, to show how the non-human takes part in becomings, such as art, often understood as exclusively human.

For Deleuze and Guattari (1987, 40–45, 502–503), there are three major strata that govern the world: the physico-chemical, the organic, and the anthropomorphic. The first can be linked to the organisation of matter, the second with life, and the third with the human (although it is actually never as simple as this).[52] Thus, 'strata' can be understood as that which regulates movement or arrests it into an organic and organised whole, if it does not stop it altogether. No wonder that Deleuze and Guattari (1987, 40) describe it as a belt. The belt holds up, restricts, often squeezing the flesh – but the belt does not eliminate movement altogether; one can still breathe, even eat. However, belts are limited too; they can break and may at some point not have enough holes. Identification, for example, is a form of stratification, as are routines of everyday life and art. A strong identification with something often wipes out the chance for new, possibly transformative directions or connections in one's life and likings; daily routines create patterns that make us focus on what we are used to, leaving no room for surprising, structure-breaking encounters. When something is stratified, it becomes commonplace and easy to communicate. Consequently, what was, above, called 'artwork' – art as an object of recognition and interpretation – is art that is stratified. Work of art, however, escapes the belt of stratification.

Yet stratoanalysis does not look only for organised, stabilised or petrified strata, be they layers of society, signification or of something else.[53] Rather, Deleuze and Guattari explore strata to escape the strata (Goodchild 1996, 156). The strata are never fully closed, there are transversal forces going through them, altering them, changing their course; the molecular, as was suggested in the previous chapter, is insistently, persistently doing its work. Like the molar and the molecular, so too do stratification and destratification always come together. In fact, no strata should be understood as inherently negative. Humans need strata, the world needs strata in order not to collapse into a state of incomprehensible chaos. To put it in more positive terms: 'Stratification is like the creation of the world from chaos, a continual renewed creation' (Deleuze and Guattari 1987, 502).

Stratification plays an important part in the emergence of the double navel painting. The painting process lasted for months, mostly because Nevado was unsatisfied with the earlier layer or phase of the painting, now all but hidden under the present figure of the girl with the double navel [Figure 2.6] (Nevado, 19 December 2004). It was because of this earlier layer, that itself consisted of multiple layers – Nevado had spent many months painting and removing layers, painting again, and overpainting – that the painting experienced long periods of arrest, out of sight, separated from other paintings, all alone on the kitchen wall of Nevado's studio. Nevado felt that at that phase the painting did not have a rhythm (Nevado, 6 March 2005); in other words, it did not have a life of its own. To paraphrase Deleuze's (2003, 86–87) conceptualisation of a similar phase typical in Francis Bacon's art-making, it was all 'given' and nothing new.

At that time, the painting was strongly governed by anthropomorphic strata; by the significance of images or, more precisely, scraps of pinup girls and a painted faceless woman, all in their white smoothing shapewear. The pinup girl in the lower part of the painting was laughing, eyes closed, mouth open, pointing her index finger towards her lips as if to highlight her erotic excitement (at being the focus of the male gaze). Another girl was more bashful, resting her arm close to her face as if to secure her bearings, shyly looking the viewer directly in the eyes. Both figures posed with arms above the chest line, exposing their curvaceous upper bodies tightly controlled by bullet shaped corsets. These fixed figures were perhaps all too recognisable as they are part of popular visual culture nowadays, infinitely reiterated in advertising – 1950s pinup girls at their best. The strong contrasts of light and darkness offered an easy route to interpreting the painting in terms of the good and the bad. A stretch of dark paint crossed the canvas in the middle from top to bottom and another diagonal stretch of black, a shred of lace from cheap underwear, cut the lower part of painting.[54] These black sectors divided the painting into segments. While the pinup girls, with their white 'Pepsodent' smiles, appeared in the well-lit sections, in the middle of the painting, where the double navel girl now poses, was a painted figure of a faceless woman, as if overshadowed by the pinups [Figure 2.6]. This layer, or this phase of the painting, was also exhibited in the installation among a series of newly created holy cards. Each of the holy cards had an accompanying maxim that originated in the daily newspapers that the artist read, and often pointed out the gendered structures of the contemporary world. The maxim on the card showing the pinups and the woman in the shadows read 'Mente estretcha' [narrow conscience], as if highlighting the narrowing work of stratification. The members of the audience could each take a card home, at no cost. The pinup card proved to be the most popular of them all, necessitating several reprints.

In one sense, at that stage, the whole painting was like a worn Marxist feminist maxim, visually declaring that advertising oppresses women, placing 'real women' in the shadow and making them faceless, while celebrating pinup girls eager to please the consumer. As mentioned, it was all given – common and already known – and nothing new, nothing surprising. That is, the painting was stratified, it was stuck. Something was needed to *destratify* the powers of representation and the related possibilities for critical feminist evaluation, so as to push the work towards something new. The solution was partly to be found in what was already there. Even though the strata, the recognisable paper scraps, dominated the painting, as did also the contrasting zones of darkness and light, they were not materially permanent, fixed for good. Like all strata, they held the potential for movement.

Forces of destratification

When I visited Susana Nevado's studio on a Sunday afternoon in late March 2005, Nevado had, so to speak, stood against 'the powers of stratification'. She announced dramatically:

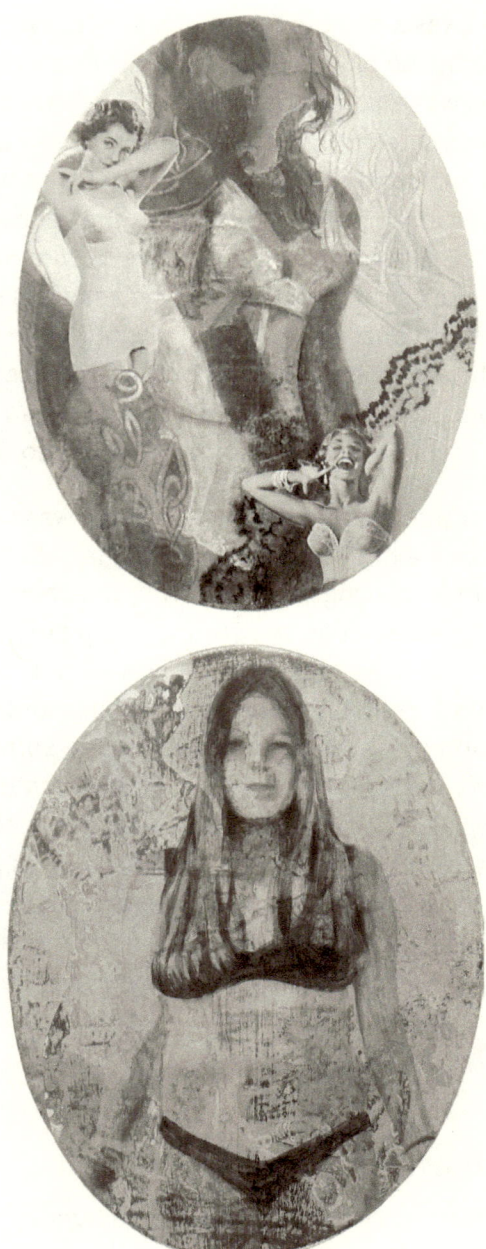

Figures 2.6 and 2.7. The double navel painting and its earlier phase. Details of Susana Nevado's *Honest Fortune Teller*, mixed media, 30cm x 21cm, Spring 2005. Photographs by Katve-Kaisa Kontturi.

> See, I've rubbed this one completely! This is the one
> I've been struggling with. ... Today I came here and
> sandpapered it from top to bottom. It has annoyed me
> so much over time. (Nevado, 20 March 2005)

Nevado had rubbed the painting thoroughly with a coarse sandpaper so that the figures had lost their obvious forms and referentiality; what was once fixed and easy to recognise was now gone. In other words, the destroyed artwork, the object of recognition, gave way to the work of art. The action of rubbing broke the surface of the scraps, paint and varnish, making them more porous, more amenable, more open to new connections.

Before the scrubbing, it was images and their significance in the anthropomorphic strata that governed the painting. This is what Deleuze and Guattari (1983; 1987; Guattari 1995) call the 'imperialism of the signifier', which they consider one of the ruling powers in Western capitalist cultures. What separates the anthropomorphic strata from the other strata is its tendency to govern the others, to impose its own laws and legacies upon everything else (Deleuze and Guattari 1987, 62–63). It behaves like a despot, a twofold despot. As Stephen Zepke puts it, '[s]ignifiance implies the autonomy of meaning from materiality in a seemingly free circulation of signifiers, but this freedom hides another despot, that of the subject' (2005, 120). For the signified–signifier pairing always requires an individual subject that wants to express something.

Nevado's act of rubbing was a way to give up the givens. First, it worked towards getting rid of the easily recognisable signs, such as the pinup girl figures from the 1950s.[55] Second, rubbing was to get rid of painting as a deconstructive, textual activity that plays games with signs within the anthropomorphic strata of signifiance.[56]

The smooth surface or space that resulted from the rubbing connected the paint and the paper scrap figures so intrinsically that they were no longer separate layers. In the heat of intensive rubbing an *inter*strata was born. What happened was that now the physico-chemical strata of the painting, the strata often seen as *sub*strata, as a kind of raw material or ground for meanings to emerge from, connected directly and reciprocally with the anthropomorphic strata, to the semiotics and significance of the painting. In this new-born assemblage 'a semiotic fragment rubs shoulders with a chemical interaction' (Deleuze and Guattari 1987, 69); in other words, '[t]he semiotic components are inseparable from material components and are in exceptionally close contact with molecular levels' (334).

Where the material and the semiotic connect, and are indeed inseparable, and content and form are not in a hierarchical conjunction either. The overcoming of the duality of content and form is part and parcel of what Deleuze and Guattari (1987, 40–72) name 'double articulation'.[57] For them, double articulations form strata. And, as they often do, Deleuze and Guattari first offer an easy explanation of double articulation by separating the first and the second articulation, but then add that beyond this obvious relation there are always more complex connections. Nevertheless, they contend that whereas the first articulation has to do with molecular flows and their ordering, the second offers a more systematic hold and a functional structure, an overcoding, hierarchisation and totalisation (Deleuze and Guattari 1987, 40–43).

It would be tempting to claim that the first articulation is about contents and molecular movement and the second about forms and molarities, or that the articulations would appear in linear format, one after the other. Deleuze and Guattari's trick, however, is to avoid this duality by arguing that strata are not simply constituted of forms and contents, of certain styles and images or figures. Rather, strata consist of content (first articulation) and expression (second articulation). But this is only half of the trick. Deleuze and Guattari further claim that there are not only forms of expression and substances of content but also forms of content and substances of expression. In Brian Massumi's (1992, 152n36) words, 'both content and expression are substance–form complexes'. Or, as Deleuze and Guattari (1987, 91) themselves put it: 'Content is not a signified nor expression a signifier; rather both are variables of the assemblage'. The paint made to form certain figures, for example, is substance of content that is overpowered by a style of painting – a form of expression. Yet, the paint has its form of content too. It has a certain chosen order: it is a certain, known-to-be functional mix of water and minerals, for example.

But the paint can also be matter of content – paint has its chemico-physical potentialities, it is a bundle of indeterminate affects. This 'active' understanding of matter resides only outside the double-pincers of articulation. Thus, in Deleuze and Guattari's vocabulary, matter appears as something that is not chosen, tamed, stratified. However, Guattari's (1995, 59–61) elaborated version of the above-described reversible quadripartite model welcomes matter along, which makes it possible to fashion semiotics beyond signification: a-signifying semiotics. In Guattari's model, matter and form connect directly in what Erin Manning and others call 'immediation' (Manning et al. forthcoming); they do not need the mediation of formed, overpowered matter, that is, substance. This, of course, entails a different understanding of both matter and form, an understanding that stresses their dynamism; matter as material flows and intensities and form as a non-stable 'diagram of a process of becoming' or, rather, as function (Massumi 1992, 14). A-signifying semiotics operates by directly (and definitely non-communicatively) 'transmitting ideas, functions, intensities, or sensations with no need to signify any meaning' (Watson 2008, 8). In a-signifying semiotics, 'form interacts directly on matter'; in other words, there is 'a reciprocal relation between material fluxes and the semiotic machine' (Watson 2008, 8).[58] This is where we have now arrived.

Particle-sign

When Nevado began to paint a new figure on the smooth, thoroughly rubbed, destratified surface, the emerging figure connected directly to the earlier layers of the painting, to the freed flow of matter-meaning particles, of paper scraps, lace, paint, ornamental tattoos, and even brush bristles. This movement had its autonomy; the artist could not possibly take over, master the multiple physico-chemical processes co-involved. At a certain phase, certain material layers reacted to each other, rejected each other, and a particle of pale pink paint from Nevado's brushstroke composing the girl's skin didn't attach to the smooth sandpapered surface and left a gap in the skin. It was through this co-emergence, the *work of painting*, that the girl acquired a double navel [Figure 2.7].

Knowing at least roughly how the double navel emerged triggers suspicion concerning its sign-value. In the palpably porous presence of the painting, the double navel does not stand out as a sign to which meanings could be attached. Instead, the double navel is inextricable from the girl's figure, as well as from the whole painting pregnant with lavish, swarming layers of material-relational action. For example, the pinup girl's once so seductive Pepsodent smile has transformed into a grimace that now gnaws the double navel girl's pink pelvic flesh. The pink painterly skin fuses with the blurred paper scrap figures, with the dense and intense layers of acrylic paint and varnish. There are no longer self-standing layers, no independent representations or signs, but an autopoietic assemblage (Guattari 1995, 108, 115–16) – an assemblage that creates itself in its own movement.[59] In the work of this non-mastering agency of the assemblage, the double navel is not so much a symbol with a general(isable) meaning as it is a singular expression of destratified matter-meaning flows, of the a-signifying *work* of art.

Put differently, the double navel is a particle-sign. Deleuze and Guattari (1987, 142, 145, 224) employ this two-part term in plural form (*particles-signs*) to emphasise its non-unitary becoming through content-matter and form-expression complexes. While appreciating all the pluralities involved, I will stick with the singular, so as to grant the term a clearer conceptual status, and also to make the positive difference between sign (of semiology) and particle-sign more apparent. In this concept, 'particle' stands for material, molecular movement, for the destratified content, and 'sign', for sign-expression, for meaning, but importantly, not in any commonsensical meaning of meaning. 'Sign' in particle-sign does not point towards a signifier, or towards representation. Rather, it has an ontological status, it connects, relates directly to material qualities, to matter in movement. In the particle-sign there is complex indexicality going on. Particle-signs have an existential relation to their referent, 'a real connection' as in C. S. Peirce's (1955, 108–109) definition of the index, which he exemplifies with, among other things, natural-cultural processes such as a barometer indexing rain or a sundial indicating time. Yet to speak of referents is too simple in the case of the double navel as particle-sign, so co-emergent is the double navel with the process of painting. Particle-sign, then, is not something that would dwell on the surface of an artwork as a separate, independent sign; it is an integral part of the material becoming of that work of art – the *work* of painting.[60] As such, particle(s)-sign(s) expresses:

> [d]estratification, a radical break with, or a line of flight from the strata that introduces something new. … [It] will appear in painting both as its destratification, as what escapes the stratifying articulations of content and expression, and as a new reality they construct. No creation without destruction. (Zepke 2005, 122–24)

Whereas in Deleuze's (2003) understanding art emerges only when the given has been destroyed, overcome, my encounter with the work of the double navel painting suggests that both givens and their destruction are essential to creation. *Stuckness*, to which I will return later, is not a failure but a way the work of art works. There would be no double navel without the givens. As Zepke claims, the particle-sign is not only an expression of destratification; it is also a creation, a construction of a new reality.

Against the lack and the lost connections that the single navel signifies, the double navel as particle-sign offers access to the abundance of material-relational movement: to the world of radical immanence where images connect with human bodies directly, without the mediating work of representations – in immediation. This is suggested by that pelvic-flesh-biting pinup girl who resides neither inside nor outside the double navel girl's body but within it, as immanent to it – similarly to the way in which the pose of María Madre de la Misericordia is incorporated into the double navel girl's posing body. Rather than signifying a 'double lack', the double navel as particle-sign points towards an open corporeality where images and various material and symbolic forces directly connect with human bodies, both those modelling and those viewing, in a continuous movement of transformation. Importantly, the double navel breaks the idea of a closed organic whole. As mentioned, the navel has an important role in the organic strata of human life. It reminds of the immediate organic connection there once was with the mother, thus reducing the origin of life to a single point, to the other end of the umbilical cord, that is, the mother. In the case of the double navel girl, we cannot be sure of her origin. The double navel ridicules the laws of organic strata as well as psychoanalysis (as a strata of subjectivation), where, so often, the lost connection to the mother equals lack – the source of anxiety and desire in modern life.

Even though the double navel caught our attention first, it is important to acknowledge that too fixed a focus on it might prevent us from noticing that it is not only the navel but, in fact, the whole stomach area that buzzes, swarms with life. This leads us to feminist debates, and to one of the most disputed arguments of materialist feminism – to women's ability to produce life within them and whether this should be seen as a constraint or as an advantage (see, for example, Firestone 1970; Braidotti 1994). Whilst we know by now that the girl in the painting has just become a mother, this is not what the painting suggests. Rather than expressing a molar becoming, the painting of the double navel girl that emerges through multiple layers, connections, offers us a sensation of how an embodied, radically immanent subjectivity works. The figure of 'the girl' fascinates Deleuze and Guattari (1987, 276–77), and for good reason: '[G]irls do not belong to an age group, sex, order, or a kingdom: they slip everywhere, between orders, acts, ages, sexes; they produce n molecular sexes on the line of flight in relation to the dualism machines they cross right through. ... The girl is like a block of becoming that remains contemporaneous to each opposite term, man, woman, child, adult'.[61]

In this sort of becoming, the human turns out to be more-than-human and the material and the meaningful coalesce directly, contemporaneous with each other: holy women, pinup girls, posing models, rhythmic brushstrokes, acrylic paint, varnish, and the shred of black lace all work 'on the same level as the real' (Deleuze and Guattari 1987, 141). The double navel painting invites reconsideration of the relevance of navel-gazing, meaning 'sign-gazing' or interpretation that so often involves making molar and moral judgments. Instead, with its vital layers that intensively extend beyond the double navel itself, the painting calls for attending to the molecular action of art. This kind of (r)evolutionary politics of painting is underpinned by the material-relational dynamics embodied in the concept of particle-sign.

In this chapter, the double navel painting has enabled rethinking of the process of art-making beyond the mastering hold of the artist and the juxtaposition of the material and the meaningful.

The conceptual suggestions of 'work of painting' and 'particle-sign' are products of neither art alone nor theory only – they have co-emerged through a zigzag movement between the two. Thus they inherently possess a quality of movement, and respect for it too. Both concepts allow the process of emergence to have *some* agency of its own, not reducible to the maker or to the power of hegemonic discourses or imageries but taking form in changing relations. This is not an individualist sort of predetermined agency, but, rather, an open co-agency, agencement. As a concept, work of painting calls for attending to the process of painting in pragmatic terms: how does the painting do what it does, how does it do its work? Particle-sign, for its part, is a more specific concept that draws attention to the way any sign is the product of a material process. What the two-part composition of the concept points out is the sign's indexical, material-relational co-emergence with the matters of art-making. These concepts – not painting but the *work* of painting, and not a sign but *particle*-sign – allow us, beg us, to appreciate art as a specific critical process of its own kind, where transformative thinking, new worlds and ways of being co-emerge through working with materials, relating them to each other, allowing them to collaborate. As concepts that enable more complex manners of perceiving art processes, in their material-relational wealth, and given the value of their specificities and capabilities, work of painting and particle-sign might open up possibilities for further collaborations between art and theory. For collaborations surely are more efficient if both parties are valued, encountered in their complexity.

Co-workings

3

Impersonal Connections

Artist Susana Nevado's studio has a special role in this and the following two chapters: it is where most of the words and practices analysed across the chapters were originally spoken, carried out, encountered, and recorded. This studio was one of the rare spaces built for that specific purpose in her then hometown of Turku. For years, this quiet, backyard facing space, in the city centre, on the fifth floor of a pinkish early twentieth-century apartment building, was most dear to the artist and of utmost importance to her art in-the-making (although by now, of course, the studio has been converted into a luxury apartment). Nevado's studio had a wall of windows, allowing light to fill the space even on the darkest days of the year. Its walls were painted white and carried marks of the work executed on them, thin lines revealing the shapes and colours of paintings painted. The floor was tiled with olive linoleum, which had been smeared with sprays and splashes of paint over the decades. It had tables of different heights covered with jars of brushes, pencils and paint, piles of material, magazines, paper scraps, books, and a collection of well-used chairs as well as an old wooden easel where some of the works discussed in the following chapters were displayed. The studio had a small kitchen too, just off the main area. This is where the double navel painting encountered in the previous chapter was stored, 'arrested', for a long time. My fascination with the space coincides with the challenge it poses to understandings of the artist's studio as a private space exclusively dedicated to lonely creation (see, for example, Jones 1996; Elkins 2000; Chare 2006, 85). Instead, Nevado's studio turned out to be a veritable theatre of multiple collaborations – but, as we will learn, of an impersonal rather than of a simply social kind.[62]

From my very first visits to Nevado's studio it was clear that the place was anything but a closed space of mysterious creation. For example, on Friday 7 March 2003, the studio was filled with vivid discussion, as besides me was present an artist with whom Nevado was going to travel to Madrid, Spain to hold a group exhibition. We were at the studio to get acquainted and to discuss their exhibition before taking off for five intensive days together. The artists explained how they decided upon the theme of the exhibition, *Azafrán* [Saffron], and what were the benefits and downsides of working together. Moreover, the theme of collaboration emerged when Nevado's colleague asked me to tell about my research project. I explained how my technique was to 'collaborate' rather than only observe the artists working, meaning that it was critical for me to stay open to their viewpoints and ways of doing – also, I was happy to help, discuss, and even model, I could add retrospectively. When Nevado asked if I was going to focus on the social dynamics of artistic practice I answered that I was more interested in the emergence and workings of the art process itself, which is not, of course, separable from the socio-political setting. The artists then turned to discussing how important it was for them to reflect on their working process with someone else, to force themselves to interact about their doings – thus clarifying the need to break the solitude and isolation of studio practice.

Whilst Nevado's colleague simply said that she would like to have 'some kind of mentor or supervisor you had when you were graduating from school', Nevado stressed reciprocity as a principle:

> It indeed helps me if I've worked at the studio many weeks by myself, and an outsider suddenly comes around. I tell [her], I've been thinking, it doesn't work in this way ... Her eyes are different [from mine as] she hasn't stared at the work for the two weeks ... Reciprocity, it is always important. (Nevado, 7 March 2003)

Practically every conversation I had with Nevado over the years that I followed her projects (2003–2005) touched at some point upon the issue of collaboration. Whether it was about getting a colleague's professionally valuable opinion, or a family member's sometimes awkward, even disappointing view on something – as in the case of reworking the Catholic figure of María Madre de Misericordia (Nevado, 5 December 2004),[63] or what someone had said on television or written in a newspaper, my material shows that studio-working in no way separated her from the world; quite the opposite. Many kinds of people continually entered her art-making: there were people, like me, who visited her studio rather regularly, while others connected via emails, phone calls, through the social media, art books and catalogues, for example. In this sense, collaboration was not just one passing theme but was vital to the way she carried out art-making. But then, even if there were people coming and going, Nevado's works of art were still, in practice, made single-handedly by her; very seldom did anyone else touch the works in progress. And even in the case of group exhibitions, it was mostly only in the beginning of the process and when hanging the exhibition that the artists met, and not during the art-making process.

Beyond individuality and identification

To think about this juxtaposition, or a continuum of collaboration and individual authorship, let us consider some basic assumptions of feminist art criticism. The claim that art-making is

not a 'free-enterprise conception of individual achievement' but
an act of multiple collaborations has been one of the founding
arguments of feminist art research since it was expressed in
Linda Nochlin's (1971) essay, 'Why Have There Been No Great
Women Artists?' In the art world, collaboration is, of course, not
only, but still strongly, a feminist issue, exercised both in theory
and practice (see, for example, Stein 1994; Jones 2005). For
instance, the exhibition *Together, Again: Women's Collaborative
Art + Community*, organised at the Brooklyn Art Museum in the
summer of 2008, brought together the collective work of feminist
art across generations. According to the curator, Carey Lovelace
(2008), one of the constitutive ideas of the exhibition was that
'feminist art laid the groundwork for' artist teams and groups
that have recently become increasingly popular by 'challenging
ideas about authorship, particularly the myth of the solo male
artist'. The exhibition pursued a celebration of this activist
movement, which shook the ways of art-making through the
1970s and 1980s, as shown in the touring feminist exhibitions
Global Feminism: New Directions in Contemporary Art (2007) and
WACK: Art and the Feminist Revolution (2007–2008). Feminism was
indeed a strong factor when artistic collaboration – making art
together in *collectives*, to share ideas, processes and authorship
– became a creative first choice as well as a political act for many
women (Stein 1994, 226). Lovelace (2008), however, notes that
collaboration did not always take place in concrete collectives;
feminist artists also exercised collaboration on what she calls
an imaginary plane. As an example of this she mentions Miriam
Schapiro's *Collaboration Series* that includes works such as *Mary
Cassatt and Me*, a painting 'femmage' that has a section of Mary
Cassatt's impressionistic painting copied in it. The work connects
two women painters of different times, creating an empowering
genealogy of women's art-making. The theme of copied paintings
reminds us how everyday life in homey surroundings both
restricted art-making and gave it a subject. On the other hand,
Schapiro's quilt-like working method connects the piece to the

long tradition of handicraft. Thus, for Schapiro, collaboration meant connections with preceding art-makers; valuing and paying homage to their work.[64]

Thalia Gouma-Peterson (1997, 37), who has written extensively on Schapiro's art, highlights the importance of collaboration in her art-making processes. Although Gouma-Peterson understands collaboration clearly in human terms, that is, as collaboration with other people, with other women, her descriptions often go beyond personal contacts, connecting women unknown to each other (see also Stein 1994, 228). She writes, for example, about double collaborations – stressing the fact that there were not only other women artists that Schapiro worked with but also anonymous women who had made the materials used in the artworks, such as doilies. When writing about Schapiro's *Collaboration Series: Mother Russia*, she goes even further in arguing for what could be called material collaborations. After listing various contacts, including collaborations between modernist Russian women artists of the 1920s, Schapiro's admiration of Sonia Delaunay's art, her family ties to Russia, and also the Russian revolutionary movement's link to American feminism, Gouma-Peterson contends that 'equally important was the central position that these women gave to fabric as part of an original and empowering formal language of their work' (Gouma-Peterson 1997, 39).

Although feminist art criticism traces the term 'collaboration' beyond its most customary sense and questions the idea of individual authorship, collaboration nevertheless remains largely person-oriented. This is quite striking, given that individualism is a key target of feminist criticism. My aim in this chapter is to combine feminist postulations of collaboration with Deleuze and Guattari's philosophy of the impersonal (cf. Neimanis 2012, 216–17). For collaboration is not always, and in fact is rarely, a direct exchange between two or more people, let alone between self-sufficient individuals. To claim that Miriam Schapiro collaborated with Mary Cassatt, anonymous doily-makers, and with a league of Russian modernists, or Susana Nevado with her artist boyfriend or with Antoni Tàpies, whose work she admires, pushes us towards a more complex and perhaps also more accurate image of the creative process than if one just insisted on independent creation. However, drawing straightforward connections between two or more individuals undermines the complexity of material-relational co-workings: 'Invoking causalities that are too general or are extrinsic ... is as good as saying anything' (Deleuze and Guattari 1987, 283).

In order to approach collaboration in its material-relational complexity, it is important to be as precise as possible, and ask – especially when it is obvious that the collaborators in question have not even met in person – what form and substance their contact takes. Looking too far afield or imagining what cannot be known might not get us far. For example, one of Susana Nevado's key collaborators is Antoni Tàpies. According to our discussions, it was on the walls of the Reina Sofia museum of contemporary art in Madrid that Nevado got closest to Tàpies' painting (Nevado, 21 January 2005). And this connection was at its most intimate when Nevado's haptically trained eyes followed the ways of brush-working in Tàpies' paintings. However, even then this intimate contact was affected, if not interrupted, by the institutional and socio-cultural situation in which the encounter took place: for example, by the hand and brush of a museum conservator, or by the light setting, or by the alarm system's determining the distance from which the work could be viewed. Moreover, this connection was affected by the educational and social circumstances that define the movement of the artist's body; the way the artist has been trained to work with brush affects what she can see and feel, and, taking the discussion further, so does the bare fact that her access to the institutions of art – schools, galleries and museums – might be limited by the class system, the country she lives in, or even by her gender.

This more complex setting lurks behind the connection between Schapiro and her collaborators, that Gouma-Peterson (1997, 39) construes with the verb 'to identify': according to Gouma-Peterson, Schapiro identifies herself with the Russian women artists of the 1920s.[65] Yet at the end of her analysis Gouma-Peterson reminds us that it was what these women *did* – how they connected to fabric, how they used it in their art – that was the more precise point of connection (Gouma-Peterson 1997, 40). Put differently, the technical and material handlings, ways of relating to the material, open up collaborations beyond the influence of and identification with given individuals. This is not to deny anyone's authorship, but to pay attention to the singular situations and creative events that these entanglements produce. It is only at first sight that these complex connections appear as personal.

Intensive connections

During the dozens of hours I spent with Nevado, chatting about her on-going art processes, she not only mentioned many artists she regards highly, but also eloquently described works she had been struck by. These enthusiastic, fervent words about the works and working methods of certain artists are my clues in following the material-relational collaborations in her painting processes.

One striking encounter she described was with Bill Viola's video-installation at Bilbao's Guggenheim Museum. The work was so astonishing, so technically perfect, so graciously exhibited that it almost made her burst into tears and gasp for breath (Nevado, 3 August 2004). Similarly, she described Damien Hirst's *Adam and Eve* installation in Tate Modern, London, as so palpably real that she could feel the wax bodies of the displayed figures vibrating under the hospital gowns (Nevado, 18 April 2004). Another bodily encounter was with Richard Wilson's *20:50* installation at the

Saatchi Gallery, where a lake of sump oil reflected the gallery's ceiling. The reflection and the iron structures of the space created a corporeal sense of the oil and its presence (Nevado, 6 June 2004). There was also the Antoni Tàpies exhibition at the Museo Reina Sofia, Madrid, that captivated her, along with some impressive old masters' works with their handling of fabric that she studied at the Prado for her *Honest Fortune Teller* installation (Nevado, 21 January 2005).

Yet not once did Nevado say that she identified with a certain artist, or that someone's work had a direct influence on hers. She did not make any causal connections between her work and that of her 'collaborators'.[66] As if against this kind of discourse, Nevado seemed to avoid drawing such lines. Instead, she fed my interest with sensations of fascinating *works* of art. What Nevado expressed was a collectivity of an impersonal sort.

If Nevado's descriptions of her encounters with other artists' works of art touch upon anything in Gouma-Peterson's (1997) take on (Miriam Schapiro's) feminist collaborations, it is the quick reference to the 'position that these women gave to fabric as part of an original and empowering formal language in their work' (Gouma-Peterson 1997, 40). For Nevado was primarily interested in the works of art, in the working techniques and material choices, rather than in the artists themselves. Intriguingly, she also described the bodily sensations of crying and gasping that the works of art induced in her – sensations that had to do with 'the formal language in their work'. She underlined the connection between technical eminence and bodily sensations by first praising the technical skills and then immediately summing up her sensations. For example, in the case of Bill Viola's work, she praised it as 'almost perfect in technical execution – so moving' (Nevado, 3 August 2004).

Nevado's descriptions call for a notion of collaboration that takes into account the material-relational execution of art. I propose the concept of 'technico-intensive' to account for this connection: the works of art as technico-intensive processes are, after all, what is most intimate in these artists' encounters. Intensity, as it is understood here, is the material-relational movement of art that cannot be quantified. It is not a question of measurable mass, weight or length, but of qualities that can only be felt. Technico-intensive might, then, seem a contradiction in terms. For technical details are often thought to be the measurable and thus also reproducible elements in artworks. Here, however, the technical is heretically understood as being inseparable from the intensities that the work produces. This relates to Gilbert Simondon's (2005) understanding of the technical as a mode that contests a normative, technocratic and human-centred stance. For Simondon, technology does not refer to human control over nature or matter, and technological innovativeness is not all about human abilities: rather, a technical innovation owes its emergence to the potential of the force fields brought together through human collaboration (see Massumi 2009b, 40). The force of the technical, then, is by nature more intensive than extensive.

When an encounter between two artists is technico-intensive it works beyond representation: what moves from one work to another are not symbols or images represented in a new work of art; nothing recognisable is directly *extended* to another work of art.[67] Rather, works are connected at the level of intensities of a working process. A particular atmosphere, sensation, individuation is what they might share. For example, when I enquired of Nevado if it bothered her that Antoni Tàpies frequently used sexualised, even sexist symbols in his art, she quite easily bypassed the subject. It did not have that much importance for her. She did not care about the vulgar visuality of high heels, slender legs, and penises carved into the matter of the canvas; she said that they belonged to the cultural context and that was that. Instead, she was fascinated with the intensive materiality of his paintings: bold strokes of paint as well as very delicate ones, canvases sometimes handled gently and sometimes ripped, torn apart, and all this inseparably connected to a variety of material objects, such as kitchen chairs and a washboard, and block letters, and those always powerful earthly colours. Above all, it was Tàpies' painting practice that she was drawn to, how he related, *connected* things – in an intensive manner (Nevado, 21 January 2004).

As might be obvious, none of Tàpies' symbols mentioned above – high heels, women's legs, or penises – found their way into Nevado's work. If anything changed in her painting, it was that more and more different kinds of materials were allowed to connect to it, to co-create a unique, intensive constellation. At the time of our discussion, she was working on a new materially-relationally rich project that combined, layered multiple materials including a series of photographs of her daughter shedding her milk teeth, and various text extracts, with the spices, turmeric and saffron, that she painted with (see Chapter 7). In this way, Tàpies connected to Nevado's works through the particular technical process of painting based on an intensive layering of materials, and not via recognisable symbols.

In this setting, Nevado's collaborative art-making is not reducible to concrete collaboration between humans. It is a rendez-vous of material-corporeal rhythms and intensive connections beyond the symbolic.[68] Nevado's reluctance to describe her collaborations in terms of identification and causal connections finds an ally in Brian Massumi's criticism of collectivity in (postmodern) cultural studies. For Massumi, cultural studies correctly realises that all expression is collective. However, he also claims that cultural studies 'takes the collectivity as already constituted, as a determinate set of actually existing persons'; thus, 'it misses the impersonal or overpersonal excesses of ongoing transformation' (Massumi 2002b, 253).[69] It is these excesses, I believe, that Nevado was dealing with when she avoided making direct causal connections between herself and her collaborators.[70]

This complex, 'non-direct' and impersonal concept of collaboration relates to Deleuze and Parnet's discussion of 'proper names' (such as 'Tàpies' or 'Nevado'): '[A proper name] does not designate a person or a subject. It designates an effect, a zigzag, something which passes or happens between two as though under a potential difference' (2002, 5). A proper name, then, is in itself movement, a contact or collective rather than a person to be identified, a petrified block of characteristics. Barbara Bolt expresses this concern by putting artists' names in quotation marks. She claims that what we know, recognise, identify as 'Ana Mendieta' or 'John Constable' is the specificity of the particular material process, 'a material work that is a work of art' (Bolt 2004a, 153). Importantly, this argumentation against identifications is not intended as moralising or condemning. As James Williams puts it: *'It is inevitable that you will identify the other but you must seek to show how this identification is illusory'* (Williams 2003, 209, emphasis in original). The agenda, then, is not to label causal connections, not to name them, but to study the action emerging between complexities which are often reduced to names.[71]

This collective zigzag setting proposes a more open model of contact and encounter than the dynamics of identification and representation that are caught in what already exists as a more or less solid formation. To put this open understanding of co-working in more practical terms, let us review Nevado's way of painting as it has unfolded in this chapter and in the previous one: in the work of painting, signs or symbols do not enter the emerging work of art as such. Connections are established at the level of process and action, through strokes, lines, colours, technicalities, sensations, intensities, and chemical reactions. As we will see in the following chapters, Nevado speaks about this repeatedly. For her, movement precedes representation.

In contrast to Gouma-Peterson's imaginary plane of contact and connection, Nevado's painting process suggests an immanent plane of composition. This is where forces both exceeding and pre-existing the personal and subjective linger. This plane is also the 'collaborative' condition of art-making: it is 'a decentred spatiotemporal "organization", a loose network of works, techniques, and qualities', where all works of art, genres, styles, forms *indirectly* influence each other (Grosz 2008, 70). This plane is not separate from the studio where Nevado works, but neither is it restricted by its walls and objects: rather, the plane takes up, intensifies what the studio offers and elaborates working as a connective 'tissue' not reducible to its parts. The material and technical forces that meet on this plane may seem very distant in terms of time and place – but this is only when they are too tightly connected to certain individuals and to their specific spatio-temporal situations. If measured with the socio-political coordinates of the art world or by counting the kilometres that separate the two artists for most of the time, Susana Nevado's collaboration with Tápies would seem a veritable impossibility, or at least highly improbable. However, if their connection is not understood extensively and concretely but impersonally and technico-intensively, then, a co-working may well have occurred.

4

Autonomy of Process

In Nevado's studio, works sometimes get stuck. There is no movement in the painting, no rhythm, everything is just too stiff, obvious. And when something is stuck, it has to be moved somehow, to get the work going – to work on its own. But being stuck is not exactly non-action. It has its own sensuous quality: the feeling of being stuck can be so absolutely irritating, frustrating, that it calls for, invites action. In his account of Francis Bacon's work, Deleuze (2003, 99) calls this phase 'preparatory work'. Paintings at this stage are often figurative, filled with figurative givens. Deleuze (2003, 87) describes this as the feeling of being encircled, besieged by photographic illustrations, newspaper narratives, by cinema and television images, by psychic and physical clichés, a whole league of ready-made perceptions, memories and phantasms. In Deleuze-Bacon, it is these clichés that have to be destroyed, so that the act of painting can begin (Deleuze 2003, 87–88, 99). In Nevado's painting this is when given images come into the picture again: they are used to move images that are stuck.

When I visited Nevado's studio in late January 2005, a big painting had been lifted up onto a table, and it was overlaid with fashion magazine covers. The stack of dusty, faded, 1950s magazines that Nevado found had been put to use. I easily recognised the figure underneath: it was me, in my black and pink underwear, posing as María Madre de Misericordia. My field notes indicate that Nevado was compelled to act as she sensed that the painting was too stiff, too self-evident – it was not working (Nevado, 23 January 2005). She introduced the magazines onto the painting to get something to happen.

> I've thrown a lot of stuff over you, all these magazines ... I'll glue the magazines, and let's see what happens then ... It'll change – I began to think that maybe it's better that I'll break it right now – that it [would] not be so obvious an image any more. And then we go on, see what happens. Later, this might become anything whatsoever. (Nevado, 23 January 2005)

Although they were surely her hands that moved the bits and pieces around and fixed them onto their chosen places, Nevado's words indicate that she did not know what would happen next and, consequently, neither did she know where the process would end up: 'this might become anything whatsoever'. This uncertainty and vagueness in Nevado's expression was something that I found difficult to understand back then. So badly did I want to know what was going on, to get a grasp of the project, that I was persistent and repetitive in my questions concerning Nevado's role: what was she planning to do next and why. I obviously had not yet found my way of following – I was stuck too, with habitual understandings of the role of the artist and ways of making. Time after time, Nevado patiently gave me the same answer: it was hard to say exactly what was happening and even harder to say what might happen. After a fair amount of repetition, it struck me: all this referred to the autonomy of process. It was Nevado who initiated the process, but then, so to speak, the process had to take a course of its own.[72] In this light, it was practically an impossibility for her to describe precisely what was going on; at least nothing beyond a yearning for motion. But there is more to this: it is hard to speak about issues for which there is no vocabulary, and that was

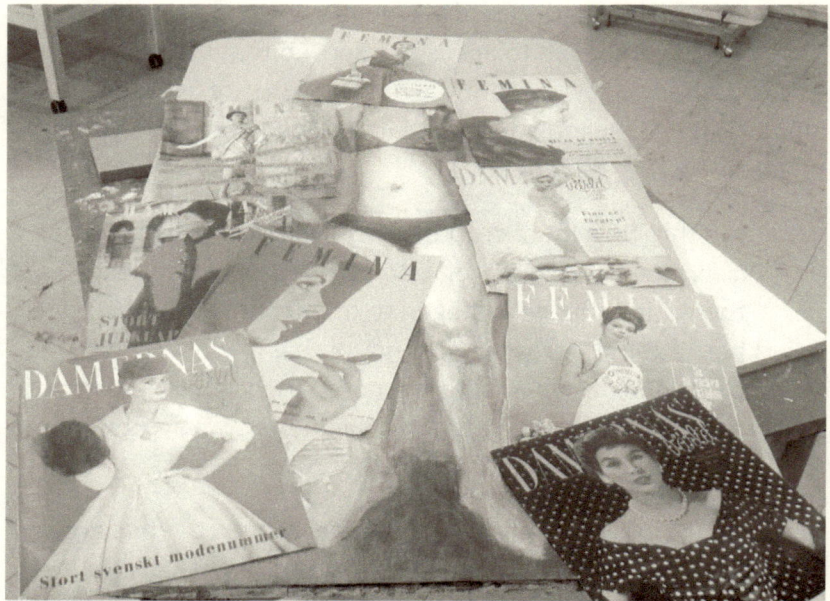

Figure 4.1. A painting covered with magazines. *Honest Fortune Teller* installation progress, January 2005. Photograph by Katve-Kaisa Kontturi.

what was going on with the singularity and unpredictability of process she was dealing with. Maybe, then, we should do what Deleuze (2003, 99) suggests: listen more closely to what painters have to say. Maybe, when we listen closely enough, attentively following the ebbs and flows, the vocabulary of process will start to build itself up.

Material images, painterly qualities

The painting covered with magazine covers had been stuck for a while. A month before, we were standing by it when Nevado said:

> Don't be afraid at all … It is now stuck in a bad way … I should get that motion into it, something like [I've done] here, to put two or three [images], to have many [of them] as if at the same [place], so that it would move more. (Nevado, 5 December 2004)

Again, images to move an image. And there was another similar case – again a woman in her underwear. That one had been stuck for a long time too, caught in the striking black and yellow, and there was a crucifix that dominated way too much. The tactic was the same: it needed an image, something, right there, to make it not so obvious anymore, 'almost whatever images' just to be left there, for quite a while, for weeks maybe (Nevado, 23 January 2005). What catches the attention here is that Nevado did not say a word about the contents of the images she worked with to get the paintings to move. Clearly, then, whether the images were clichés, 'givens' (as in the case of those magazine covers), or not, it was not what they represented that mattered; was important. Instead, it was all about very concrete things, images, two, three or many, in the same place. Just images, projected slides, scraps, whatever. As she said when working with an earlier project: I want 'to paint a little there, add some layers, and to see what happens then' (Nevado, 22 May 2004).

In Nevado's work of painting, then, images are not useless, only there to be destroyed, although their representational role does not have much value at this stage. It is the material process, not the representational one, that Nevado focuses on during the process of making. To emphasise the importance of materiality, images should here be understood as pictures, not only as symbolic or representational images but as 'complex assemblages of virtual, material, and symbolic elements' (Mitchell 2005, xiii). Maybe, when understood as pictures, images are easier to conceive of as being equal to any other material elements of art-making, and not above the others in their 'superior' realm of signification. In Nevado's painting, images as pictures are not only virtual images, or ideas inscribed into the matter of the work of art; they are themselves of moving, doing matter. For example, when Nevado asserts that what images do – 'what would happen then' – is not in her hands, she refers to some level of autonomy, to a material agency of their own. Here images as pictures are not clichéd objects, givens that communicate something. Rather, they are material collaborators, co-workers in the creation of a work of art; they move the process precisely because of their material(-agential) capacities – as in the emergence of the double navel in the project *Honest Fortune Teller*. Yet this does not mean that pictures had no representational value to Nevado; surely they were chosen thematically in the beginning. It is only that in a certain phase of the process their material purpose became more prominent, stronger than their representational function.

Even when Nevado describes the images she uses, she does so in the material terms of the 'haptic' rather than in terms of what they visually represent or contain. Haptic, according to Deleuze and Guattari, who derive it from art historian Alois Riegl's thinking, is connected to 'close-range' vision: it 'invites the assumption that the eye itself may fulfil ... the non-optical function' (1987, 492). Hapticity, then, designates the specific function of touch unique to the sight itself.[73] Deleuze and Guattari remind us that '[a] painting is done at close range' (1987, 493). At close range, what can be seen and felt are volumes, textures, colours, contrasts. It is only from a distance that representations can be recognised. In Nevado's painting processes, images as representations never come first. Representations are not privileged: like all the other materials – the paint, varnish, brush(work) – images appear, rather, as yet another set of material particles.[74] When beginning a painting for an exhibition titled *60°27'06"N 22°16'38"E* at the Wäinö Aaltonen Museum (hereafter WAM exhibition), Nevado explained:

> The starting point, was ... in the beginning, that there'll be a kind of contrast ... But I don't know how that will evolve. I found old postcards of a church in Mallorca. A very frilly kind of a picture of these angels. Everything that has to do with Catholic religion, [has] an overabundance of stuff: gold, statues, and stuff ...

> So, the starting point would be this picture. I've visited this cathedral, but I haven't seen this [painting] ... This is just at an early stage; it might be that these [angel figures] will go away and text will appear. The idea would be that there's a lot and that it would be simple. (Nevado, n.d. August 2003)

What comes first is not images but something even more abstract and yet still a material partaker: the *contrast* – a resonance between different elements in painting. It is frilliness relating to the visual-haptic plenitude, 'an overabundance of stuff', that is the most important thing, not which angels are present, whom they represent, or which Bible stories they reference – Nevado had no idea about these issues during the process. These aesthetic qualities could, of course, be given a symbolic meaning: the visual richness, 'a lot', 'an overabundance of stuff', could refer to the wealth and power of the Catholic Church (and through that even to the Crusades and imperialism and other forms of white robbery and violence perhaps). However, during the process of making, these elements are treated principally as haptic, painterly qualities.

Consequently, the idea that there would be 'a lot and that it would be simple' is a painterly idea, that is, an idea connected to a material-relational process of painting in the making. It is a matter of painterly expression that there should be 'a lot' even though it should be 'simple' too. Remarkably, the completed, exhibited painting still had the angel figures, but the way they were painted did not render them recognisable: gold and brown shades folding, merging into each other, the brushstrokes blurring the scene rather than shaping the figures clearly. Yet, paradoxically perhaps, it was these painterly qualities and the material action of images that had made the blurred figures, representations if you like, emerge.

The painterly way of making sketched above does not entail Nevado's brushing aside the symbolic altogether. It is just that the painterly elements are prioritised during the working process. Replying once again to my insistent question about what it was that advanced a certain painting, in this case the black and yellow portrait just mentioned, Nevado explained:

> There are many stages [in the process]. For example, when I started the first [painting], I wanted to have some kind of colour there. And then when I had that colour, I needed to get some texture there … I had painted some decorative details up there, and I wanted to start with that … I was wondering what kind of solutions I can make now, when there's no contrast at all although there is transparency. Then I thought that these colours should change altogether … I began to change [the colour of] the drapery, and the first thing after I changed that I had to change the [colour of the] body then, and then that of the bra too.
>
> Then I wanted something that would be in front of everything, so that the [figure of a] woman would be behind, and the body on a different layer, and then I wanted a layer again before everything else … and then … yet another layer.
>
> The fourth layer I wanted was these underpants I've put here. These were once bought from a so-called sex shop; I got them as a gift. I was thinking, I'm painting fabric [clothing], and putting that fabric [there too]. Why not?! Of course, underwear is, or how do you say, knickers, it is a symbol too, I don't know if it'll be too kitsch. It's somehow a funny idea that a painting has pants. [Laughs.] Suddenly I thought of them as a bit of a joke. There should be a bit of humour. Then, they

[the knickers] produce quite a lot of contrast. That red [colour]. (Nevado, 23 January 2005)

Whereas Nevado begins with the painterly qualities of colour, texture, contrast and transparency, she is not unaware of, and does not deny, the symbolic value of underwear. Also, there are many recognisable figures in the painting – in the middle, a woman in underwear, María de Misericordia's cape on her shoulders, a Catholic sacred heart pierced by swords, the head of a woman with a 1960s hairstyle sneaking in the upper corner, and two stickers of girls in historical outfits – but these do not appear in Nevado's description of the process. What has relevance here is the rhetorical order of her argument: she both begins and concludes her discussion with the painterly details of texture, contrast and colour, whereas symbolic value is only touched upon in the middle of her description [Figures 4.2 and 4.3]. She is a bit worried about the knickers being too kitschy, and then talks about the humour they introduce, but finally closes saying that the red colour offers the desired painterly contrast.[75]

Describing the process, Nevado speaks about layers, in layers. There is the knickers layer, one she wanted to add where the arm is, then an extra layer, and still one layer more. But these layers are not in hierarchical order; there are no higher or lower layers in terms of value. They simply add *motion*, density, intensity. They make the work of art move, live. Nevado's role is to assist in this, to collaborate. The connectedness of layers – their collaboration – is also present: a change in one layer often calls for a change in the other layers too. Images do not work alone; there are no images as such, images in themselves, nor are there 'more material' elements that mediate somehow more virtual images, ideas. What these layers create is not an iconographic puzzle, a problem to be solved, but an event in which painterly elements form new agencement, which can, of course, later attain representational significance.

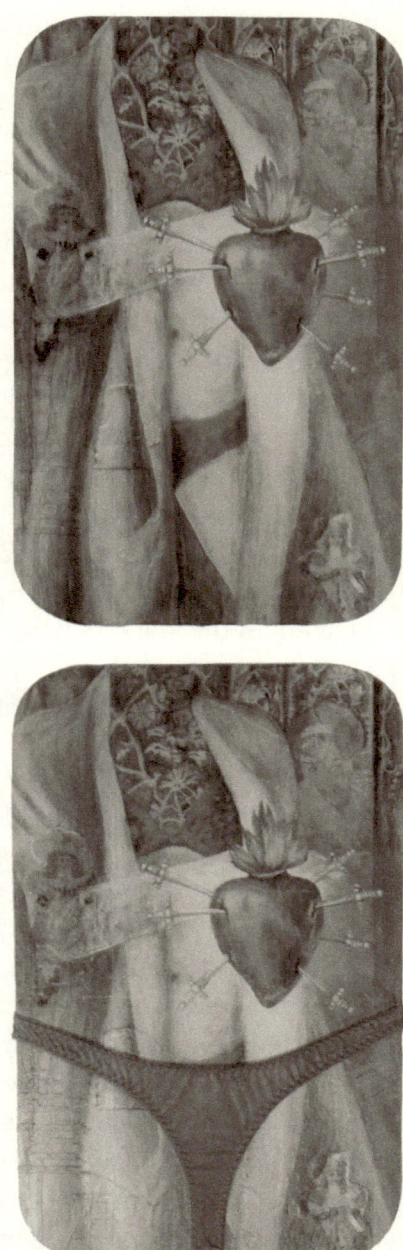

Figures 4.2 and 4.3. Painterly contrast: a painting with and without panties. Details of *Honest Fortune Teller*, 67cm x 38cm, Spring 2005. Photographs by Katve-Kaisa Kontturi.

Ideas in change

In the essay 'Painting the Voice of Grain', Brian Massumi (2006, 201–13) approaches Bracha L. Ettinger's hazy, drifting, spectre-like paintings in their materiality and attends to their events of emergence. Like Nevado, Ettinger uses images, photographs, in her painting processes, where faces and figures become unrecognisable. Massumi's observations resonate with Nevado's way of painting: during the making of the works the symbolic meaning of the images plays hardly any role. Ettinger's working method of stopping a photocopier in the middle of the copying process, which leads to messy copies on the move, is a major force in her art-making: when the beads of ink have no time to fasten, the copy is suspended in its becoming. The work, however, is not trapped in the binary of copy and original. Instead, the act of stopping the machine, intervening in its usual procedure, creates a space for something beyond the binary, still haunting the logics of representation and meaning-production. In this process, Ettinger relinquishes 'her painterly will' (Manning and Massumi 2014, 60). While the will is gone, painterly qualities gain power, taking over the artist's ideas.

In Ettinger's project, this deliberate, yet gentle destruction of recognisable representations, that leaves the images hovering, wafting in a state of material becoming, connects to her conceptual creation of matrixial borderspace. The 'matrixial' refers to the womb, to the intrauterine, but also more generally to a connective tissue, organic and inorganic alike, where meanings dwell in their incipiency. That is, not in a symbolic or identifiable form, but in their material, molecular and transsubjective phase. This makes for an interesting comparison – and companion – to Nevado's image-filled painting processes, which we have come to see in material-relational terms rather than simply as symbolic motion: in terms of colour, resonance, contrast, texture. What Massumi claims about Ettinger's works holds true in Nevado's case too: 'as the artistic process wends it[s] way toward the gallery, toward exhibition, it begins to reconnect with existing systems of reference: symbolic and discursive systems such as myth, philosophy, art theory, psychoanalysis, and any number of others' (2006, 210). There are phases in the process of making, in the process of painting, where symbolic and discursive systems do not count – but then titles are often needed, a press release must be sent off, the work has to be reconnected to operate outside the studio. This is not to say that the studio is a place, a sphere, in which everything is de-connected, brushed away, rubbed apart. The painting's studio-life is all about making connections, but not connections that are mediated primarily by hierarchical laws and practices of meaning-making. Instead, these connections are immanent and imminent, direct. Thus, in Susana Nevado's studio, ideas are not re-produced. Bracha Ettinger's words strike the point: 'Painting does not reproduce an idea, it is an idea' (Massumi 2006, 202).

An idea, then, is not content for expression. In the work of painting, the two are thoroughly connected: it is an idea in process, becoming content-expression. As Deleuze suggests in his text on the creative act: 'Ideas have to be treated like potentials already engaged in one mode of expression or another and inseparable from the mode of expression, such that I cannot say that I have an idea in general' (2007b, 307).[76] Although an idea is something Nevado mentions throughout our conversations, it is always surrounded with a liberal measure of indeterminacy, murkiness: there are no ideas to be represented, only potentials – 'initial', 'original' and 'basic' ideas – before they transform, re-form in the course of the process.

When Nevado described a group exhibition piece that she was working on, she was very careful to stress the vagueness of her idea. For her, an idea is closely connected, if not equal to the process of making, to the process of becoming. Notably, almost everything she says about her ideas connects to the ways of making and the materials involved in that process:

Autonomy of Process 93

I've got an idea for that Ama Gallery exhibition. But let's see how it will take shape. There are always these practical problems. That material does not work, or the idea is not what I wanted. (Nevado, n.d. August 2003)

It is in the stage of an initial idea, or [rather] evolving from it. At least I know that I want something that'll be torn and that has multiple layers. The multi-layeredness, that is what Europe is about ... [I want] that there would be so much of it [layers] that it is confusing. But I don't know how it will evolve. (Nevado, 22 May 2004)

This is my original idea, but I don't know how it will work out. As you have probably noticed, sometimes these ideas evolve in some other direction. (Nevado, 6 June 2004)

So this is the initial idea and I don't know how it will materialise. There'll be something beneath that or something. So that basically you almost don't notice anything, but you notice that there is something weird. But let's see, I will read and look and [do] such [things]. (Nevado, 6 June 2004)

The idea is that it will become manifold, pictures, planes and then the circle. (Nevado, 3 August 2004)

This is the basic idea from which it would then develop forwards. (Nevado, 24 October 2004)

The idea is to mould [it], it will probably change and then it will eventually become something else. It is something that you are not able to know in advance. (Nevado, 5 December 2004)

Giving the active voice to the material process instead of 'I' mastering the making, and Nevado's repetitive expressions of 'not knowing where it will end' refer to the same phenomenon. They stress the autonomy of the process: 'idea' as an evolving event that is not solely in Nevado's hands. What Massumi says about performance artist Stelarc's status in the performance events he creates makes sense here: 'He has no mastery of the situation, no effective control over which ideas the spectators verbalize, or over how or if they subsequently connect. And he seems entirely unbothered by the fact, even pleased at the range and unpredictability of responses' (2002b, 119). Likewise, in her performance of painting, Nevado does not describe herself as the fully volitional agent of the process – it is ideas that will become, evolve, change. It is not she alone who makes them become, evolve, change. She has an initial idea; she 'reads and looks' – and paints too. What she does obviously connects to the process but does not determine, master it. Her doing, her movement, such as reading, *can* change the process, bring something to it. But there is no guarantee that it will. The process of art-making is a joint, and, as such, an unpredictable co-composition.[77]

One more citation. Nevado says: 'I've been painting and painting, and in this way, it has transformed into something altogether different' (Nevado, 21 January 2005). She does *not* say 'I changed it by painting it'. And the expression is similar every single time she speaks about the process of creation: I can do certain things, but I do not know where the process will go. 'You cannot paint ideas, or if you want to do it, it is better to write on the canvas in letters "this is my idea"' (Nevado, 16 June 2005), she explains and laughs, implying that 'doing ideas' consciously and intentionally will not lead anywhere. It is the process, the work of painting that becomes the idea: the painting is thinking in the act of painting, in colours, textures, resonances.

The 'autonomy of process' mapped out above does not equate to the traditional notion of autonomy of art, which separates art from social engagement and only celebrates aesthetic values. In the heat of working, in the heat of emerging, all sorts of particles from different strata – chemical, social, and symbolic alike – merge, come together, and find their rhythm in reciprocity. It is not, then, autonomy from the social or from the symbolic that I am suggesting in connection with Nevado, with art processes followed. It is just that when connected in art-making, matters of art create their own mutual movement that might be called autonomous. In short, there is autopoeisis when something 'starts to work for itself' (Guattari 1995, 132). This is how ideas emerge through the co-workings of Nevado's painting. They are immanent to the process in the making. There is no guiding idea that would master the process, nor an individual behind it. We might also call this sort of collaboration 'co-poeisis', to cite Bracha Ettinger (2006, 109, 159). 'Co-poeisis' emphasises even more effectively the aspect of collaboration; it reminds us that there are always multiple participants in the process.

Immanence of art-making

In Nevado's practice, images and ideas – often understood as things that *predetermine* and *direct* art processes through their association with the 'superior' realm of signification – turn out to function rather differently: what counts is their relational materiality, and hapticity, images as pictures; images as material-relational aggregates along with and equal to other partakers, co-workers in the painting process. This is not to say, however, that Nevado's paintings are separate from the realm of signification, it is just that even when there are representations to interpret in her works, these are not only born of intentional workings to produce certain kinds of representations. Rather, they are immanent to the material process of art-making, coming to being, co-composed in colours, contrasts, resonances, rhythms of painterly qualities. Neither do ideas pre-exist the process, but evolve in the specificity of process; they too are tied to the materiality in the making, evolving, emerging relationally.

The outcome of this is that since images and ideas have no predetermined, intentional function but are rather allowed to work, or put to co-work on their own, the process acquires a certain autonomy. In other words, both ideas and images are immanent to the process.

Whereas this chapter has 'materialised' both images and ideas, often understood in terms of transcendent rather than immanent qualities, there is still a lot to address in Nevado's painting processes on the immanent plane of composition. Reference has already been made to various ways of *composing*: of putting images in layers, of painting and reading. Yet how this happens in the actual working process has not been addressed in detail. I will now turn to manual labour in the collaborative processes of co-composition and reflect on its importance in terms of emergence and in detaching images from their figurative task (cf. Deleuze 2003, 97–98).

5

Manual Labour

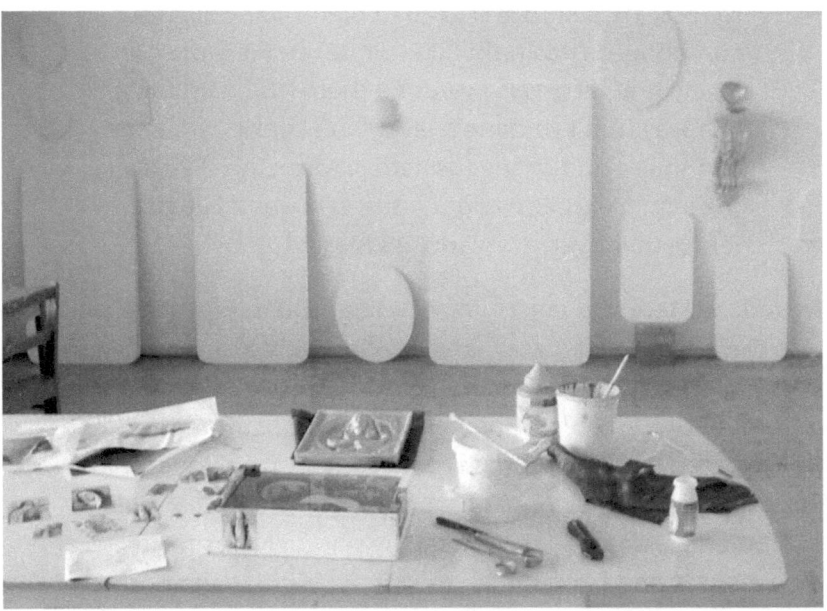

Figure 5.1. Blank canvases at Susana Nevado's studio. *Honest Fortune Teller*, October 2004. Photograph by Katve-Kaisa Kontturi.

In the beginning, there was a blank canvas, in fact, a series of them. When I visited Nevado's studio in late October 2004, to my surprise I encountered a full series of white canvases of various sizes and shapes on the floor and leaning against the wall; they were to become part of the installation later named *Honest Fortune Teller* [Figure 5.1]. I was surprised because, by this time

I had learned not only that Nevado usually works in layers, but that she also adds layers over her own (older) paintings. Five months later, when the canvases had acquired multiple layers, it turned out ... well ... that those canvases never really were blank. They were recycled and came from earlier works of art that were exhibited at Ama Gallery:

> That is, they come from another work of art ... [I]t is recycled material, which is always important! But the reason I wanted them to be white is that I wanted to force myself to start with a blank [canvas]. It's somehow difficult, that it is white, and it is pretty funny that, after all, I've done them [the paintings] in a way that I've done a layer, and continued, and continued and changed them. In principle, I've done the same, that is, I've done the same and I've begun far further even. (Nevado, 23 March 2005)

Nevado's interest in layers, in recycling, and in reprocessing was the outcome of a year-long special course for professional visual artists that she undertook in 2003–2004. The course had a tremendous effect on her working method: afterwards she only worked with recycled, second-hand or found materials. For example, in the works of art made for the *Family Album* exhibition at Ama Gallery, old family photographs from Nevado's own albums and from those bought at flea markets both in Finland and Spain entered the painting process again and again. In the *Honest Fortune Teller* installation, the canvases themselves were recycled, alongside a pack of found and second-hand objects, wallpaper, dolls, frames and picture stands, and of course those ubiquitous figures of María Madre de Misericordia emerging through the continuous painting, re-painting, over-painting – through *painting in layers*. While there is a lot of recycling involved in Susana Nevado's art, the same figures are not repeated identically over and over again. Not even once.

Nevado underlines this as she retrospectively pieces together the painting process of *Honest Fortune Teller:*

> It's about evolving, not about stopping ... It is not repetition [of the same] although there is that virgin [again] ... It's about evolving, it continues, in another mode. (Nevado, 16 June 2005)

This chapter deals with painting not as work of simple repetition but differentiation: repetitions vary, purposefully and inevitably. Because painting is about evolving. And evolving, as we will learn, is hard manual work.

Acts of un-recognition

For Nevado, recycling entails transformation. This is also what Judy Purdom claims in relation to Nancy Spero's dancing, leaping, tumbling female figures on the move: '[t]here is repetition but never duplication' (2000, 171). And it is not because the figures represent movement, but because they are on the move, transformed by Spero's manual labour of printing, stamping and collage; printing, overprinting, reprinting – 'inevitably then each piece is a singular production with its own peculiar material and composition' (Purdom 2000, 169). Often, Nevado's work of painting involves even more complex repetition. Think of her reworking of those fixed figures of pinup girls and holy women, for example – they add an extra layer of movement. For it is obvious that the figures are on the move because of the *continuous*, layered doing, their composition in layers that group, crowd and sometimes isolate, differentiate the figures. This is not simple reproduction: it is 'the movement of the process(ion) not progression or proliferation' (Purdom 2000, 171). In other words, it is recycling as differential repetition, 'repetition as real movement, in opposition to representation which is false movement of the abstract' (Deleuze 1994a, 23). For Nevado, working in layers is a differentiating tool: painting, overpainting, repainting, painting with paper scraps, photographs. This repetition is not only physical, but ontological in kind (Deleuze 1994a, 293). The movement here is 'ontogenetic', it is inseparable from its coming into being. To change, to crack the fixed image by insisting on its intricate movement is to say 'no' to recognition. Recognisable figures are halted, belted – stopped. And, as Nevado insists, painting is not about stopping.

The recognition of symbols, colours, things, is a repeated theme in Nevado's descriptions of her art processes. But the theme is always approached in its insufficiency; there has to be more than just recognition. What she is really interested in is un-recognition: how to confuse, how to make it so that you really cannot know, recognise.

> Many [people] have said [to me] that you don't need anything else, white wall, the tiles in this way [in circle, marking the countries of the EU], and you don't need anything else ... It could be a symbol, but I'm not satisfied with it. (Nevado, 6 June 2004)

> It's somehow a funny colour [purple], 'cause you can't know if it's dried blood or blueberry soup. (Nevado, 18 April 2004)

> The layers should be very transparent. I would like to have a bit of abstraction there, if you understand? So that I would get that [yet too] integral body to crack. So that at some point you don't quite recognise what it is. (Nevado, 5 December 2004)

> It's a bit like a game; you note that there are various [faces], but you can't know; can't recognise who it is. (Nevado, 5 December 2004)

> I've been thinking that there would be many figures. Let's see how it will evolve ... If the virgin's body will

also appear, that is, the figure from that holy card, if
a part of it will emerge ... This is a bit like a collage,
something's maintained, something's covered – I
want to do a painting in the same manner. (Nevado, 5
December 2004)

For Nevado, painting creates figures that are not recognisable. To achieve this, she practices various acts of unrecognition: she bypasses symbolic signs, chooses colours without self-evident reference points, paints with collage-like techniques and adds abstract elements. In a way, these acts of unrecognition are about ruining recognition – to paraphrase Dorothea Olkowski's (1999) conceptualisation of the ruin of representation. 'There is a bit of a game' (Nevado, 22 May 2004): you think you can recognise but then, really, you cannot.

Notably, the acts of unrecognition only make sense in connection with certain art processes: it is the singularity of the process that is at issue here. For example, purple is not an ambiguous colour in all circumstances. On a recycled antique soup plate, however, it gains a more ambivalent resonance. And when that plate is surrounded by a dozen other plates decorated with anatomical figures such as pelvic bones and muscular tissue, as well as photographs of naked women's bodies, as in Nevado's installation displayed at the Caisa Gallery in Helsinki 2003, the colour easily connotes blood [Figures 5.2 and 5.3]. Moreover, colour is always connected to texture; what we see as colour has a haptic quality inseparable from the process of making. It is precisely this colour-texture combination that creates confusion. In this case, the purple texture was acquired by transferring a photograph via a gel medium onto a white stoneware plate. Hence, to be exact, it was in the conjunction of that 'gel image' and the stoneware that the unrecognisable purple occurred.

The paintings with faces moved, blurred, transformed and deformed by manual working make for yet another case of

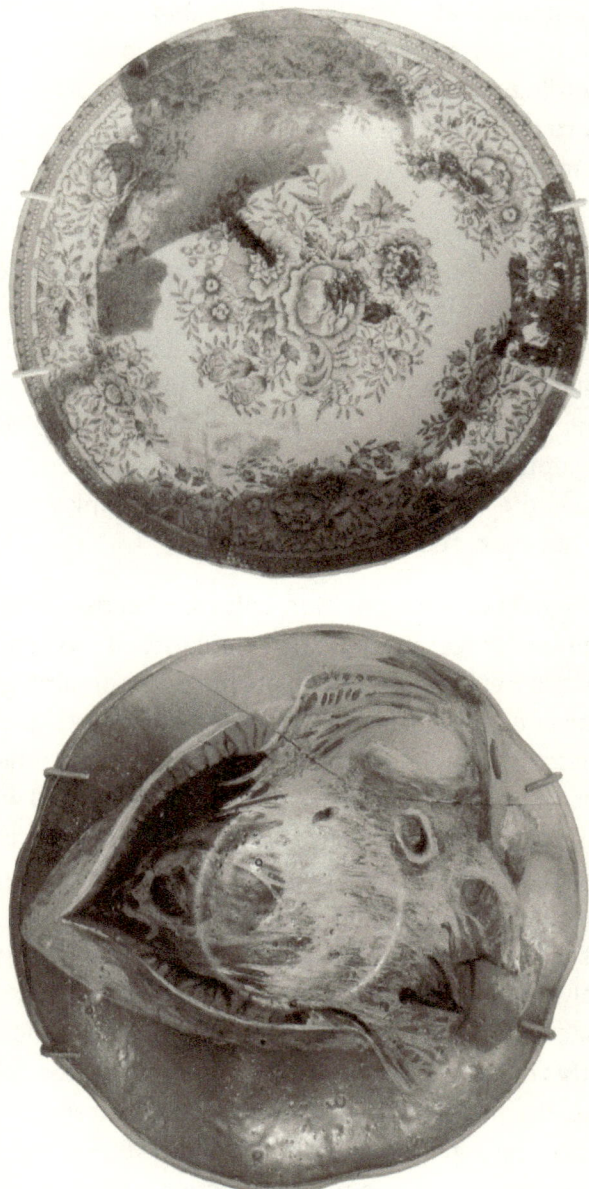

Figures 5.2 and 5.3. Un-recognition I: Layered plates. Details of Susana Nevado's *Invisible Spirit* [Espíritu Invisible], mixed media on second hand plates, size variable, process documentation of *On the Other Side* exhibition at the Gallery of the International Cultural Centre Caisa, Helsinki, April 2004. Photographs by Katve-Kaisa Kontturi.

unrecognition. The identifiable human face, as an arena for ever-persistent interpretation, scrutiny and control is indisputable: for example, there are strict rules for what passport images should look like, as they must be recognisable to authorities that control access. There are also numerous political and advertising campaigns based on faces, a long history of analysis of facial expressions, and more recently also *Facebook* as a means of knowing and connecting people. Deleuze and Guattari (1987, 167–91) use the term 'faciality' [*visagéité*] to describe this phenomenon that subordinates the human face to the powers of identification, subjectification and representation – to recognition.[78] For them, de-facialisation describes acts that 'break through the walls of signifiance, pour out of the holes of subjectivity' (Deleuze and Guattari 1987, 190), rendering faces unrecognisable. This movement is at work in Nevado's eagerness to 'de-facialise': multiple layers and transferable images not only render the models' faces unrecognisable but set them in constant motion by connecting them to other heads, such as that of María Madre de Misericordia elaborated from the holy cards [Figures 5.4, 5.5 and 5.6].

Again, lively layers are doing their work, ruining recognition; the work of unrecognition.[79] Deleuze and Guattari (1987, 302) provocatively claim that painting is the very deterritorialisation of the face. For them, painting must go beyond recognition, that is, it must uproot the face from its usual territory (of recognition). This deterritorialisation always requires at least two territories – 'one never deterritorializes alone' (Deleuze and Guattari 1987, 174, 306) – provided, in this case, by multiple layers connecting, for example, the Catholic holy card tradition and the 'real-life' face of a woman who posed as María Madre de Misericordia. In Nevado's art, elements that are applied to disturb recognition will not do this by themselves; it is at the intersection of various 'techniques', such as gluing paper scraps onto the acrylic paint filled canvas (to 'crack open' too recognisable Virgin figures) that adding abstract elements works. In sum, in Nevado's art, it is the manual act of layering and of letting layers do work of their own that produces unrecognition, differential repetition, something unexpected:

> I don't know how many layers I will still do, there are already at least three layers. I will, I guess, still add up to five or six layers, and it will emerge, and become different all the time. (Nevado, 5 December 2004)

Getting physical

It is not automatic or guaranteed getting the layers to co-work. Nevado's descriptions of the painting process emphasise this, with her repeated use of verbs related to struggling and battling.[80] Deleuze also does this often in *Francis Bacon: The Logic of Sensation* (2003, 99, 101–103, 106): there are battles on the canvas, intense efforts of both a spiritual and manual kind, frenetic dance … It is not an easy job to get the materials to collaborate among themselves, and with the artist. The germ of rhythm must be found (Deleuze 2003, 102).

> It wasn't an easy job, I struggled with it for almost a year. (Nevado, 27 May 2003)
>
> I've been struggling with them enormously … But I really believe that when I've painted more, the paint will begin to speak. (Nevado, 5 December 2004)
>
> I've been struggling with it almost for one and a half months … I've been rather hostile since I haven't been able to gain the rhythm, and also, the hostility in itself causes such an effect that it doesn't come easy. (Nevado, 6 March 2005)

For Nevado, struggling concerns finding a contact, a mutual understanding, co-rhythm with the materials, including paint and the painter's mind–body aggregate. This is what collaboration

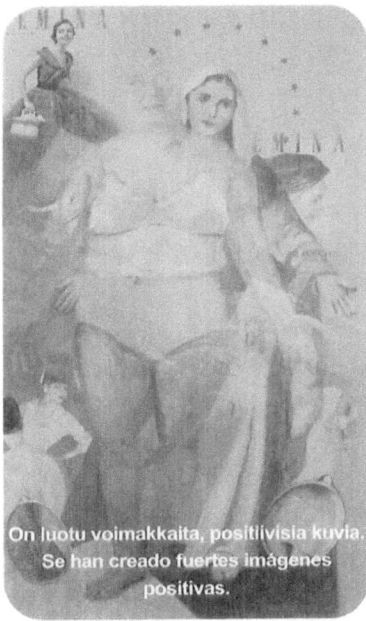
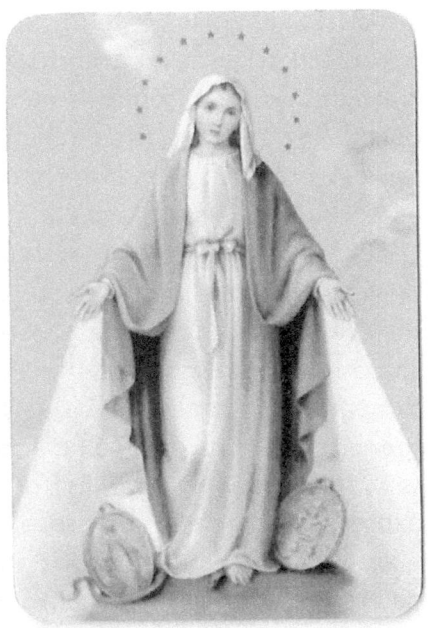
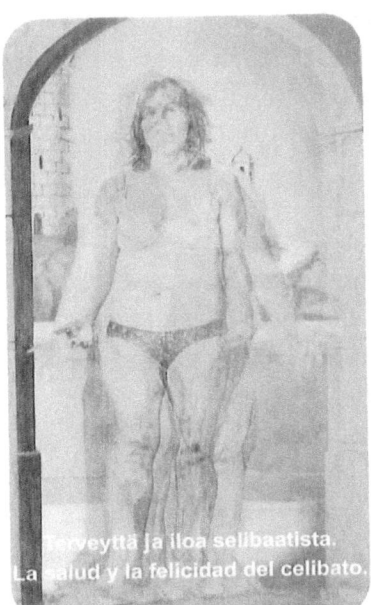

Figures 5.4, 5.5 and 5.6. Un-recognition II: The original holy card of María Madre de la Misericordia and the 'de-facialised' holy cards based on paintings from Susana Nevado's *Honest Fortune Teller* installation.

entails, to get the work going. 'Stuckness', addressed earlier, is part of the process; it is the struggle expressing itself, when the co-rhythm is yet to come. Painting is not just a simple process of applying paint onto something but is about getting the paint to work with the artist, with her brush, with the surface.[81] The artist does not just use the paint: 'The model is not one of utility but of struggle – a "hand-to-hand combat of energies"' (Massumi 1992, 13).[82] This quotation serves here as a key to the event of 'woodworking', through which Brian Massumi sketches a challenging complex of content and expression, and form and substance (1992, 10–21), helping us to further rethink the relations of painter, paint, and brush.[83] Relations of wood, tool, and woodworker are far from simple: there is content, expression, form and substance on all sides.[84] The wood is not only a raw material, a substance, but a substance with a determinate form. Nor is the wood mere content for expression executed by the woodworker. It is also the expression of multiple natural (sun, rainwater, rich soil) and cultural (forestry) forces that contribute to its emergence. Wood is not the passive object of the woodworker's actions, although the force of the wood's qualities is certainly weaker than that of the tool in the hand of the woodworker.

Massumi draws attention to the need for a woodworker to be sensitive to the 'signs' of the wood, to its *qualities* of texture, elasticity, durability, to its directions, tensions. These qualities are not just properties or visible perceptions; rather, they envelop a potential: 'the capacity to be affected, or to submit to a force' (Massumi 1992, 10). The woodworker has to have certain knowledge of what a wood can do; otherwise they will not form a functional assemblage in terms of creating a table, for example. Barbara Bolt (2004a, 84) stresses that these contacts, linkages between materials, tools, and the artist must be made anew every time. Every event of making is different, *singular*, the dynamism it will acquire cannot be known beforehand. The paint might be more liquid, the canvas more porous, the

Manual Labour 107

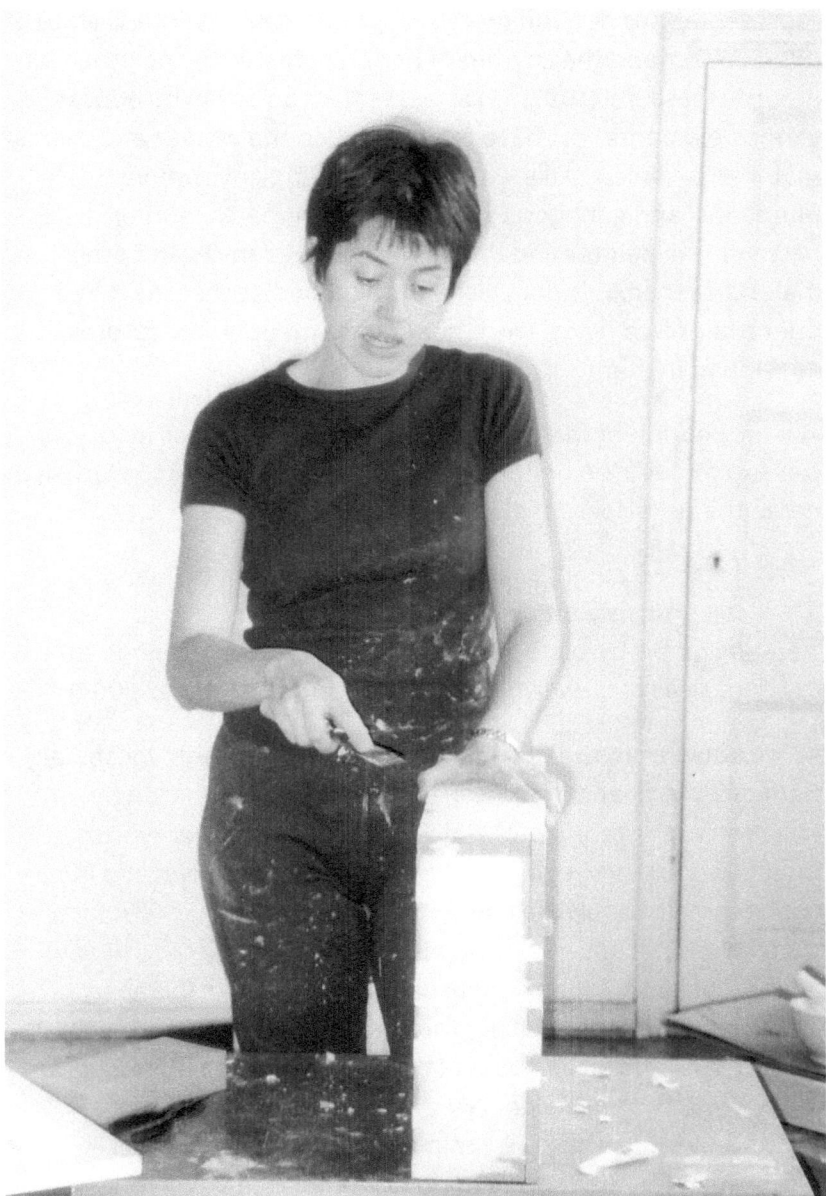

Figure 5.7. The woodworker – Susana Nevado at her studio. *Room to Move* exhibition for Titanik Gallery in the making, Turku, March 2004. Photograph by Katve-Kaisa Kontturi.

representations at hand more recognisable, the painter's state of mind calmer and the rhythm of her body faster, or the other way around. Massumi (1992, 15) stresses this too as he introduces various elements that have their effect on the worker and the material: technical skills, education, working environment, intentions, and genetics, to name a few. In the encounter between the painter and the paint (and the canvas and other materials), then, it is not clearly defined bodies that meet but rather force fields, with their pasts and potential futures enveloped in them.

The conception of the painter and the paint as forces lead Nevado to describe her attempt to get the paint(ing) to work with her in the physical terms of *sports*.[85]

> I started but it got stuck in a rut. I'll return to it, and it'll probably break down altogether, and build up again bit-by-bit. But it is not that moment yet, since I'm basically still warming up. (Nevado, 5 December 2004)

As we know from the previous chapters, in Nevado's vocabulary 'being stuck' means that the art process is still too strongly attached to the realm of the already known. In other words, it is not a *work* of art yet; it is not *working on its own*. Nevado has not been able to release it with her collaborative actions: for she is 'still warming up'. A warm-up is necessary to succeed in any physical activity. A warm-up usually consists of an increase in (bodily and mental) intensity through joint flexibility, enhanced by exercises and stretches that together aim at opening out the body, activating its energy system, and making it more elastic and more able to sustain the forthcoming effort. The warm-up enables the body to do even more, to go beyond its normal everyday duties. In collaborative art-making, which brings together various capacities both human and more-than-human, an expanding warm-up to 'oil' the elasticity of 'joints' and linkages is even more crucial. Whereas in sports a warm-up exercise is needed for a safe performance, in the realm of art, intensification is an indispensable procedure for a *work* of art to find its rhythm, to work.

Importantly, both in sports and in the arts a warm-up should be conceived of as part of the actual exercise, and not as preceding it: warming up turns into training – into 'working out' a work of art:

> It's not easy at all. It takes an awful lot ... and not only technically ... I've begun with these smaller ones. Doing them I could get a bit of training to [deal with] that bigger one; they demand an awful lot of work. (Nevado, 5 December 2004)

When Nevado speaks about the need for training to deal with 'that bigger one', it is almost as if she were dealing with weightlifting: pumping iron rather than painting. In both cases the task is to get one's body to adjust to the movement, rhythm, and resistance by starting with smaller challenges. Rehearsal, time, and patience are needed. Another example of this approach is Nevado's comparison between doing an aerobics class and practising painting: if you have not done an exercise class for a long time, it takes time for your muscles to adjust to the movements, to remember the movement, the rhythm, and the same goes for painting (Nevado, 23 January 2005). Thus, for Nevado, painting is a physical task, manual, and not only mental labour. This is what was suggested earlier: 'when I've painted more, then the paint will begin to speak'. Whilst Nevado uses a language-oriented expression regarding getting the paint 'to speak', it is the intensity of the manual labour of painting that makes the paint speak. This is important, as it is often 'the paint that gives a solution'. She continues:

> Of course I've often felt very irritated if I haven't been able to make the paint speak. For it can be a whole day that nothing happens; the colours don't communicate

> with each other or with me. Then, it is better to stop.
> (Nevado, 5 December 2004)

Whereas Massumi (1992, 11) writes that a woodworker must follow the grain of the wood, to work *with* it, it is a painter's task to follow the qualities of paint. And whereas it is the woodworker's job to bring the qualities of wood to a certain expression, such as a table, the painter faces perhaps even more challenging a task: she must collaborate with the paint (and other materials) to create something new. What the woodworker and the painter have in common is that it is not simply their intention or will that defines the process, the creation. Instead, creation necessitates collaboration with and not a mastery over the material. This is when 'a [wo]man discovers rhythm as matter and material' and where 'it is no longer inner vision … but manual power' that directs the process (Deleuze 2003, 108).

As Bolt (2004a, 84) highlights, these linkages between the artist and her materials have to be made anew every time she paints. Nevado takes up this point as she reflects upon her relationship with different materials. Her exhibition at the Topelius Gallery in Helsinki displayed painting-collages on various materials including canvas, mdf-board and steel. When talking with an exhibition visitor about her steel works, she said: 'I'm probably more courageous, stronger to[wards] those materials' (27 May 2003). When I asked her to explain it more clearly, she went on: 'You can do whatever you please with these, they were found in a garbage bin'. In contrast to the steel, she explained that the canvas is so loaded with traditions that it creates barriers to creativity.

The shred of black lace from the double navel painting (Chapter 2) that was 'under arrest' for a long time because it was so absolutely stuck, offers another, more intimate example of Nevado's struggle with materials. The shred of lace crossed the painting diagonally, dividing it into two segments, separating the pinup girl and the 'real life' woman from each other. It made the space *striated* in a literal sense. The lace was rough, cheap, of the kind that irritates the skin, makes it itchy. However, Nevado's explanation of keeping the painting 'under arrest' did not draw any particular attention to the lace. Rather, she claimed that it was the overall appearance of the painting that was stuck – the representations of women were indeed too stereotypical (Nevado, 5 December 2004). Nevado was frustrated, even angry. It was only a few months later, and in connection with another painting in process, that the role of the lace started to gain significance, and the possibility arose that it could actually have something to do with the painter's anger. Nevado explained that the lace was cut from a corset bought at a so-called sex shop, a disliked gift from a former boyfriend. 'It was not so much a gift for me but for him', she stated (Nevado, 21 January 2005). In allowing the lace to enter the process she had, voluntarily or otherwise, invited a whole array of affective, material and cultural forces enveloped in that piece of fabric to collaborate with her.

With the pinup scraps, the black lace created a perfect visual whole with a strong reference to the subordination of women in terms of Marxist feminism. But as the idea was to create something new and not just repeat, this was not enough for Nevado. As it happened, she ended up *manually* sandpapering the painting and the visual whole, and consequently the lace lost its recognisable character. In this state of destratification the visual – the eye – no longer governed the painting. However, it would also be too simple to claim that the manual, the hand alone, governed the process now. The destratification allowed a new kind of collaboration to emerge, a dynamism among the materials, the hand, and the eye. Deleuze calls this the haptic: 'if there is still eye, it is the "eye" ... linked to an immense agitation of matter' (2003, 137). The painting that emerged from the stratification and destratification continuum was pregnant with matter, as the paint and the remains of paper scraps and lace visibly connected with the (representational) figure, as if under its painterly skin. The manual work scrambled the recognisable visual representations; co-working with the layers of painting it transformed the visual whole into the haptic assemblage where the lace, that earlier had seemed to create a barrier to creation, was neither tamed nor erased, but acted as a participant in the work of the work of art.

What 'getting physical' makes apparent here, then, is that in the material and bodily processes of painting, the working procedure is never only mechanical, schematic – it does not somehow reside in the painter's body ready to be applied on whatever surface. No collaboration is given: every event is singular and the collaboration always has to be negotiated, warmed-up, struggled with anew.

Affirming, learning

Let us further consider Nevado's handling of and co-working with the black lace that had its irritating history, both in her personal life and, more widely, in terms of hierarchic gender difference. As noted, the lace that was probably responsible for delays and difficulty in the process of making the piece was not completely destroyed or altogether removed in the process, contrary to what one might assume. Rather, it was transformed, made unrecognisable, and in its transformed form it was allowed to participate in the creation of the piece – it became a material-symbolic participant in the emergence of the double navel girl, as it remains a part of the girl's painterly skin. This exemplifies what is typical of Nevado's work of painting: the layers beneath the most recent one are not overpainted for good, left behind forever, but are allowed to live their life, to stay active in one form or another. This is painting as an affirmative practice.

In her elaboration on Susan Hiller's *Painting Blocks* (1984), cut and sewn from the artist's own, turn-around canvases, Rosemary

Betterton makes an interesting observation concerning affirmation. She suggests that by transforming earlier works into new ones Hiller allows the paintings 'to participate in life', to continue living. Hiller does not treat the earlier works as objects to be 'entombed' in museums or in some dusty storage space, but instead allows them to work on (Hiller, cited in Betterton 2004a, 83). Betterton makes another interesting note in reference to Hiller's *Hand Grenades* (1969–1972), works filled with ash from paintings that Hiller had burnt. She claims that this 'material transformation ... enacts a new moment of becoming' (Betterton 2004a, 85). For Betterton, transformation and becoming oppose the modern understanding of painting as melancholic *mourning*.[86] In this way, Hiller's practice of remaking her paintings suggests a refusal to mourn the past and, instead, give it a renewed, affirmative agency in the present and for the future.

Nevado's painting practice follows a similar dynamism. While the example of Nevado's practice provided above concerns affirmation within an individual art process, I witnessed several events that show how affirmation, as differential recycling, encompasses her practice more extensively. 'Affirmation' also belongs to Nevado's own vocabulary: 'I transmit; I affirm ... I have a pretty strong will to do things' (Nevado, n.d. December 2003). Elizabeth Grosz, one of the feminist philosophers who have most profoundly argued on behalf of affirmative practice, contrasts it not only to mourning and lamenting but also to critique as a negative practice (see Kontturi and Tiainen 2007, 246–56). Grosz claims that one can easily make a negative reading of, for example, Deleuze, Spinoza and Darwin, since these 'founding fathers' do not have many positive things to say about women. Yet she insists that, without Deleuze, for example, there are many things that would remain unsaid. Following Grosz, there are many things that would not have been able to emerge if Nevado had not used stereotypical materials such as lace in her art and, also, if she had been satisfied with making critical representations, images that are perhaps reiterative, yet stratified, recognisable. Affirmation assumes transformation. To affirm is not to affirm the same thing (that is to confirm) but to allow transformation to enter, to join the process.

To return to more practical considerations, let us turn to Nevado's own words. In her affirmative understanding, works of art live continuously and this becoming occurs, above all, in terms of self-differentiating matter:

> I think that a work of art lives on continuously. And if you use them again, it is a kind of continuum ... it is about evolving not about stopping ... I feel a work of art can live forever [but] it could be that you never have to return to it, or then, for example, you paint something else over it. It never comes to an end; [and] it is never what it was on my [studio's] wall. (Nevado, 16 June 2005)

However, the transformative continuum, becoming, also extends beyond particular exhibitions:

> I've been thinking that these works, which are going to Wäinö Aaltonen [Art Museum], have already been there once. They are recycled material, a part of the work which was exhibited there in the year 2000. It's exciting ... that they are returning there. (Nevado, n.d. December 2003)

Although this chapter has emphasised that Nevado works in layers – even in terms of layered materials from earlier exhibitions (as above) – this does not mean that she would do nothing but keep repeating this practice. One of the principal characteristics of Nevado's artistic practice is that she does not cling to what she is used to. She is willing to learn, and for her, learning means trying out new collaborators, working differently, with a different rhythm – it necessitates engagement, elasticity, and persistent hard work. In other words, 'learning means composing the singular points of one's own body or one's own language with those of another shape or element, which tears us apart but also propels us into a hitherto unknown and unheard-of world of problems' (Deleuze 1994a, 192).

Nevado's way of working in layers has continuously changed as she has experimented with new materials and techniques: she has extended the life of her old paintings by painting on them, or rather *with* them, but she has also used a gel medium called 'Medium' to transfer and connect images to various materials and has tried miniature painting, decorating antique plates for the Caisa exhibition (Nevado, 18 April 2004).[87] The layers themselves consist of multiple materials: of photographs, spices, scraps, recipes, varnish, paint, and clothes, to give a few examples. In Nevado's practice, learning takes place at the level of exhibition planning, but also as a continuum from one exhibition to another: 'Already in the Ama exhibition, there were these various layers ... I'd like to carry this out and bring together my previous thoughts' (Nevado, 1 August 2004). Interestingly, Nevado's description of the connections between her earlier exhibition(s) and a forthcoming one was not a straightforward evolution from one point to another, but something more vague. Thus, even when it came to learning there were no precise directions, just a desire to continue, to learn something different, to differentiate: 'It is a step forward, [not] to a next phase, but forwards' (Nevado, 22 May 2004).

While Nevado's technique of affirmative and future-oriented layering might be rich and sometimes even abundant in its variety, her way of doing could be perceived, in Irit Rogoff's words (2001), as being 'without'. In Rogoff's usage, the term 'without' indicates dedication to change and singularity, courage and the capacity to sustain in a situation of continual transformation. This is also what Warwick Mules (2006, 78–79) emphasises in his article on creativity, singularity and techné, in which he discusses how William Turner had to *un*-learn certain techniques in order to create something new. Nevado's openness to learning is, then, an affirmative and courageous commitment to continuous change. Let me end the account of Nevado's practices of learning and affirming with a quote: 'The driving economy of all her work is to recycle, to loop back to earlier projects and experiments, sometimes even failed ones, to regenerate them and make them into something new' (Fer 2006, 285).

6

Zigzagging Art and Life

In Susana Nevado's exhibition at the multicultural Caisa Centre in Helsinki, May 2004, art and life assembled in multiple ways. At Caisa, Nevado displayed a long wall filled with reworked, redecorated antique plates of various sizes, titled, somewhat mysteriously, *Invisible Spirit* [Espíritu Invisible]. All the plates were second-hand and many were gifts from friends and colleagues who had inherited them – for example, as I did, from their grandparents. The plates had had a long life, an extensive history before their newly acquired lives as works of art. While at a distance the plates did not appear as anything uncommon – they looked like a set of collector plates, carefully hung in a dynamic constellation – a closer look revealed that they had unusual decorations: strongly textured, layered images of human body parts, organs, muscular tissue, pelvic bones, and Fallopian tubes covering, connecting with the original ornamental decorations [Figures 6.1, 6.2, 5.2 and 5.3]. There was a softly contorted female body with multiple sclerosis, a condition eventually resulting in death, and a post-coitus body stained by menstrual blood, ambiguously presenting both life and death – coitus as the possibility of new life and menstrual blood as a sign of the lost chance of reproduction [Figures 6.1 and 6.2]. Both of these plates had a connection to Nevado's body, not only because she had worked on them single-handedly, but because the softly contorted body was her sister's, and thus intimate to the artist

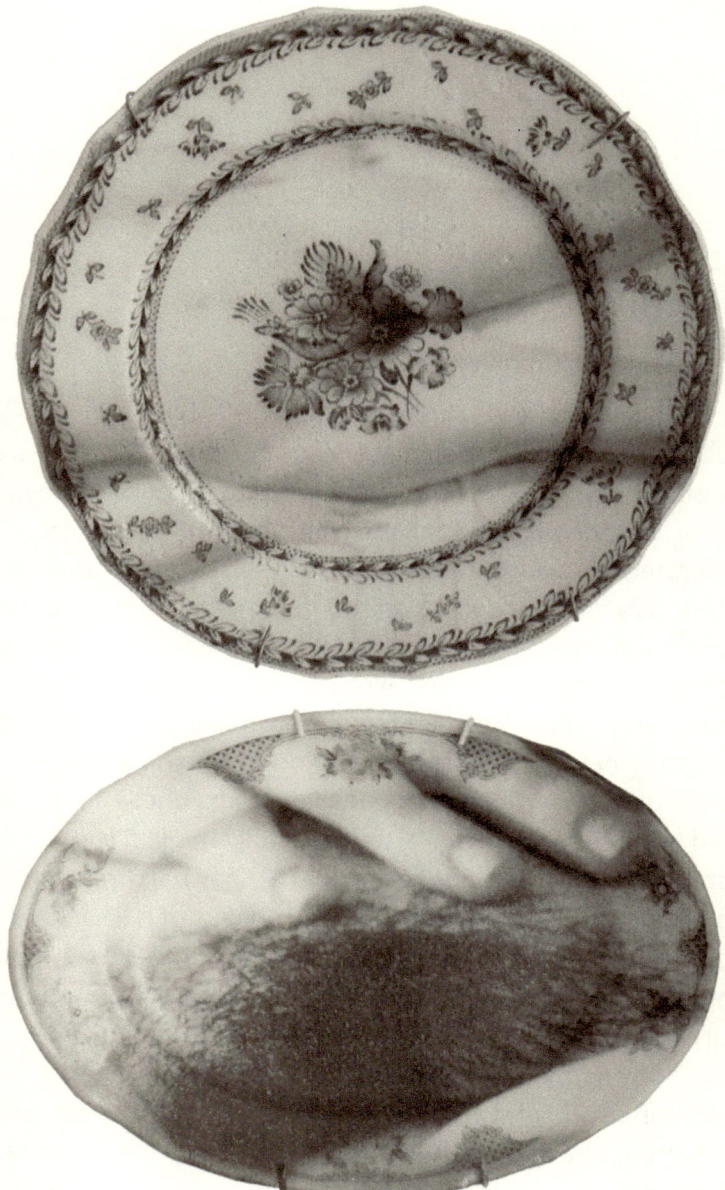

Figure 6.1 and 6.2. Assemblages of art and life. Details of *Invisible Spirit* [Espíritu Invisible], Spring 2004. Photographs by Katve-Kaisa Kontturi.

also in terms of genes, and the post-coitus body was her own – as much as a body can ever belong to just one person.

As complex compositions of art, life, and death, these plates present the task of this chapter: to reconfigure the art and life theme typical of traditional art-writing. While the heroic tales of great (male) artists celebrate the extraordinary lives of already passed-away geniuses, here, life acquires a more nuanced, yet thoroughly differential meaning: life is considered as an ongoing force, becoming in itself, not reducible to the life of any single human being, extraordinary or otherwise. As already discussed, a work of art cannot emerge without a rhythm, a life of its own. Still, unquestionably, Nevado has a particular life of her own, surrounded, supported, enabled by family members, friends, colleagues and others, both in Finland and in Spain, and she has her work as an artist and as an art teacher. It is this kind of full-lived life that has intrigued and inspired feminist art and theory, resulting in the widespread claim that art in its expression is subjective and culture-bound rather than universal or transcendental.

Here, the second-hand plates, with their inventive life (t)issues, call for rethinking the entanglements of art and life in a more complex and impersonal manner. 'Zigzagging' is the verb that I propose to emphasise the non-causal, non-linear, non-dialectical conjunction of the two. The thought-image that Deleuze (1994a, 119) offers for 'zigzag' is lightning, a flash or strike of lightning during a thunderstorm: there is, surely, a connection between them but the connection is not visibly identifiable.[88] Where does the spark of light, the flash come from?

Before the flash there was only potential – an intensive field of charged particles. But the flash never resembles, represents, or even reproduces this field (Massumi 2002a, xxiv). Rather, it is a culmination (but not the end) of an intensive continuum. Analogously, the artist's lived life is not represented or reproduced in her art – and although there might be a seeming resemblance, there is still an intensive transformative process between the two: the process of art-making.

This is how Nevado herself articulated the transformative continuum between her art and her life just before she started work on the Caisa exhibition and immediately after it:

> I can no longer differentiate between what is my art and what is my life ... I don't think I'm bohemian, perhaps it's about my attitude towards life ... It is such a rich [life] that you can connect many things ... You have something in your mind, a process you're working at. You want to gain something, to assemble these things. (Nevado, n.d. December 2003)

> I think I live in and through art ... They are not at all separate things. And if they were to be differentiated by force it would be catastrophic, I reckon, since my whole lifestyle is making art. (Nevado, 6 June 2004)

In praising the richness of being able to connect so many things, Nevado celebrates the close connection of her art and her life. The verb she uses here is to 'assemble' – to bring and fit together, to make elements co-work. In Deleuze and Guattari's (1987, 40, 337) definition, an assemblage always has two sides: one facing strata, in which case the binary of content and expression still holds, and one opened up by creative lines of flight that flee from the pincers of the strata. As Nevado speaks so strongly for a continuum and the inseparability of art and life, it is relevant to think about this a bit more: what sort of process could allow a creative flight from the constraints of the strata of the everyday without getting rid of those matters altogether?

Deleuze and Guattari (1994, 170) apply the term 'style' to a creative process that transforms lived everyday life – feelings and perceptions – into impersonal affects and percepts. And style is, of course, an assemblage in itself, constituted of energies, ideas, particles and bodies in movement. There are many styles, ways of co-composition, and Deleuze and Guattari (1994, 171–73) focus on 'extracting' and 'saturating'. Both of these processes, originating in chemistry, allow for transformation without the loss of connection to what was before. Or, if and when the stratified, molar connection is lost and gone, it is the molecular one that is sustained. Elizabeth Grosz elaborates on this sort of molecular connection that allows for continuums:

> Perceptions and affections, forces lived in everyday life, can only be wrenched from this ... context to the extent that the natural and lived are themselves transformed, the virtual in them explored and strange connections – that have no clear point or value – elaborated with considerable effort and risk to the normalized narratives of the everyday ... The material perceptions – the bodily relations between states of things and subjects – become resources of the unliveable percept; materials of affection – our sufferings, joys, horrors, our becomings, the events we undertake become our possibilities for inhuman transformations. (2008, 78)

In other words, the transformation taking place in the process of making turns lived experience into something new that, in its turn, casts its effects and affects back to our lives, changing them, allowing them to become more-than-human. Thought of in this way, Nevado's connection to her sister's sick but beautiful, boneless-looking body, as extracted and saturated onto a plate, is far from being a straightforward one. In the process of extracting and saturating photographic residues of her sister's life, Nevado's feelings towards her sister and her sister's approaching death have transformed, and acquired a permanent material support (the plate, the paint, and so on). In Deleuze and Guattari's (1994, 168) words, they now form a monument.

Yet this is not a personal memory plate, to support a formed memory, to respect or sublimate something almost already gone. Nor does this particular plate stand out as a monument in itself – it belongs to a larger constellation; it is accompanied by, if not countless other plates, then at least so many that they cannot be taken in at a single glance. Over thirty plates, with their respective imagery of bodies, body parts, muscle tissues, pelvic bones, and organs such as ovaries, textured and moved – transformed – by acrylic paint, the gel medium used for transferring photographs, surface cracks, and traditional picturesque decoration, create their own 'lifecycle': life on those plates, or rather the life of the plates, the life of the work of art, emerging from the rhythm that co-composes the pieces. This is how 'personal' human life is extracted and saturated, transformed into the more-than-human life of the assemblage.

I

'To give birth' to the life-saturated plates was a long and also technically challenging process, especially as Nevado aimed to be as precise in her work as were the anatomy textbooks she was inspired by (Nevado, 11 April 2004). Although she had precise models to use and although there was a serial quality about the creation of the thirty plates, she described the process as being far from industrial:

> This is a very slow, time-consuming process ... I think that this is not a factory ... [laughs]. They'll [works of art] be born when they'll be born, as quickly or as slowly as they will. (Nevado, 18 April 2004)

In *Anti-Oedipus,* the first part of their oeuvre *Capitalism and Schizophrenia*, Deleuze and Guattari (1983) build the political model of the factory in order to fight against the hegemonic powers of the nuclear-family and the psychoanalytic idea of the unconscious. In their next volume, *A Thousand Plateaus* (1987),

Zigzagging Art and Life 123

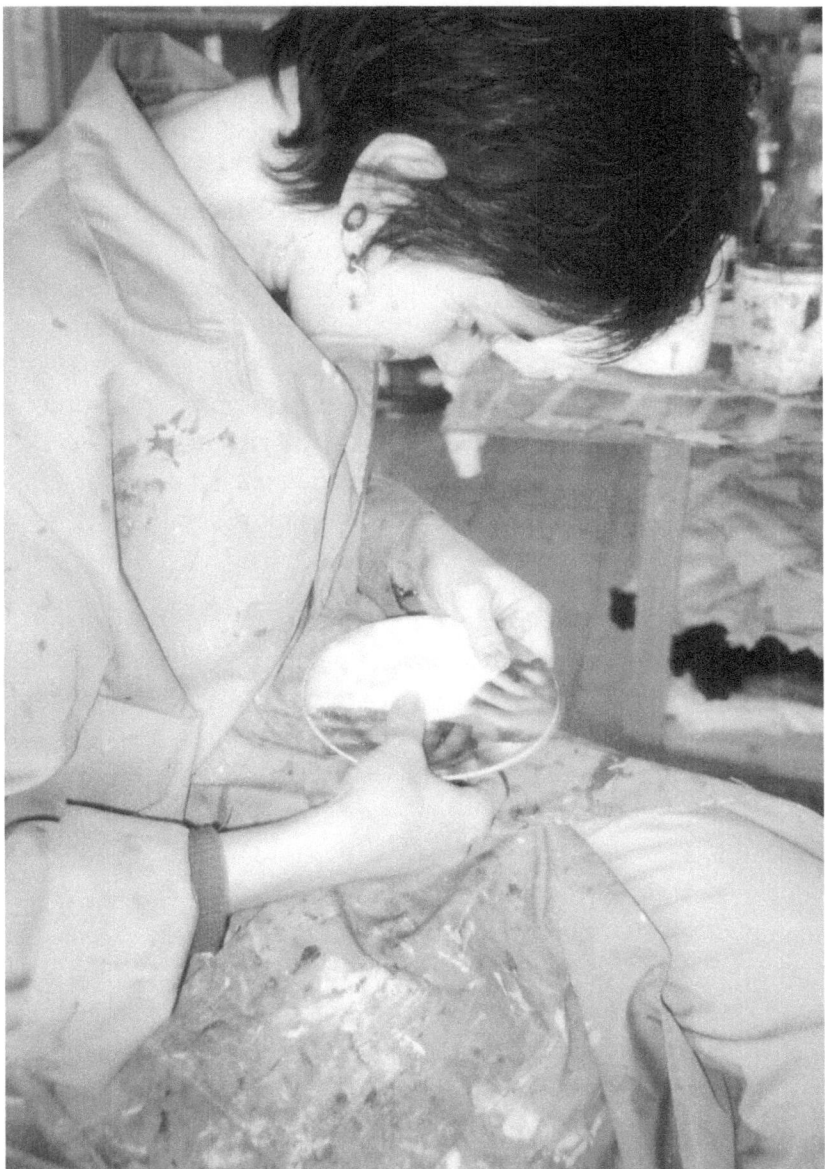

Figure 6.3. Not a factory – Susana Nevado at her studio. *Invisible Spirit* [Espíritu Invisible], Spring 2004. Photograph by Katve-Kaisa Kontturi.

they move to the creative idea of machinic assemblage that offered them, as Deleuze (2007a, 175–79) notes retrospectively, a far more complex and also inclusive arrangement that, importantly, does not stand against pre-existing forces but aims at inventing new fields. In this light, Nevado's humoristic refusal of the factory model makes sense: the factory is too simple a model for the complex processes of making she is involved in. Nevado's way of painting lacks the two obvious attributes of a factory: a tightly scheduled production process and pre-determined ideas for the products. While in factories there is no space or time for intensive continuums culminating in transformative flashes, creative assemblages thrive on them. Maybe, then, to think about Nevado's way of extracting, saturating, life to art, the concept of machinic assemblage is worth considering.

In his essay on Gérard Fromanger's photogenic art, Deleuze (1999, 64) comes up with the concept 'painting machine' [*tableau-machine*]. This concept helps Deleuze to pattern how Fromanger's painting process works: 'how to bring the painting to life' (66). While the artist-mechanic sets the machine to work, it is the connections they enable but do not master that make the work of art (65–66) – this is how we have learned to understand Susana Nevado's work of painting too. This is a procedure that involves multiple connections: conjunctions, disjunctions, and eventually transformations – 'the change[s] the painting produces in the image' (77). In Fromanger's case, the change that transforms 'the givens' is handled principally in terms of colours, 'hot and cold', that is, in terms of painterly *qualities* (see Chapter 5). But the contrast alone is not enough to bring the painting to life. Extraction, rather than abstraction, is the key practice here (76). To extract daily life, images, givens, in a (painterly) way that allows sensations to occur, trembling across the visual whole. This, according to Deleuze, produces life for tomorrow instead of phantasms that only mortify life (75, 77).

The painting-machine, as any machinic assemblage, works in its connections. While the concept, in itself, is critical of human mastery, humans are, of course, still involved. Fromanger, for example, works with a photographer, and there are always multiple co-workers involved in Nevado's processes. In fact, the Caisa exhibition was a joint one too, and this time literally so. In the other half of the exhibition room, Nevado's former partner had his own minimalist, strongly textured, material paintings displayed. The title that brought their works together stated ambiguously, *On the Other Side* [Toista puolta], as if to emphasise the differences in their styles, and yet to draw them together. While Nevado clearly states that the forceful separation of her art and life would be catastrophic to her, this does not mean that she would yearn for a total union, in terms of combining partnership and collaborative art-making, for example.

This became obvious when she was amused by a short newspaper review declaring 'the very active Susana Nevado – this time with Leonardo Nieva' (Nevado, 6 June 2004), for she knew that the list was a long one – she had of course worked with many people: Susana Nevado *and* Leonardo Nieva, Susana Nevado *and* Heli Kurunsaari *and* Sari Koski-Vähälä *and* Paula Ollikainen, to name just a few colleagues she had exhibited with in small-scale group exhibitions and (to judge from our conversations) whose opinion she valued. The list could easily be continued, adding her daughters and their friends who helped tear off the wallpapers for the installation in Titanik Gallery, and the professional craftsman needed for the background tiling of the *Honest Fortune Teller* installation. Susana Nevado *and* her daughters, Susana Nevado *and* the tiler, Susana Nevado *and* her mother *and* numerous other people that continually pop up in her explanations of her working process. And of course, Susana Nevado *and* Katve-Kaisa Kontturi, for our research collaboration. Colleagues and friends, family members, partners. In short, art and life – and although Nevado was amused by the critic's choice of words, she immediately added more seriously: 'It is really hard to differentiate between your art and life' (6 June 2004).

Deleuze and Parnet's pondering upon the conjunction 'and', which has been repetitively employed above, grants collaboration the needed creative twist as well as stressing its ambiguous in-between nature: 'What the conjunction AND is [is] neither a union, nor a juxtaposition but the birth of a stammering, the outline of a broken line which always sets off at right angles, a sort of creative line of flight? AND ... AND ... AND ...' (2002, 7–8). But as mentioned earlier, despite the number of people entering into her machine, with a few exceptions, Nevado worked alone in her studio. Deleuze and Parnet, however, point out how this solitude is extremely populated, which beautifully sums up what has been at issue throughout the three preceding chapters: various transformative co-workings between humans, but also, and crucially, beyond the human.

> When you work, you are necessarily in absolute solitude. ... But it is an extremely populous solitude. Populated not with dreams, phantasm or plans, but with encounters. ... You encounter people (and sometimes without knowing them or even without seeing them) but also movements, ideas, events, entities. (Deleuze and Parnet 2002, 5)

II

For Nevado, the creative zigzagging and encountering that Deleuze speaks of is more generally tied to a certain way of making art, to a certain way of *relating*. Referring to her move from traditional rectangle painting to painting installations, she states:

> A couple of years ago ... when I [only] made paintings, it was somehow restricted ... It is lovely and enjoyable

to work as you can combine many elements/actors and many things, and you can collaborate. (Nevado, n.d. December 2003)

Thus, for Nevado, installation is the form of art that calls for assembling and collaboration. To make painting installations, to assemble and collaborate with the materials entering the machine, Nevado's painting machine works in layers. If Deleuze and Guattari are interested in destratifying the strata, to allow for lines of flight to crack open the already known, Nevado's painting machine layers to de-layer. It is in the breakage of separate layers, in layers producing confusion, un-recognition, or in the multiplication where single layers become undetectable, that a work of art gains a life of its own. It is in the layers undoing themselves that Nevado finds the delight of making. According to Deleuze (1999, 76–77), without joyfulness – the delight in the process of making – it is impossible to bring anything to life.

And … and … and is also the structure of layering: add a layer, three, four, five of them to make something emerge. A layer of the technical preciseness of an anatomical image, of miniature painting, a layer of conventional flower decorations, a layer of women designers' undervalued artistry, a sick body, a healthy body, a productive body, a represented body on an old plate with a crackled glaze. A material-relational installation taking shape in the layers of practice.

Layering, then, is a way of dealing with a 'rich life', as expressed in the beginning of this chapter: to make the most of it, to open it up, even more, to evolve. Her enabling layers to work on their own also indicates that Nevado does not want to assume a fixed position; she is a co-worker, a companion to a multiplicity of elements in the process. She is not the one who runs the process, but one who allows new connections to occur and affect the process of making, beyond processes of recognition and identification. 'An immigrant artist in Finland' is one of those fixed positions, identifications, that she rejected – a title suggested to her by a TV reporter who interviewed her about the Caisa exhibition (Nevado, 6 June 2004). For Nevado, layering is not an epistemic choice of creating a place whence to express herself. Rather it is an ontological practice of affirmative learning: a way of becoming with this and then that, and then …

If anything, Susana Nevado's painting machine is a layering machine. For the principal quality of this machine is, after all, not its capability to paint but to assemble, relate, and transform different *materia,* be it living, moving, representational, semiotic, or symbolic – to co-create fresh compositions, new life, by layering. This is what the previous chapters have offered access to with their discussion of impersonal connections, contrasting, co-vibrating qualities, autonomous processes, differential repetitions, and affirmative practices, all highlighting the transformative continuums of art and life, making art alive and life art; events of making that are not all the same, but singular – because each co-worker brings along his or her or its own immanent field of intensity. In Grosz's words: 'art engenders becomings, not imaginative becomings … but material becomings … in which life folds over itself to embrace its contact with materiality, in which each exchanges some elements or particles with the other, to become more and other' (2008, 23).

Sensations

Prelude: An Oral Triptych

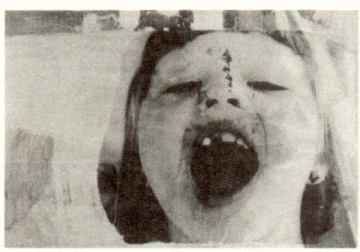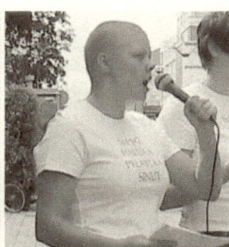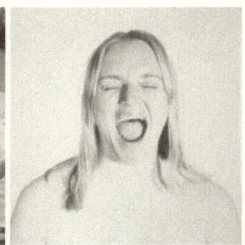

1. Susana Nevado, *D2I*, 2003, detail, mixed media, 30cm x 21cm. Photograph by Marjukka Irni.
2. Marjukka Irni, *Sappho Wants to Save You*, 2006–2010, detail.
3. Helena Hietanen, *Sketches*, 1999–, detail. Photograph by Eva Persson.

Oral passages

A mouth is a way to enter a body, to transform a body, to connect bodies. Think of eating: how junk food moulds contemporary bodies in the documentary film *Super Size Me* (2004); how Christians take the Holy Communion, ingesting the body of Christ and drinking his blood to renew and strengthen their connection to God;[89] or, how the children observing *Heaven Machine* so excitedly, eagerly munched its beams of light.

But a mouth does not only take in, it gives, expresses in words, warps and grunts. In this chapter, mouths grimace, preach, and scream. In Susana Nevado's installation of mixed media paintings and a vitrine of milk teeth, titled *D21* (2003), the pleasures and pains of growing up are expressed through a grimacing mouth with a row of teeth in striking transformation. Preaching is a charismatic vocal-bodily expression through which gender-becomings vary and vibrate in Marjukka Irni's *Sappho Wants to Save You* (2006–2010). In a series of photographs documenting the surgical procedure that sculptor Helena Hietanen underwent when recovering from breast cancer (1999-), she screams, mouth open but full of flesh.

In each of these works of art, the mouth is a passage between the inside and the outside of the body, ultimately presenting a direct relation between the two.[90] In her *Mouth Mantra* (2015), Björk sings that the mouth is a tunnel that enables, but where movement can also get stuck. As the accompanying music video viscerally shows, taking the viewer inside Björk's singing mouth, the mouth's surfaces, cavities, and crevices are sensitively yet powerfully palpating, expressing tissues, none of which ever works alone. They pulse and halt, flow and get stuck in relation to the inside and the outside of the body – the environment of oral expression. One can easily lose one's voice if there are too many tangled tensions between the body and the environment – in a body-environment. But these tensions are not inherently negative. Indeed, if affirmatively sustained, or graciously left behind, they can lead to change, to a new expression. In fact, tensions are indispensable for change: bodily transformations are rarely smooth and predictable – shedding milk teeth, negotiating sexual orientation, or battling breast cancer are complex affective processes, and intrinsically relational in their quality.

The triptych form

Thinking-feeling with these three works of art, side by side, one after the other, forms an oral triptych where mouths initiate a variety of direct relations, that is, unmediated conjunctions and immanent connections, in the events of experiencing and creating art. The mouth is the passage that all the art-encounters of the following chapters begin with and are linked by. It is through open – grimacing, preaching, screaming – mouths that these artworks lead us to a collection of decaying milk teeth that prompt molecular memories of endurance and sustainability (Chapter 7), to relational events where standing still is only possible by moving continually (Chapter 8), and to sculpting one's flesh by incorporating images into one's body (Chapter 9).

Why compose a triptych, one might ask, and of separate works of art even, to make a claim about direct relations? First, the three complementary examples provide an opportunity to fashion direct relations in a more multi-faceted way than grasping only a single art-encounter would allow. Another crucial issue is the allusion that the triptych form carries: the three-panel structure has a long history as a traditional, religious form of art, especially across the Churches of Christianity. In their different ways, all three artworks of the present oral triptych refer to Christian religious practices. The left panel of the triptych, Nevado's grimacing mouth, acquires its affective power in relation to the Catholic tradition of relics. The installation includes a wooden case that displays decaying pieces of the human body – shed milk teeth – through a window frame. The middle panel, the preaching mouth, is extracted from Marjukka Irni's *Sappho Wants to Save You* installation that not only critically revises the Christian slogan 'Jesus wants to save you', but also revolves around preaching – the preferred form of revelation since the Reformation. The right panel, the screaming mouth, takes us back to Helena Hietanen's art. This panel is from the series *Sketches* that comprises religious imagery of the artist posing as Christ and was once meant to be exhibited at the ruins of a Gothic revival church in Berlin, Germany. But there is more to triptychs and religiosity than this. To make sense of this complexity another triptych, a theoretical one, follows. It consists of three parts, as triptychs do.

A theoretical triptych

Panel 1: Figures of Sensation

In *Francis Bacon: The Logic of Sensation* (2003), Gilles Deleuze's analysis focuses on triptychs. Following Deleuze, a triptych is not merely a narrative structure that forms a biblical story by bringing together the figures and events represented in its three panels. Instead, in a triptych figures themselves emerge through complex forces and rhythms that are distributed across and flow through the whole composition. Bacon's triptychs are the art of figures: popes, monsters, Christs, queers of London's underworld; figures in transformation, contorted by forces: infernal, celestial, terrestrial, and thus exceeding the limits of their representation. For Deleuze (2003, xiv), Bacon's art is extraordinary in the sense that it breaks figuration by elevating the figure itself to such dominance.

If there is anything spiritual in Deleuze's study of triptychs, this spirituality tends to be visceral, not transcendental but purely immanent. In Deleuze–Bacon, there is no faith in the almighty God, yet there is faith in life as a cosmic force that has an element of eternity to it. This life force appears to humans as vibratory sensations, and it is visual art, alongside the other arts, that makes these direct relations perceptible.[91] Art does not impose a grid on forces; it moves with them, follows them, harnessing them to intensify them into sensation.[92] Forces greater than the human twist bodies in Bacon, make them spasm in Michelangelo, and elongate them in El Greco – the major references for Bacon's art (Deleuze 2003, 9, 25, 130, 160). In Nevado, her daughter is caught up in the process of growing up; in Irni, Sapphic figures preach, stutter, and subtly vibrate in their becoming; whereas in Hietanen, a body is struggling with the forces of cancer – life lethally splitting its cells. While these figures might not be as contorted as in Bacon's paintings, in their singular ways they still make perceptible something not (yet) commonsensically sensed: the violent pleasures of growing up, the micro-movements of gender and sexuality, and the complex experiences of breast cancer.

Panel 2: Affirmative Radical Immanence

In her call for postsecular spirituality, Rosi Braidotti (2006b, 254–59) redefines spirituality as a topology of affects. The topology of affects – the world emerging through affective encounters and relations of impersonal forces – suggests a spirituality not tied to Christian ideals. There is no God behind it all, yet there are forces greater than the human and not controllable by the human: gravity is an obvious example, natural catastrophes another. Contesting the popularity of neo-eschatological visions of catastrophe and redemption, postsecular spirituality expresses faith in the future (258). Braidotti calls this affirmative, eternal life force 'zoe'.[93] Here, spirituality does not refer to a mysticist notion of life as pure becoming empty of all meanings (255). Rather, spiritual practices, and indeed all practices, are always embodied and embedded: 'they do not take place in a flight from the flesh, but through it' (255). The abandonment of (Christian-related) transcendence is at the heart of this spirituality that rests on radical immanence. Radical immanence is about entering into direct relations, emerging, becoming in those relations that are the subject's future (257), or rather its end as a self-contained entity: a vitalist-relational venture that affirms change.

As a materialist philosopher, Braidotti never ceases to emphasise political agency and the material circumstances in which life is lived. For her, in the wake of Foucault, the conditions that negatively oppress can also offer lines of flight.[94] She believes that it is possible to constitute empowering and affirmative relations directly and creatively out of the material world (Braidotti 2008a, 15–16). In the works of the oral triptych, the practices of Christian religion – teeth relics in Nevado's installation, charismatic preaching in Irni's *Sappho Wants to Save You*, and transfiguration in Hietanen's breast cancer portraits

– are approached affirmatively to show how the affective connections, sensations they offer can bring about new, more varied and more sustainable bodies. Abandoning transcendence and carving out the lines of immanence is what radical affirmation is about.

Panel 3: Against Theology, Horizontally

In *Art Encounters Deleuze and Guattari*, one of the statements Simon O'Sullivan makes is posited 'against theology' (2006a, 28–31). According to Deleuze, 'any organization that comes from above and refers to a transcendence, be it a hidden one, can be called a theological plan' (1988, 128). Like Braidotti, O'Sullivan speaks vigorously of the world as 'a plane of immanent connectivity and complexity' that 'operates without points of transcendence' (2006a, 28). This is 'our world "seen" without the spectacles of representation' (2006a, 28) and without a mastering principle that would order everything in the name of God's law.

To study art in the name of radical immanence necessitates a new relation to art: a more direct relation in which the researcher opens up and encounters art as a parallel body-process. In this direct relation, affects are felt as sensations that connect bodies – horizontally – without a judgmental godly eye that studies its subject from high above, but rather from mouth-to-mouth, from body-to-body.

7

The Grimacing Mouth

In describing how practically everything she does in her life interacts with her art-making, painter Susana Nevado employs the verb 'ingest'. For Nevado, an act of ingestion – in other words, the bodily process of swallowing, that entails taking something in through the mouth – enables the linking of everyday experiences and turning them into art.[95]

> Of course, everything I do alongside [art-making] interacts with my art-making. ... I don't know, maybe it's the only way I can somehow ingest those things. [That is] in a different way, when there's a possibility of creating something new. (Nevado, n.d. December 2003)

As Nevado emphasises, ingestion makes possible the handling of everyday life in a creative, productive way. From one angle, ingesting everyday experiences into art is what the portrait with the grimacing mouth is all about [Figure 7.1]. The mouth belongs to the artist's then six-year-old daughter, Paula, and crystallises something elemental in the process of growing up. There is a burgeoning independence in her daughter's face, an emerging own will revealed by the protesting mouth. Paula's startlingly uneven row of teeth catches the attention, so severely is it affected by the process of growing up, of losing milk teeth and growing new, permanent ones. From the artist's viewpoint, what is swallowed in the grimacing mouth, then, is a changing relation between a mother and a daughter: baby girl is growing up.

While being a mother is something that Nevado regularly ingests in her art-making, another issue that many of her works deal with is the power of the Catholic Church and its continuing influence in the lives of the people brought up in secularised Spain. The mixed media installation *D2I* (2002), of which the 'grimacing mouth' is a part, brings these ingestions together; it digests Nevado's experiences of motherhood and Catholicism and transmutes them into something new.[96]

D2I works with a series of documentary photographs that Nevado took when her daughter Paula's milk teeth were being shed. In the installation, the grimacing mouth is accompanied by fourteen other portraits, that come in two rows, as (human) teeth do [Figures 7.2 and 7.3].[97] Each of these portraits re-works the documentary photos through a variety of colours, rhythms, and materials. The box-shaped 'canvases' made of plywood are filled with approximately life-size heads with mouths strikingly open, showing a row of teeth in transformation. The heads and the teeth gain and lose form in and through reddish, bloody browns, sturdy, spicy yellows, blacks and whites, strokes at times rough, at times fine, and surfaces worked in multiple layers. These are transfer portraits copied with gel medium once, twice, sometimes three times, and then elaborated, fabricated into painting-assemblages with strokes of acrylic paint and repeated acts of rubbing, scratching, ripping, and re-painting.[98] Conceptually, the painting-assemblage emphasises the visual–material complexity of the artwork, but also its affective openness – assemblages are relational be(com)ings.

In *D2I* the teeth operate as the visual–material focal point of the work. Against the black abysses of the open mouths, the teeth stand out; they catch the eye, and the other senses. Moreover,

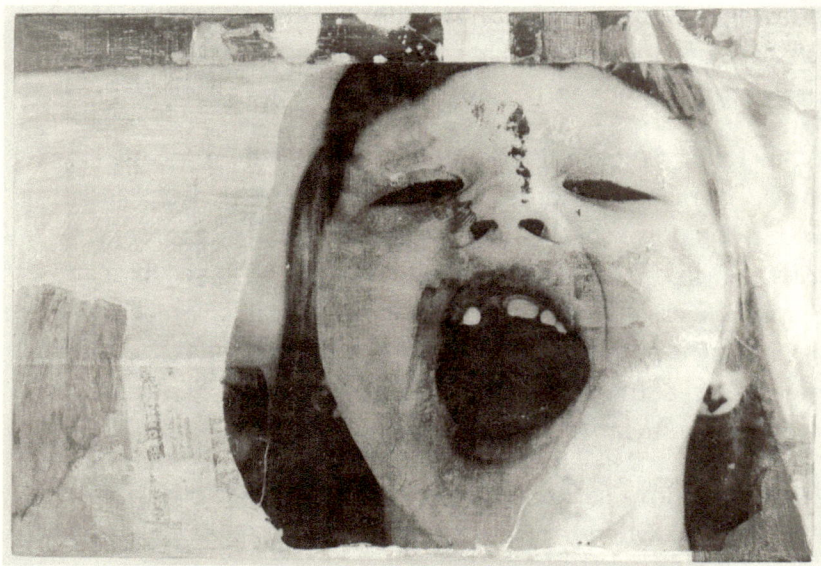

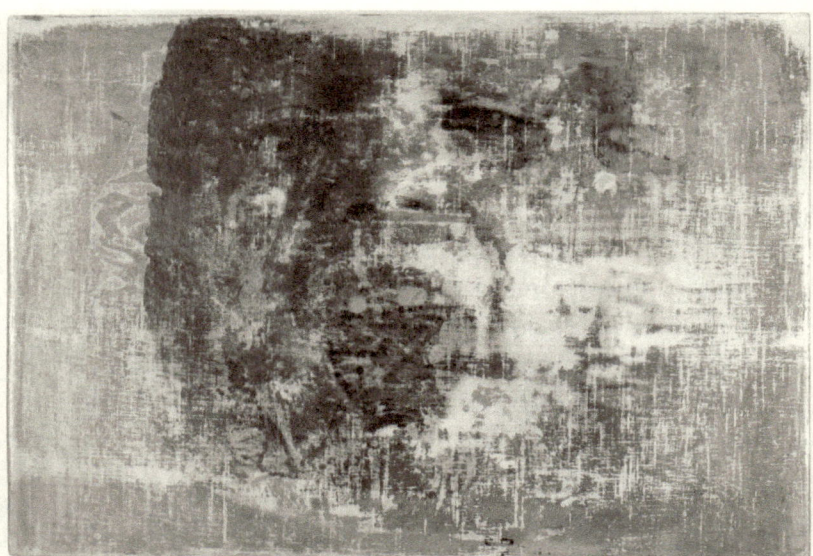

Figures 7.1 and 7.2. The grimacing mouth and the reddish, bloodish brown mouth. Details of Susana Nevado's *D2I*, 2002, mixed media, 30 x 21 cm. Photographs by Marjukka Irni.

the title of the installation suggests a focus on the teeth. 'D2I' is a clinical term used in dentistry to describe the first upper front tooth on the left (in clinical discourse 'D' stands for a tooth, '2' for the upper left quadrant of the jaws, and 'I' for the first tooth of the quadrant). In every piece of the installation, the D2I has a more or less different shape and colour. There is change, but no completion of the process: the row does not grow perfect. The installation refuses to present dental transformation in any linear manner.

If the installation documents anything, it is the unruliness and happy unpredictability of the process of growing up, presented in the varying compositions of facial expressions and the teeth in transformation. There is also a wooden vitrine carrying seven milk teeth on a crimson velvet cushion [Figure 7.4]. The teeth in the vitrine are those missing from Nevado's daughter's mouth as shown in the portraits, offering corporeal evidence of her growing up.

Affective remembrance of growing up

It is tempting to think that the teeth in the box would provide a more direct corporeal contact with the process of growing up than do the painted portraits. Although such a hierarchy is not followed here, there is no reason to deny that the milk teeth – even when seen through the glass window of their box – have an exceptional affective appeal [Figure 7.4]. The bone of the teeth is dense with cracks, some of a capillary kind, some more severe, almost splitting the teeth in two. The blood in the root canals has turned brown, and the teeth have acquired a yellowish, aged tone. This subtle and slow material transformation of the teeth, their organic decay, equips the work with a powerful connectivity: in their current stage the teeth simply have a more porous surface than when they were still shining with plastic-like brilliance. The way the teeth are displayed only emphasises this connectivity. The lower parts of the teeth, once embedded in the gums, are not hidden in the crimson cushion but are fully shown in their frail and visceral variability as the teeth are arranged in a circle with roots pointing outwards, upwards. The smooth dense velvet enhances the effect as it contrasts with the crumbling shapes of the teeth. It rarely becomes as obvious as here: materiality in motion is cracking the form.

Staring at those primal teeth arouses visceral sensations: the body shivers, goosebumps rise. As the teeth connect with the viewer's body, affect the body, they might awaken 'forgotten' potentialities of the body: something that does not actualise itself in everyday duties, something that is not actively re-membered.[99] What are (potentially) actualised in an encounter with *D2I* are bodily processes from the years of transition when one's own milk teeth were being shed. The viewer might recall commanding the tip of the tongue to excavate a loose tooth, pushing it with precision and effort; feel child fingers gently wiggling the loose tooth back and forth, and some frustration as the tooth does not come out but only wobbles. And eventually, when the time has come, boldly pulling the tooth out. What a cracking sound the final pull-out leaves resonating in the head's cavities! Then an iron-tasting burst of blood in the mouth, accompanied by an urgent need to spit out that bloody saliva. Afterwards, a proud, happy feeling that the tooth is finally gone. Look at the portraits of the little girl's face in the installation; look at your own face [Figure 7.5]. No mourning for milk teeth. No looking back, no sense of lack. This is a moment of joy.

It is crucial to note the change in tense in the above description-encounter. At the end of the paragraph, no past tense is needed: this kind of sensuous remembrance creates affects that are in the here and now; affects born, made alive, actualised in the encounter with art. Rosi Braidotti (2006b, 165–69) calls this kind of remembering 'affective'. Affective remembering belongs

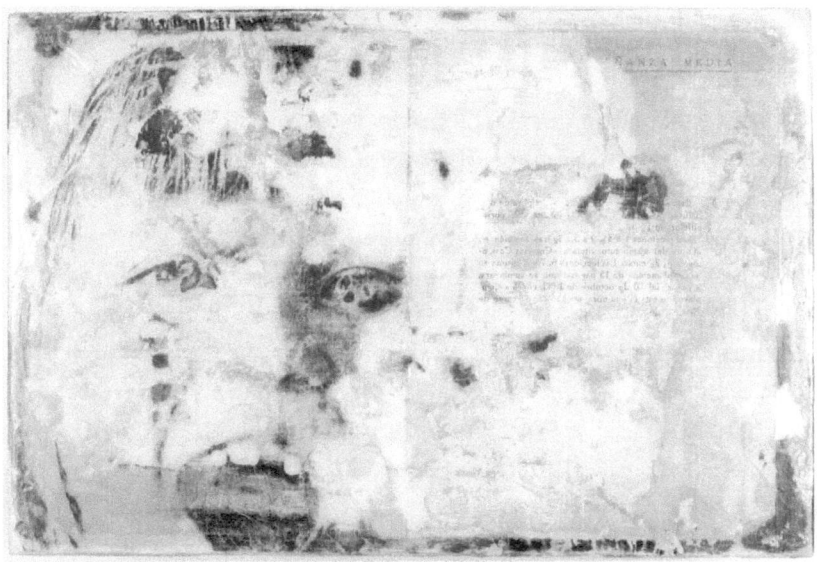

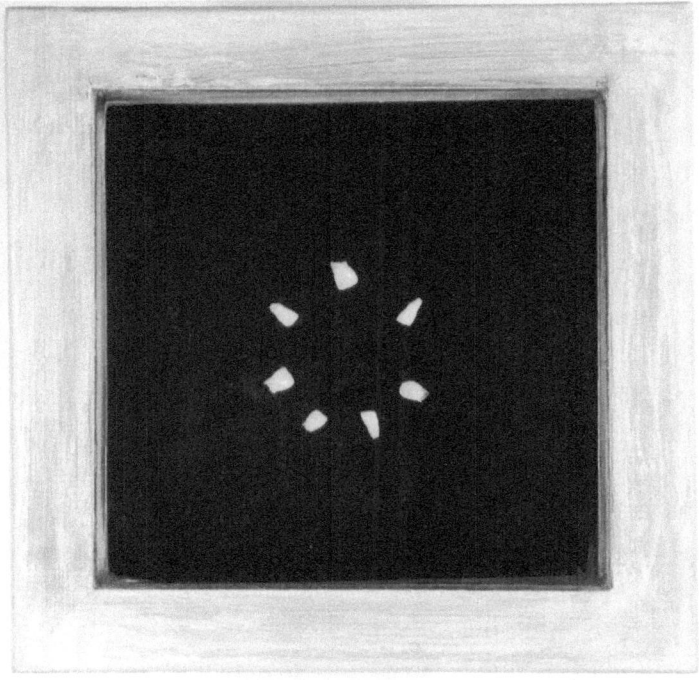

Figures 7.3 and 7.4. The spicy mouth and the relic box. Details of *D2I*, 30cm x 21cm and 17.5cm x 17.5cm. Photographs by Marjukka Irni.

to the realm of molecular memory that is a counterpart to molar memory.

Molar memory, the dominant memory of a majoritarian linear and logocentric subject, or of a nation-state with its milestones, great men, and characteristic psychic structures, works through the necessity to conform to and identify with existing laws, histories, and socio-cultural expectations. Molecular memory, in contrast, encompasses an 'empowerment of all that was not programmed within the dominant memory' (Braidotti 2006b, 167). Molecular memory, then, is fluid, flowing, an unruly transgressive force; a nonhuman agency that 'dislodges the subject from a unified and centralized location' (Braidotti 2006b, 167).

Importantly, affective remembering does not just revive some originary affects that one had (almost) lost. Rather, affective remembering is a productive act. It is a re-invention of the self through affective sensations. Art has a crucial role here, for it holds the potential of creating previously unrecognised and unknown affects (Deleuze and Guattari 1994, 175),[100] and makes them felt.

In modern Western culture, the interpretation of dreams (see, for example, Freud 2006, 397–403) – which in itself connects to a particular understanding of subjectivity – offers a conventional explanation for loose(ning) and shedding teeth. Dreams concerning teeth appear to be remarkably common. What popular interpretations of teeth dreams persuade us is that dreaming of losing one's tooth/teeth connects to the experiences of childhood, and tells about the fear of change, fear of growing up, the pressure to act like an adult, reflecting feelings of powerlessness and an inability to take control. In short, wobbling, falling teeth signal that the foundations in one's life are shaking, somehow coming down, failing the subject. Thus, a loosening tooth emerges as a threat to the 'order of things'.

The Grimacing Mouth 143

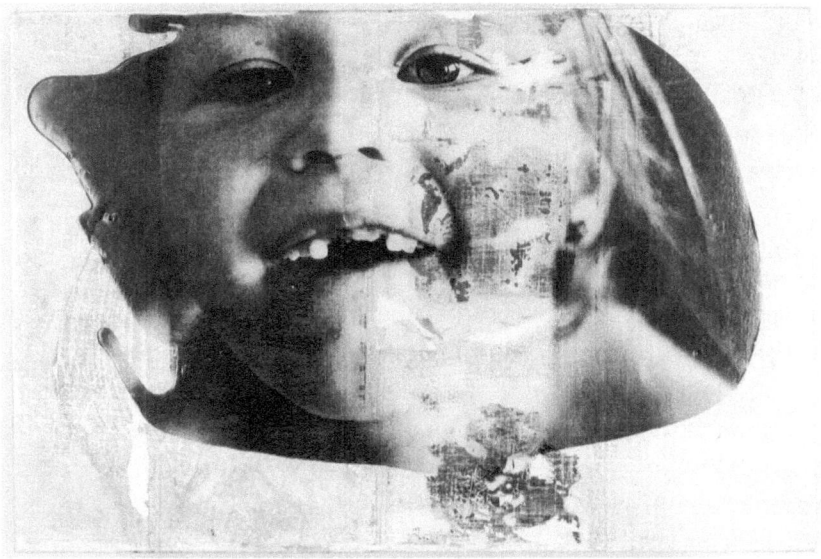

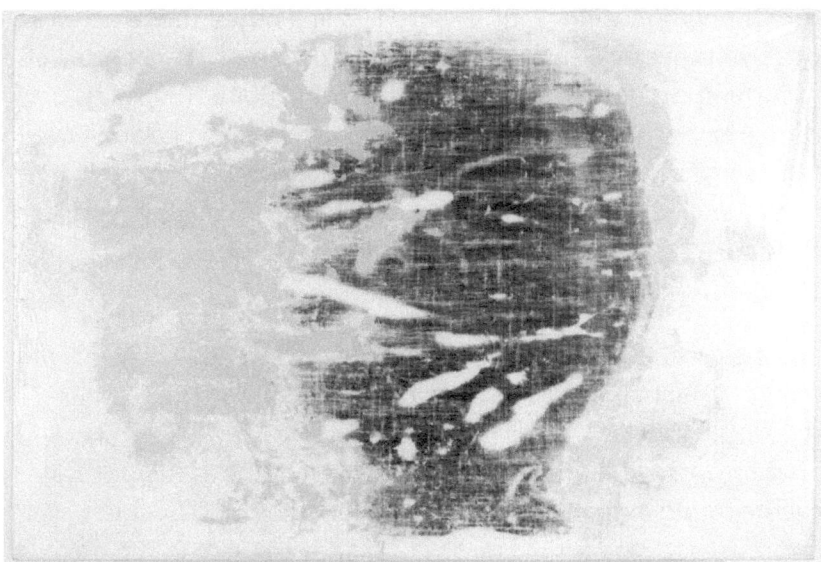

Figures 7.5 and 7.6. The joyful smile and the sandpapered smile. Details of *D2I*. Photographs by Marjukka Irni.

Ultimately, what interpretations of this kind suggest is that a bodily transformation such as shedding teeth stands out, not as a positive event, but as one that should be met with fear. At the same time as this interpretation offers a dominant, molar structure for reacting with fear and negativity to one's childhood memories of shedding teeth, it also suggests a corresponding subjectivity: a melancholic subjectivity built on loss.

The process of molecular remembering with which *D2I* engages the viewer proposes something different. In many of the assemblages the little girl's face gleams with joy, suggesting that the orientation towards change has a more positive feel to it than the majoritarian storyline would allow [Figure 7.5]. The shed teeth are not represented only as 'lack', as an empty place in the little girl's row of teeth. Instead, they are preserved in a box. It is molar memory that suppresses the possibilities of seeing the wobbling, shaking, and eventual falling out of the teeth as a positive event by freezing memories into its molar structures of mourning and loss. However, as Braidotti (2006b, 169) suggests, remembering in 'nomadic mode is the active reinvention of a self that is joyfully discontinuous, as opposed to being mournfully consistent, as programmed by phallogocentric culture'. As stated, no mourning for milk teeth. No looking back, or sense of lack. The teeth are still here.

It is the co-existence of the portraits and the teeth – organic things – that makes the installation rich with more joyful than mournful affects. The portraits and the teeth have a strong relation, interdependence even. What is missing in the portraits can be found in the box. Yet the teeth are not merely direct references for the portraits. There are seven teeth in the box, but only a few empty spots for them apparent in the mouth in the portraits. No portrait makes an easy match with a particular tooth or its position.

This irreducibility is related to the multiple material layers in and through which all the portraits emerge. Therefore, the painting-assemblages are far from being just bare documents of what was happening in Paula's mouth at a certain time, at a certain age.[101] They are not just traces of the past. Material layers – some poured over the canvas, having the feel of a heavy oil-like liquid, some composed in a patchwork manner, some just slapped on and appearing merely as stains of paint, others sandpapered until almost bare – are working Paula's face, re-working it, working over it, creating it [Figures 7.5 and 7.8]. Strong and sturdy yellows, reddish browns create a bloody effect, and a crowd of yellowish and greyish shades mould both facial expressions and features, making her anew in every portrait, showing her in constant change. The development of Paula's front teeth is not followed chronologically. There is more to these portraits than just a capturing of linear time, of what happened. Call it a messy type of remembering that 'does not even aim at retrieving information in a linear manner' (Braidotti 2006b, 167); a messy remembering emerging in and through the work of art, through bodies connecting in a parallel manner.

Relics and rituals of transition

Both the rich, multi-material affectivity and the appearance of the box in which the teeth dwell connect the installation to religious practices and discourses around relics. The box of teeth, with its velvet cushion and glass window, resembles a reliquary, a case holding a holy relic, a fragment of a deceased saint or something that was close to a saint's body, such as clothing. Although Paula's teeth are evidently not as old as relics often are – several hundred, if not thousands of years old – their exposure to time is already evident. They are what is left of something: relics. Relics are effective through conveying the (retained) power of that to which they have lost their material connection. For example, in the Catholic Church, relics are often understood to bear the spirit and the benevolent power of the deceased saint.[102]

Throughout the history of Christendom, the equivocal nature of relics has provoked considerable controversy: their dual character, incorporating both divine, 'transcendent' powers and material existence – the body that before consecration could have belonged to any one of us – makes relics a site of contact between the earthly and the spiritual (Miller 2009, 2, 64). Depending on viewpoint, this transitional in-between nature has been seen as 'dangerous materialism' associated with 'a pagan idolatry' (Belting 1994, 298), or as allowing the possibility of bringing the divine presence to the human through a 'sensuous experience' (Miller 2009, passim). Whereas in Christian practices relics bring together the divine and the earthly, the spiritual and the human, thus constituting a site of contact between different realms, *D2I* forms a site of contact between art and everyday experience, past and present.

While Nevado's daughter is no longer a child, neither is she 'gone' in the same sense as a medieval saint, whose earthly body, soon after death, was cooked – the bones and minor body parts such as teeth and joints (the holy matter) being then separated from the dead meat to be carefully stored in cases specially designed for them (see, for example, Park 1994, 1–13; Walker 2011, 131–32). As Paula certainly is not a consecrated saint, what is it, then, in the six-year-old's teeth that needs to be restored, connected with, remembered?

***

An interesting characteristic of relics is that they rarely come on their own: from the later stages of ancient Christianity onwards, the cult of relics has been accompanied and supported by rich visual and/or textual rhetorics, such as poetics based on ekphrasis, skilfully crafted ornaments, and colourful paintings (Miller 2009, 63–81), or, in modern times, simply by printed

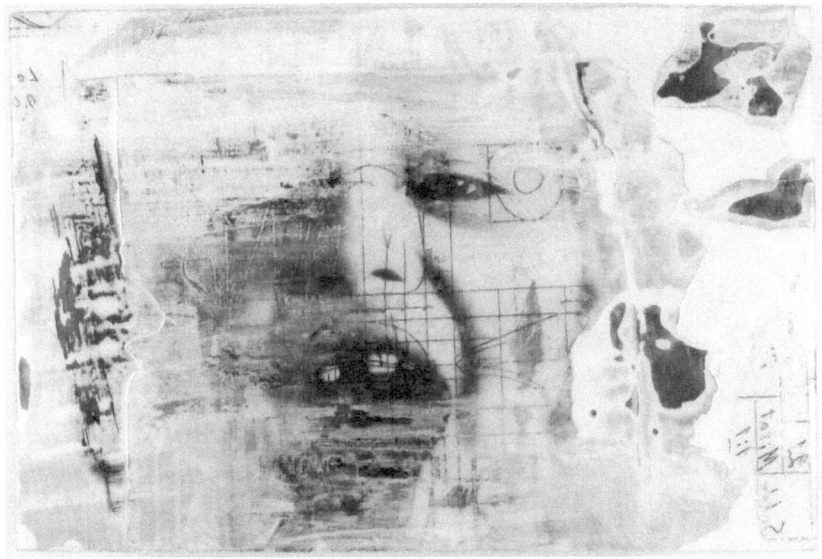

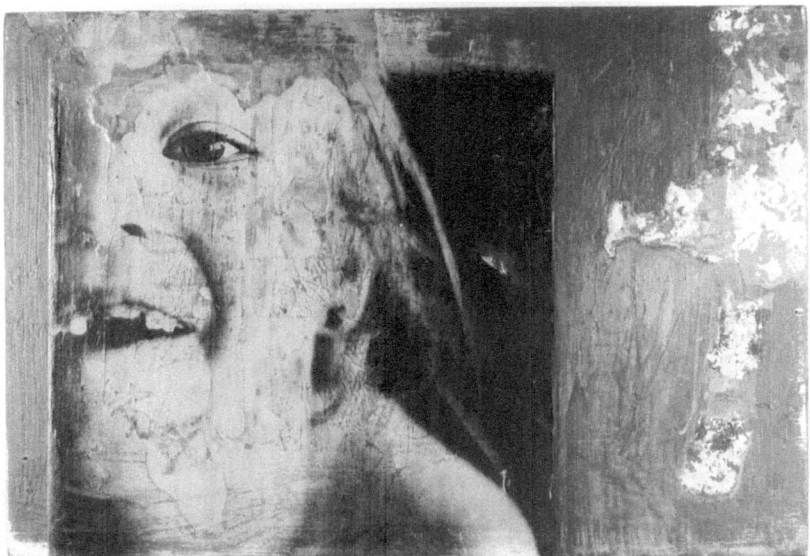

Figures 7.7 and 7.8. A joyful monster. Details of *D2I*. Photographs by Marjukka Irni.

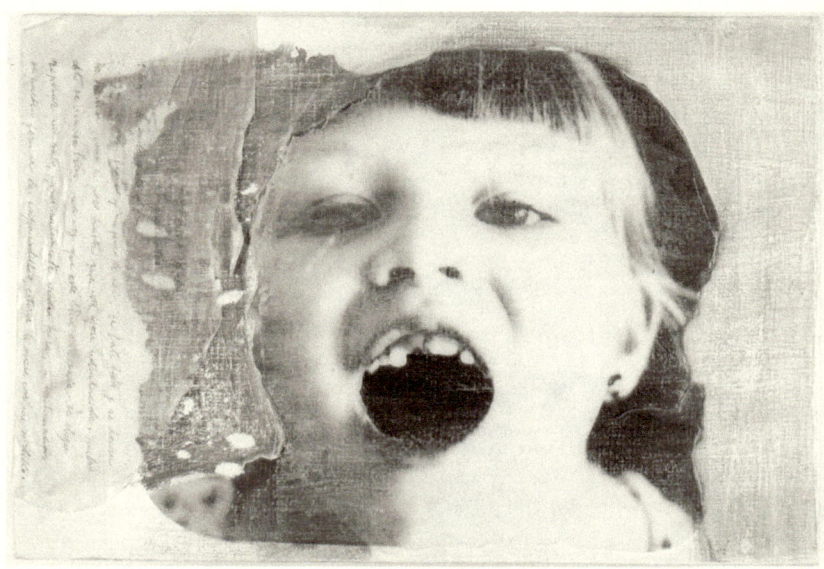

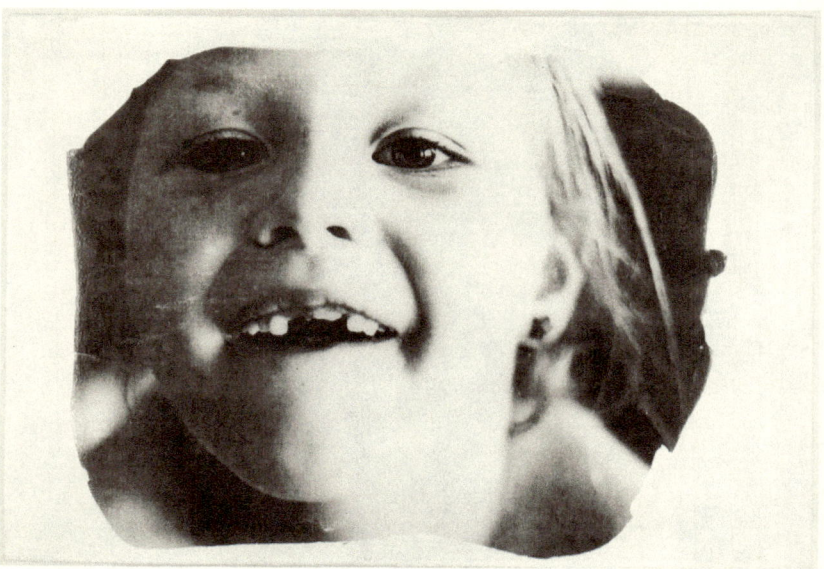

Figures 7.9 and 7.10. The portrait with the recipe and the little girl sustaining change. Details of *D2I*. Photographs by Marjukka Irni.

holy cards depicting saints and describing their deeds. In other words, aesthetic objects, such as beautifully carved and detailed reliquaries, have been seen to furnish the relic with at least part of its affective power. Accordingly, Nevado's *D2I* creates affective remembrance through the co-existence of 'teeth relics' and the visual art of painting-assemblages.

Both relics in general and Nevado's *D2I* installation in particular are processes with strong material presence as well as affective powers[103] – consider how, in the Catholic view, relics have the power to help people, heal the sick, and save lives, and how *D2I* might arouse affective memories in the audience. Both have ephemeral and fading, rather than permanent, existence in this world – teeth and bones slowly crumble, their organic composition decays. The qualities of impermanence and affectivity affirm transformation; they are the antithesis of stability.

But both relics and *D2I* are also about transformation in another sense: they fashion change from one order into another. Relics negotiate between earthly and heavenly bodies, they are of something that was human and became holy; in Nevado's installation, a child is growing up, acquiring adult teeth, entering into a new world, into a new form of existence.

Rituals concerning fallen-out milk teeth are transitional processes that relate not only to growing up but to relics. There are various local forms of this transition ritual: the tooth is placed under the child's pillow or in a glass of water next to the child's bed so that a tooth-fairy may take it away during the night. Thus, the tooth is (willingly) given, or taken away, for it no longer belongs to the child's life. The tooth must be left behind; otherwise the child does not grow up. Often the tooth is replaced with a coin – and so the child is introduced to the adults' world of monetary exchange: something is lost, something gained in exchange, preferably something more valuable. *D2I* does not seem to assign, or relate to, such an exchange practice in any way. Rather, it refers to a different kind of ritual, one akin to religious practices concerning relics.

What the Catholic understanding of relics offers is not an exchange economy. Rather, the relic is a site of continuing contact and reciprocal encounter. This notion echoes ancient Christian (and pagan) beliefs in relics as nodal points linking different realms – the earthly and the transcendental, the sensuous and the metaphysical – hence also subduing the potential dichotomy between matter and spirit (Miller 2009, 2, 64, 102). One could see, too, a correspondence between the Catholic practice of cherishing the material-spiritual connection that relics allow, and the way the milk teeth are often stored by Spanish mothers in small boxes specifically designed for them, or are made into artworks in which they form petals of a flower, as Nevado's Mexican friend described to me (Berber, 19 June 2009).[104]

A noteworthy characteristic of material remembering is its gender-specificity. Material remembrances and lived experience are the focus of many feminist works concerning bringing up children. One of the most notorious works in this vein is Mary Kelly's *Post-Partum Document* (1973–1979) that studies her son's early development from the mother's point of view – assembling everything from soiled diapers to diagrams of the content of his faeces, and from the baby boy's first fumbling efforts to write letters to the mother's typed diary notes. While Nevado's *D21* focuses on an episode a bit later in her daughter's life and is also narrower in its temporal perspective, it still encompasses more than just the exfoliation of milk teeth. At the age when a child's milk teeth are being shed (that is, approximately between the ages of five and seven), there are other major changes too.[105] The child is expected to grow more independent, to enter the school system, and to learn to read and write.

The *D21* portraits signal Paula's budding will in the midst of the transformation she cannot but submit to. She is making faces. Her hair is a bit of a mess, the fringe apparently self-scissored, the look in her eyes not obedient but happily unruly. At times, the painting-assemblages express a bit of monstrosity [Figures 7.7 and 7.8]. The roughly worked multi-layered portraits transform the child's eyes, nostrils, and the mouth into black holes; elsewhere, rubbing has made her face disappear into the play of shadows [Figure 7.6]; in the process, the face is at times de-facialised, sometimes rendered almost, sometimes altogether unrecognisable. Mostly, it is her mouth that appears deformed by the processes of transformation she is experiencing. The growing teeth do not form a perfect row. In the portrait that opened this chapter there is brownish red paint staining her mouth like blood, in others, black shadows, scratched and ripped-off sections, all suggesting that losing teeth is a mutilating experience [Figure 7.2]. Yet, in many other portraits the girl appears to be insistently happy. There is joy in her eyes and in her facial expression; the grimace is imbued with a smile. She is not avoiding the camera, turning her head away, but boldly taking pride in showing the change she is going through. There is no evidence of the horror of losing teeth that figures in adult dreams, or in psychoanalytical interpretations of them.

In the installation, the process of transformation the child is undergoing appears also through various, hard to read text excerpts. Among other things, there is a dirty, very well-worn book page, another upside down, a dispersed crumbled hand-written recipe for puff pastries [*empanadillas*],[106] and a dampened, 'swollen', faded out letter with slightly spread ink on it [Figure 7.9]. In their hardly readable, soiled and, at times, apparently decayed state these textual excerpts suggest that reading is not a self-evident skill – and entering into this new domain of cultural knowledge is not necessarily a smooth process either. In Kelly's *Post-Partum Document*, there is a whole episode dedicated to the process of stepping into the realm of language. However, whereas in Kelly's work her son's entrance into the realm of language finds its culmination in his ability to write his last name – his father's name – at the age of precisely four years and eight months (Saarikangas 1997, 110), in Nevado's *D2I* the child stays in the state of wonder, in the state of acquiring new skills.

The monument of enduring change

The happy, excited expression on Paula's face will not change, it will stay there as long as the material lasts – enduring beyond the process of growing up [Figures 7.5 and 7.10]. It is, enshrined, monumentalised there forever, ready to encounter its viewer: 'sensation is now forever tied to this smile, this yellow … in its absolute singularity' (Grosz 2008, 74).[107] What are monumentalised are not (solely) Paula's or her mother's personal emotions, but affects beyond any particular individual, affects created, negotiated in the work of art. These affects, even the joyous smile, are indebted to or, rather, supported by the material qualities of the piece, by the brushstrokes, the re-worked transfer medium, the varying thicknesses and fluidities of matter composing the work. So connected they are that it is hard to say, 'where in fact the material ends and sensation begins' (Deleuze and Guattari 1994, 161, 166).

The multiple smiling faces spread across the installation propose that Paula is not lost in transformation but happily sustained in the change she is going through. Maybe she reminds us that we have all endured such changes ourselves; we have the experience of enduring constant change built, coded into our bodies. Rosi Braidotti (2002; 2006b) has perhaps most persistently argued for a subject who could sustain their sense of limits and endure in the contemporary world of fast changes, continual transformations, metamorphoses and mutations. Crucially, she has argued for a subject who can be sustainable without readily, unproblematically, adopting the commercial practices of profit-bound capitalism, to buy this and that, to stock up and cash in, to keep up with change, to adjust to change. The ethics of sustainability that Braidotti fashions is grounded on very different principles: on the subject's or any being's propensity for life – for life as a force that cannot be owned but that can be lived by giving oneself 'away in a web of multiple belongings and complex interactions' without self-destruction (Braidotti 2006b, 215). The subject must find balance in giving away and in sustaining their limits, enduring change. If the relic teeth of Nevado's installation with its fifteen painting-assemblages call us to remember something, it is that sustainability and endurance are intertwined in the process of growing up. This is suggested by a new figuration acquired in the joyous smiles of the girl sustaining the change.

As this chapter is approaching its end, it is time to return to ingestion. Unless the viewer-participant 'ingests' the work of art, allows their own system of being and thought to open up to that of the other, to connect with that of its parallel-body, not much really happens, gets digested. Without ingestion – both Nevado's and mine – the grimacing mouth would have stayed a grimacing mouth, and the unruly, enduring happiness infused into the portraits and encountered in the relic teeth could not have emerged.

8

The Preaching Mouth

A woman with a shaved head and no make-up preaches with a powerful, demanding voice. She is wearing a white T-shirt that states 'Sappho wants to save you' [Figure 8.1]. What comes out of her mouth is as stereotypically lesbian as her looks: *The Woman-Identified Woman* manifesto (1970, 1) by the American activist group Radicalesbians:

> A lesbian is the rage of all women condensed to the point of explosion. She is the woman who ... acts in accordance with her inner compulsion to be a more complete and freer human being than her society ... cares to allow her. ... The perspective gained from ... the liberation of self, the inner peace, the real love of self and of all women is something to be shared with all women – because we are all women.

This preaching video is the core element in Marjukka Irni's artwork *Sappho Wants to Save You* (2006–2010), an installation that also encompasses six life-size photographic portraits of women posing in 'Sappho wants to save you' T-shirts. The installation relates to a community art project that Irni organised with local Gender Studies departments in Turku, Finland. Many of the employees at these departments felt annoyed by the young and fiery Christian converters, a man and a woman, who preached their religious message in a patriarchal order – the woman following the man – at the pedestrian area in the centre of Turku. The aim of the art project was to turn the shared annoyance into something positive and affirmative. The major event of the project was a performance involving bilingual public preaching in the name of Sappho, and a rally of fifteen women that moved through the pedestrian area as a united front, so as to claim the space as their own.

Through its different manifestations – demonstration march, preaching, and installation – the *Sappho Wants to Save You* project not only criticises stereotypical conceptions of gender, it also proposes subtler, nuanced, open formations of gender as a process of relational becoming. In the above excerpt of the 1970s manifesto, becoming is expressed in relation to the inner self and to the society that restricts the individual. The direction is clear: to become a freer and a more complete human being. But in Irni's artwork, relationscapes of sexual becoming multiply: they reach beyond the individual with inner will and the regulating, restricting powers of society. In *Sappho Wants to Save You*, sexualities emerge material-relationally, for example, in the intensities of bodily acts such as preaching or posing, as well as in the line-up of the slowly-moving, space-taking all-woman wall.

Starting with the preaching mouth, this chapter engages with the intensive and vibrational variations that open sexual becomings beyond the prism of (subversive) identity politics through which they are commonly analysed. This does not mean that *Sappho Wants to Save You* does not have explicit references to sexual identity, and, more precisely, to lesbian identity politics. The references are obvious in the manifesto, including such statements as: 'To be a woman who belongs to no man is to be invisible, pathetic, inauthentic, unreal. ... As long as we are dependent on the male culture, for his approval, we cannot be free' (Radicalesbians 1970, 3). The stereotypical lesbian looks of the preacher further confirm lesbian identity, as do the T-shirts with the historical reference to the Greek poet, Sappho, from whose home island of Lesbos the name for modern-day lesbians is derived. Moreover, the fact that the project was an all-women gathering supports the overall lesbian theme.

With all these references, *Sappho Wants to Save You* could be said to work as an outspoken advocate of the lesbian identity politics that flourished in the late 1960s and 1970s concurrently with other radical social movements, including the Anti-War, Black Power, Jesus, and Student movements. What made these movements attractive was that they introduced a new kind of politics that emphasised the personal as political (Doy 1998, 106–15). To stress personal connections, some of the 'Sapphic' demonstrators wore personalised T-shirts stating 'Your mother' or 'Your sister', while others identified as lesbians by wearing T-shirts with likenesses of well-known lesbian thinkers and artists printed on them. In so doing, they related to the identity politics central to the radical social movements, which stressed politics as one's chosen cause and community, where everyone mattered in the collective effort towards changing the world. A Finnish radical leftist song of the time crystallises the personal as political by asking: '[w]hom do you stand for, whose flag do you carry?' It continues, claiming: 'There won't be justice without a battle. And no battle without a united front' (Chydenius and Oksanen 1968).[108] With the preaching of the *Woman-Identified Woman* manifesto and the demonstration taking the form of a Sapphic front, *Sappho Wants to Save You* summons the spirit of this radical identity politics aptly indeed.[109]

However, the artist stresses that the project was made with a twinkle in the eye: the lesbian and religious gravity of the project was at least partially parodic (Nissi 2007). Following Judith Butler (1990) and her book *Gender Trouble: Feminism and the Subversion of Identity*, the lesbian perfection of *Sappho Wants to Save You* is performed. According to Butler, there are certain historical limitations that make genders possible, and parody arises from performing them iteratively – with a parodic twist (1990, 177). To understand parody, contextual knowledge is needed. In this regard, parody works similarly to irony: there is a necessity to distance oneself from the actuality of the event experienced and to think what the parody in question refers to, what it parodies (Colebrook 2002, ix–xix). To 'get' the parody of the project, it is relevant to give an example, to acknowledge the popular phrase, 'Jesus wants to save you', that was spread more or less globally by the Christian peace movement, the 'Jesus movement', and, interestingly enough, parallel with the heyday of lesbian radicalism in the late 1960s and early 1970s.

But there is more to this work of art than historical references or possibilities, no matter how subversive their performance. Careful atten*dance* to how *Sappho Wants to Save You* emerges as a work of art invites one to perceive rather future than past orientated openings: suddenly those lesbian stereotypes stutter and stammer, allowing for more varied sexual becomings. Each section of this chapter focuses on openings emerging material-relationally in the work of art: first studied are the complexities of preaching as an affective bodily performance, then the auto-organised, collective practices of the women's bodily demonstration, and, finally, the subtle micro-movements of posing and installation display. This is to carve out sensations of sexuality and gender variety beyond recognizable identity politics, and also beyond individual choices and the personal.

Affective preaching

To make it more widely shareable, the Radicalesbian manifesto of *Sappho Wants to Save You* is delivered bilingually, by two readers, one after the other: sentences in Finnish are followed by English translations – this is how the Christian preachers that the performance criticises proceeded too [Figure 8.1]. This kind of immediate translation is common in spiritual sermons held at international religious conferences. At these conferences, the evangelic idea is translated not only literally or orally, but also by way of bodily movements (Coleman 1996, 121). This highlights the performative nature of the preaching event: bare translation of words is never sufficient. The spread word is not a textual 'message', but a spiritual process emanating directly from God. Contrary to the faithful mimicking practised in mass sermons, the bilingual preaching of *Sappho Wants to Save You* highlights the singularity of each bodily expression, of each embodied performer. Each preacher's body has its distinctive rhythm and bearing, its singular support technique for the voice to emerge – relationally. The varying ways of expression make the manifesto different each time too.

The woman preaching in Finnish has an intense look in her eyes; her articulation is sharp and strong; bodily posture firm and secure, effortlessly supportive of voice production. The potent preaching flows through her body with admirable ease. The one who preaches in English as a second language struggles slightly; there are pauses that take a little longer than they should, and a bit of bodily jerking suggesting that considerable effort is being put into the performance, to make the manifesto heard and felt.

The singularities of the two performances suggest that preaching is unmistakably a bodily phenomenon. Here, the body is not a passive 'venue' for the godly content. Instead, a preaching body does a lot; it expresses in a vibrating relation to muscles, tissues and nerves throughout the body, from top to toe. Not only does the voice resonate in the nasal and oral cavities, but toes, feet, legs, the core, relate the body to the ground, to its environment, doing their work in balancing the posture, making the words flow.

The affectivity of preaching relates to the conception of bodies becoming in their relation to other bodies, which encompass human and more-than-human, organic and inorganic, such as

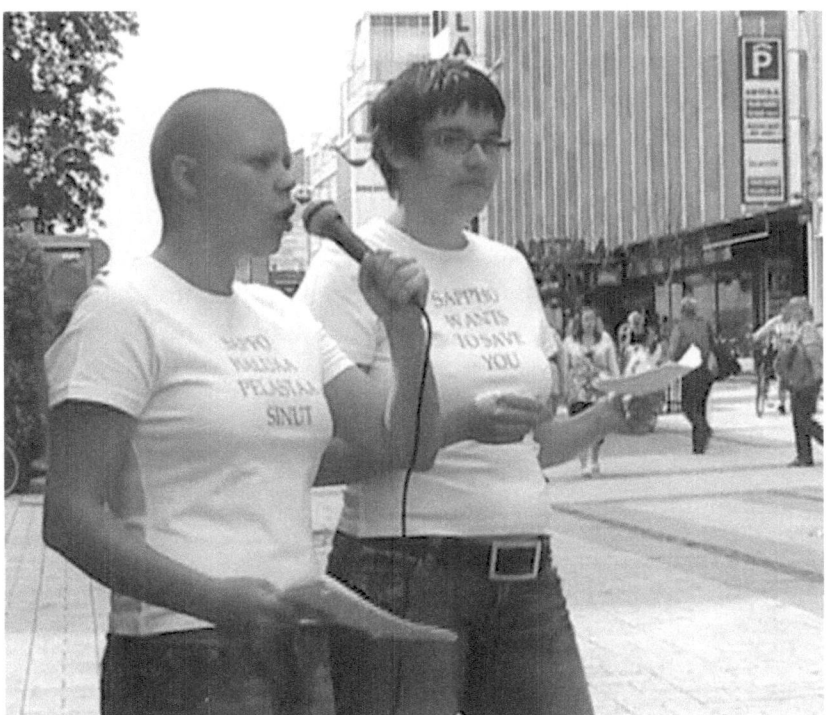

Figure 8.1. The preachers. Frame enlargement of Marjukka Irni's *Sappho Wants to Save You* video, 2006.

a vibrational sound. Brian Massumi and Erin Manning (2014) designate settings where bodies are in a dynamic relation to each other, 'events'. Affects are relations that make an event emerge, they hold it together, relationally. Affects are qualitative changes, felt as intensities in, or rather in between bodies. Events are always singular – they happen between specific bodies and their relations. Alter or adjust one element, and the event becomes different. Yet it is possible, as Massumi (2015, 109) claims, to experience collective events, where bodies, each in their unique way, relate to, perceive and process the same 'cue' – such a singular preaching voice. No preacher without a body, no preacher without surrounding bodies. No event without change. No event without becoming.

This is to say, that preaching is a material-relational event per se, and as an event it is always more than a mouth that voices, articulates. An example: if one does not understand either of the languages the preachers utilise, then one is more inclined to attend to the affective emergence of the manifesto, feel and relate to the non-verbal qualities of articulation – to the body in motion – to try to follow its movements, tones, pauses, slowing downs and accelerations. And even if one does comprehend one or both of the languages, that does not eradicate the affective force of bodily articulation. It only renders it less perceptible.

According to David Morgan (2007, 204, 217, 222–23), charismatic orality is a central power in preaching events. It eventfully, *energetically* occurs across bodies, moving through and via tones, gestures, choreographies (Morgan 2007, 223; see also Bennett 2010b, 28). Like electricity, charisma needs a circuit to circulate, spread its powers; to get its forces to flow. Charisma's circuit are the bodies attending the preaching event, making its emergence possible.

Even though, for Morgan, the (human) body is the fundamental medium of charisma, he specifies that today, media, including television and radio broadcasting and digital recordings, extend the body. While the media of so called 'tele-evangelism' multiplies relationscapes of the body, it does not weaken intensities felt relationally. What the producers and distributors of recordings of preaching events and services claim is that the sacred word retains its affective power when recorded or saved; and that these products are popular precisely because through them affective events can be revisited again and again (Coleman 1996, 121; Morgan 2007, 225). As Simon Coleman (1996, 120–21) explains, tele-evangelism provides its recipients with presence and immediacy, and the production process supports this. The way in which Irni's preacher video is shot and produced is quite similar to that of religious event recordings of tele-evangelism. In *Sappho Wants to Save You*, the camera focuses on the two preachers and only occasionally a few reaction shots of the audience are included, just as is the case in 'real' religious preaching recordings. Moreover, there are no interruptions, no discontinuities, not even a list of credits to point out that this is a re-presentation, and not a live recording.

In the art world, performance and installation works have gained a similar reputation: 'Instead of *representing* texture, space, light and so on', they are to be experienced directly; '[t]his', Claire Bishop claims, 'introduces an emphasis on sensory immediacy, on physical participation' (2005, 11, emphasis added). In tele-evangelism, 'direct' physical participation can be experienced by placing hands upon the radio or television receiver so as to relate to the voice of the preacher (Morgan 2007, 223). In this way, the viewer becomes a participant, touches the spirit, and is touched by it. In the case of contemporary art, bodily participation is seldom achieved by touching the work itself, yet bodily participation is central to the expectation of sensing the work in the body. However, whereas religious event recordings tend to technically smooth out sound distortion, so 'that the Word can flow unhindered' (Coleman 1996, 121) and hence be encountered as directly as possible, in *Sappho Wants to Save You* the second preacher stumbles through her speech, and the somewhat jerky and stumbling mode of expression is not hidden or edited.

To paraphrase Brian Massumi (2002b, 40–41), the smooth, polished flow of words does not necessarily account for a higher affective connectivity or offer a more direct relation to the listening bodies than the stumbling, fumbling expression, but rather the opposite. The case of the former president of the United States of America, Ronald Reagan, proves this. Reagan was immensely popular and won the confidence of the masses, despite the fact that he was widely known, and mocked, for his lack of clear expression, for 'invalid' articulation. This suggests that Reagan's success was not based on his verbal fluency or the exactness of his words. Instead, his struggle with words amplified their connectivity: jerks and pauses opened the speech up so that a wide variety of people found him irresistibly appealing. It was not by the power of ideology or coherent political content, but affectively, that he connected with the people, connected the people and thus re-connected the nation. Consequently, it is important not to idealise free flows of preaching but attend to those tiny movements that disturb the perfect expression, make it more bodily affective. Such talk resonates, stutters more, its singularity has more contact surfaces than the polished flow of words (see Deleuze 1994b). This is to say that even if the content of the manifesto might have been precipitous in its lesbian identity politics – in claiming that 'lesbians are the rage of all women', for example – the way that this content was made felt through the two preachers delivering it in their singular ways in fact opens it up much more radically. Allowing affective stumbling to have its effect on the contents made the manifesto queer – positively troublesome, disobedient to a recognisable lesbian identity.

Passive activism

The affectively open preaching event was part of a public performance, and was preceded by a quiet, small-scale demonstration march: a slowly moving wall of lesbian women who just walked rather silently through the busy pedestrian area, without a particular choreography to emphasise their agenda, without shouting any political slogans to underline their message [Figure 8.2]. The front had no single spokeswoman, yet it was sufficiently coherent – but not violently so: it allowed other people to pass through it, only to immediately reunite.

The lesbian front of *Sappho Wants to Save You* follows the ways of the feminist history of women's passive, peaceful, bodily demonstrations. There are two practices of passive demonstration that I want to bring up here: the Greenham

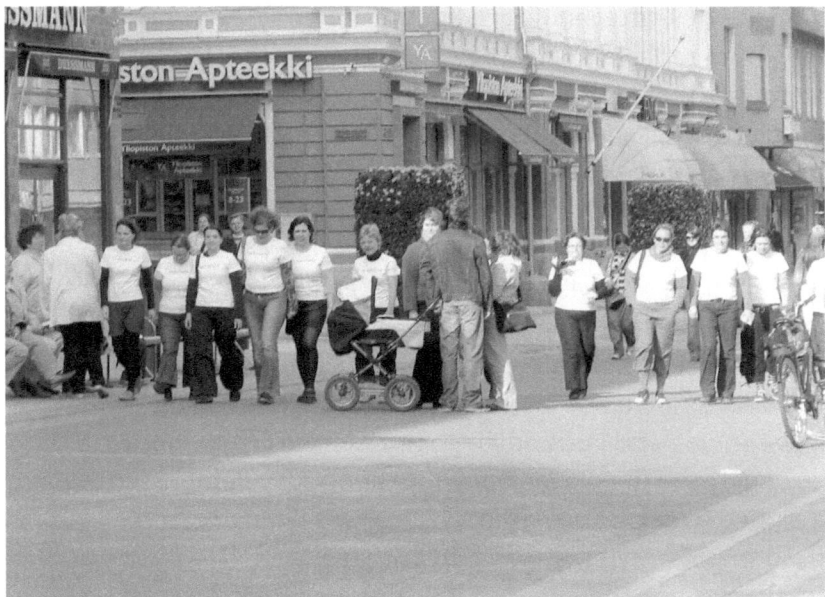

Figure 8.2. The demonstration march in Turku, *Sappho Wants to Save You* (Lesbian Missionary) community art project with the Gender Studies departments at the University of Turku and Åbo Akademi University, May 2006. Photograph by Taina Erävaara.

women's peace camp in the UK (1982–2000), and the Argentinian Las Madres de Plaza del Mayo (1977–).[110] The Greenham women, taking their name from the location, camped for almost two decades by the fences of a US nuclear base in Wales, to protest against storing nuclear weapons there (Roseneil 1995; 2000). The camping was not a planned event but the seamless continuation of a peace march against the storing of missiles. The march was so peaceful, indeed, that it did not gain much media attention. To get more publicity for their cause, some of the marchers handcuffed themselves to the fence surrounding the base, at that point without having any further purpose (Roseneil 1995). However, the women decided to stay until something was done, and soon the peace camp became permanent.[111]

The Greenham women's ways of practising activism were emphatically non-violent: they did not want to protest the violence of war technology by acting violently, as this would only have repeated what they criticised. Instead, the Greenham women protested peacefully, and became famous for passive blockades (Roseneil 1995, 63–64): the women blocked the activities of the 'war machine' with their bodies. They discharged their everyday duties and lived their lives year after year where it was forbidden to live and where it certainly disturbed the military base's activities. They also organised mass events that in different ways made affirmative use of the collective body of women. For example, the 'embrace the base' event gathered together over 30,000 women, who surrounded the base, embracing it and each other. Their claim was, 'together we are strong; break the nuclear chain'. Other bodily demonstrations included dancing on missile silos, collective singing and chanting.[112]

Radical feminism, including that of the Greenham women studied by Roseneil, challenges the rules of patriarchal organisations that alienate human bodies and emotions by dividing lives into a series of duties assigned from 'above', whether the authoritative institution is the army, religion, or capitalist economics (Roseneil 1995).[113] As the *Woman-Identified Woman* manifesto preached by the Sapphics of *Sappho Wants to Save You* suggests, women must free themselves from the traditional, sexist roles that subordinate them to men and to the economic, political, and military functions of patriarchal institutions. The manifesto incites collective auto-organisation: 'It is the primacy of women relating to women, of women creating a new consciousness of and with each other, which is at the heart of women's liberation, and the basis for the cultural revolution' (Radicalesbians 1970, 4).

Rather than being armed with weapons, it could be suggested that the Greenham women were armed with their own 'lived temporality', with the immanence of living. They did not allow their time to be hierarchically governed from 'above', it was made collectively their own as they created their daily camping rhythm with no electricity or running water supply – essentials of modern housewifery (Roseneil 2000, 90–91). The way the participants of the Lesbian front of *Sappho Wants to Save You* proceeded was, likewise, self-organised and independent of the capitalist structures of the shopping district: Sapphics walked together quietly in their own rhythm in the midst of a pedestrian area busy with weekend shoppers running errands to 'keep up with the system'. This was also 'a being-together experience – not too serious' – as one of the Greenham protestors had claimed.[114] Indeed, one of the participants of the *Sappho Wants to Save You* demonstration made a statement that similarly emphasised co-relatedness when describing her experience of marching and blocking the commercial district with the women's united front, lightly claiming: 'Oh we just walked and chatted together' (anonymous march participant, 20 November 2009). Hence the collective organisation into being-togetherness and making their own time was a crucial part of the activist practice against the patriarchal surroundings that both the Greenham women and the Sapphics of the *Sappho Wants to Save You* demonstration exercised.

In her ethnographical study *Lived Temporalities: Exploring Duration in Guatemala*, Julia Mahler (2008, 65–78) calls this kind of time, that captures the immediacy of everyday life, 'passive time'. Passive time is not hierarchically governed by structural, institutionalised authorities but has the immediacy of lived temporality. The concept relates to Gilles Deleuze's passive synthesis of time, which he introduces in *Difference and Repetition* (1994a, 70–85).[115] It captures the way in which the time modes of past, present, and future encounter and transform each other in an eternal return. Passive time does not emerge linearly or chronologically, or as a result of an active reflection such as historical analysis. In passive synthesis, past, present, and future synthesise through affects, intensity, and bodies in becoming.

Although passive time can seem to stand still, it is rich with intensive movement. Passive time cannot be quantified or hurried up: it is a qualitative, relational mode of becoming.[116] Another phrase for this kind of experience of time is 'event-time' (Manning 2013, 106–107; 2016, 81–83, 122–23). As Erin Manning (2013, 106) specifies, event-time subverts linear clock-time, it is a kind of 'no-time'. As there is no time to control the process, the process will compose its future in relation, immanently. From the perspective of event-time, it is not particularly relevant information that the Greenham women camped next to the nuclear weapons base precisely from 1982 to 2000, nor is it essential to be aware of how long the demonstrators of *Sappho Wants to Save You* marched. It is *how* they did it and what kind of an event emerged and was felt that means the most.

Many of the passive actions that Mahler depicts connect to intensive temporalities of the everyday that do not benefit from modern resources such as electricity, tap water, or supermarkets. To tend, guard the fire to get the wood burning, is one such passive event. Patience and time are needed to allow the wood to light, for the wood to be affected by the fire, and then to get the fire to last, hold out, long enough for food to be properly cooked. This was what the Greenham women experienced too: at the camp, the fire was a vital source of energy and warmth, where meals were prepared, and around which meals were consumed, plans discussed, and life stories exchanged – and keeping it going was, simultaneously, hard, delicate, yet time-consuming work (Roseneil 2000, 94).

While the Sapphics of *Sappho Wants to Save You* did not tend a fire, nor did they perform any other time-consuming household tasks, their resistance carried another tenor of passive time: religious processions that connect living people to the dead and the divine, across time and bodies (Mahler 2008, 100–102). The slowly moving, generally quiet, but at times chatty Lesbian collective wall disturbed the busyness and the conventional choreography of the shopping district where people hastily run their daily errands. Ignoring the consumer habits of the post-capitalist market place, the Sapphics followed, took and made time and rhythm of their own – while their bodies connected to the feminist history of passive demonstration and all the way back to the Greek 'Goddess' Sappho and her 'sisters'.

Slow, space-occupying moving resistance is also what the Argentinian women's group Las Madres de Plaza de Mayo [Mothers of Plaza de Mayo] is known for. The group was established soon after the first mass-kidnappings during the military dictatorship from 1976 to 1983. Madres and their sub-organisation, Las Abuelas [grandmothers] de Plaza de Mayo, demanded that their 'disappeared' children and grandchildren be returned, and to make their cause visible to political decision-makers they started to gather in front of the main government buildings of Buenos Aires, the capital of Argentina. As the local policemen pointed out that their group gathering was illegal, the women started to slowly walk one behind the other, and eventually formed a moving circle around a monumental obelisk erected, paradoxically, for peace. The women wore white headscarves, which later became permanent signs of the women at the square, as white headscarves were painted around the monument. While their symbols stay there all week, speaking for their cause, it is the women's weekly quiet demonstrations that have made the biggest impact on the public, on decision-makers and fellow citizens. In their practice, the affective, intensive power of moving bodies has exceeded the representational power of painted scarfs (cf. Brunner 2015, 182–88).

Following Mahler (2008, 72–73), what is built on by the passive actions of the Greenham women, Las Madres de Plaza de Mayo and the Sapphics of *Sappho Wants to Save You* is that in their practice intensive slowness and repetition offer a leap from actual time to passive time which shows life's potentialities, beyond everyday experience yet arising from the everyday. Yet, passive time does not lack activity. Rather, passive time is active in its relational emergence, and this may well have political consequences also.

Through their persistent, time-consuming, non-violent passive activities, both the Greenham women and Las Madres de Plaza de Mayo have gained a lot; their passive actions have attracted media attention, made their cause not only visible but felt. The first missiles of the Greenham base were sent for destruction in 1989 and the base was closed in 2000. The list of achievements of Las Madres de Plaza de Mayo is impressive: several hundred of the 'disappeared' children have been recovered and given the possibility to rework their stolen identities; Las Madres have also been nominated for the Nobel Peace Prize, and many women's groups around the world have adopted their tactics. Although at the level of structural political changes *Sappho Wants to Save You* is not, by any means, comparable to these achievements, the three groups have more in common at the level of the affective: relational intensities that emerge in women's passive group demonstrations as well as in the manifesto preaching may have radical and far-reaching effects. Whereas the long-term passive resistance of the Greenham women and Las Madres de Plaza del Mayo has resulted in crucial structural changes, *Sappho Wants to Save You* moves its viewer-participants and the identity positions involved in a way that might potentially transform perceptions and understandings of lesbianism and sexual identities. This is what Sasha Roseneil (2000, 321) suggests about the Greenham Commons women's peace camp too: it 'queered lives and, just a little, queered the world'. To consider the affective micropolitics of *Sappho Wants to Save You* further, to further queer the queer, let us turn next to the installation version of the work.

Queer politics of the imperceptible

In the *Sappho Wants to Save You* installation, the slowly walking front of Sapphics is expressed in six full-body portraits that fill the exhibition space in front of the manifesto video. The bold, confident, and powerful portraits oscillate in the air, minutely, molecularly moved by exhibition goers but also by their technical construction: the fabric of the screens is light enough to be affected by the currents of air created by the audience and the air-conditioning, for example, and their wired hanging system flexible enough to respond to the aerial variation, the metal laths on the top and bottom of the screens not too heavy to resist the movement [Figure 8.3]. So much is the constellation of the installation prone to affective movement that during one iteration of the installation, the portraits were constantly turned around by the power and movement of the air. During this event, the brave lesbian portraits became faint ghosts as they could be perceived only through the slightly transparent fabric.

Consequently, lightness, flexibility, and weight should not be perceived as merely technical or formal details indifferent to the meaning of the work. Rather, they should be regarded as art's two-way bodily capacities: as a capacity to be affected and a capacity to affect (Deleuze 1988, 123). In this way, the affect economy of art emerges in relation to form and technicalities, and not only in relation to 'content', to what kind of image – poignant or otherwise – a work of art represents. As it is understood here, form is dynamic, and not a static or neutral see-through participant in the work (Manning 2009, 15–16).[117] In other words, form is not a fixed construction but filled with incipient potential for movement, and images exist only in this movement. Thus, dynamic form is an ontological issue. To highlight how important it is not to disregard the technical qualities of a work of art, but to consider them in terms of movement and change, I suggest calling this ontological quality of art 'technico-affectivity'. Technico-affectivity is the more-than of technical. Erin Manning (2013, 32–35) names this sort of technicality 'technicity'. For her, technicity is not reproducible, it is something that emerges in relation, and thus is always open to the future, to what it is yet to come.

Let us visit the installation again with a focus on technico-affectivity. In the portraits, women pose in rather solid positions [Figure 8.4]. They stand legs more or less apart, to indicate a strong, firm position; two stand with arms akimbo, two have their arms protectively crossed. If perceived as representations, the Sapphic figures, with all their effort, appear to stand still; they are well aware of and are guarding their place in society. However, when the minutely moving, technico-affective materiality of the installation is taken into account, the still bodies sway despite all this effort [Figure 8.3]. The portraits are in constant delicate movement – their dynamic form gives no opportunity for such fixed (lesbian) positions to stay still. But there is more to it.

In her extraordinary little essay titled 'Mover's Guide for Standing Still', Erin Manning (2009, 43–47) proposes that the effort to stand still is a rather hopeless endeavour. Manning's subtle descriptions of what kind of an event trying to stand still actually is make it obvious that we do not ever stand still in our lives. To sum up: to stand still you have to move. Standing still requires constant corrections. These are not conscious corrections. They are micro-movements that move through the feeling of standing still. Posture is not about stopping. Posture is dynamic and constitutive of the body's tendencies for reconfiguration. Whereas the images as representations seem to stress fixed identity positions (although in a manner that is almost too straightforward, and therefore parodically performative), what the installation presents as an event is something else. Seemingly still, stiff posers sway in the air almost imperceptibly.

The Preaching Mouth 171

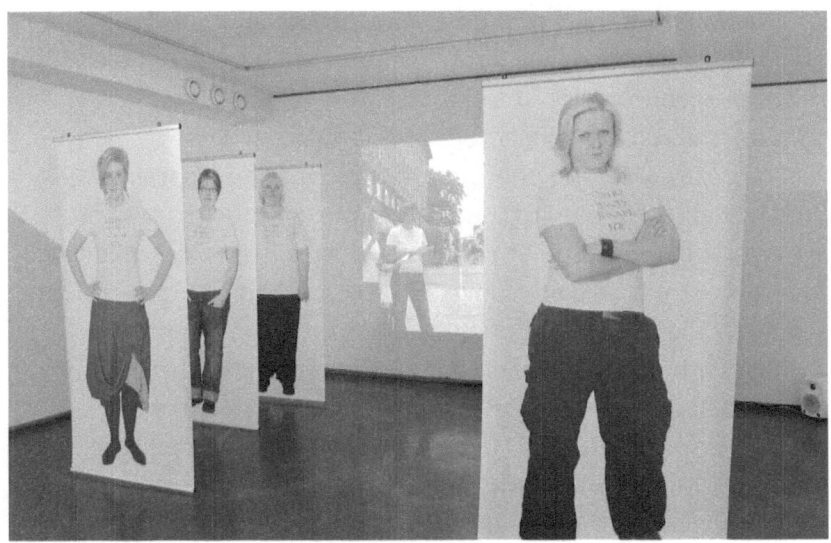

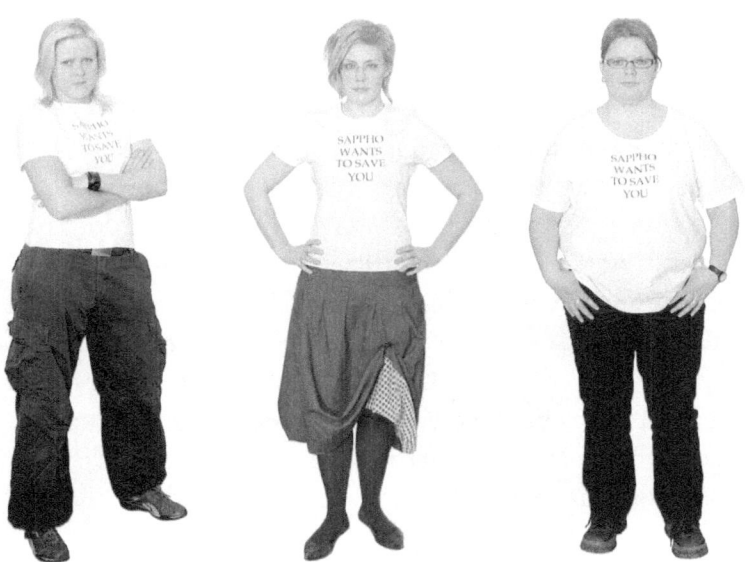

Figures 8.3 and 8.4. *Sappho Wants to Save You* installation at *Zigzagging from Art to Theory – and Back* exhibition, curated by Katve-Kaisa Kontturi. Titanik Gallery, Turku, November 2010; and portraits for *Sappho Wants to Save You*, July 2006. Photographs by Marjukka Irni.

As I happen to be one of the persons posing in those portraits, I begin to re-member my body – remember in my body the uncomfortable feeling of trying to stand still in front of the camera. What may have accentuated my experience is that I had to pose twice; the photos had to be re-taken as there were technical difficulties with the camera during the first session. As Manning writes, the effort of standing still requires vigorous, careful balancing – controlling movement, contradictory though it may sound, by moving. Also, standing still can put one in contact with other bodily movement-feelings: the nose itches, hair tickles the chin, one feels an urge to scratch one's back …. No matter how perfectly composed one's posture might seem, it is not a solid position but a series of almost imperceptible micro-movements – and, as such, an endless process. Thus, the endeavour of standing still is an obvious failure to begin with: it simply is not possible. Nor, for that matter, are fixed identity positions. There is always something on the move, however hard one tries to fix a position, an identity.

Although the solidly posing Sapphics might at first glance suggest a connection to the lesbian identity politics that builds around recognition, the politics of *Sappho Wants to Save You* does not, in the end, work towards the affirmation of a pre-constituted identity group such as lesbians. Rather, it suggests that the very positions we think we 'own' or occupy are not stable, but ever-changing phases of continual movement. As the swaying, quiet movement of the body-screens intimates, this is a politics of imperceptible forces. Elizabeth Grosz defines the politics of the imperceptible as follows:

> Politics can be seen as the struggle of imperceptible forces, forces in and around us, forces in continual conflict, forces including those mobilizing pleasure, pain, and desire … Instead of a politics of recognition, in which subjugated groups and minorities strive for a validated and affirmed place in public life, feminist

politics should, I believe, now consider the affirmation
of the politics of imperceptibility, leaving its traces and
effects everywhere but never being identified with a
person, group, or organization. (Grosz 2005, 193–94)

Grosz claims that affirmative politics of the imperceptible does not undermine feminist politics but reinforces it by opening it beyond the scope of the recognisable, what is already known, and hence queering it further. It is not the bodies per se that require recognition or validation for their activities; what must be attended to are the impersonal forces that traverse any seemingly fixed position or identity, thus uncovering their permanent instability. Accordingly, what the minutely moving Sapphics of *Sappho Wants to Save You* call for is for queer politics to re-direct its focus to the pre-personal micro-movements that constitute any subject, or work of art. For if there was interest in these micro-movements, it would become evident that 'sexuality, and identity itself, are fundamentally mosaic-like fields composed of aligned but disparate elements, energies, goals, and wills' (Grosz 2004, 195). This would allow for a larger variety of sexualities, thus expanding the horizon of sexual difference towards 'a thousand tiny sexes' (Deleuze and Guattari 1987; Grosz 1993; 1994).

When differences multiply beyond recognition and becoming-imperceptible, prevalent understandings of minority and majority – dependent on the very concepts of identity, recognition and visibility – are contested. Becoming-imperceptible, by allowing oneself to open and change in relation to forces, intensities, affects, is to become without a presupposed, already established goal: this is not about progressing from a minor position to a major one, or the reverse (Deleuze and Guattari 1987, 469–73).[118] Whereas becoming a minority always occurs in relation to a majority, becoming-minoritarian is a self-differentiating process that does not relate to or find its power in the battle against the majority: 'The power of the minoritarian is not measured by their capacity to enter and make themselves felt within the majority system, nor even to reverse the necessarily tautological criterion for majority, but to bring to bear the force of non-denumerable sets, however small they may be, against the denumerable sets, even if they are infinite, reversed, changed, even if they imply new axioms, or beyond that a new axiomatic' (Deleuze and Guattari 1987, 471). The minoritarian politics of becoming-imperceptible proposes that affective micro-movements traverse both marginal and normative, majoritarian identity positions – which are never really as established as they are often thought to be.

In her essay 'Queer Aesthetics', Claire Colebrook (2011, 25–28) calls this kind of becoming 'passive'. Colebrook suggests that becoming has become a normative and dominant concept in the contemporary theories of art and subjectivity that tend to value change over stability: in this way becoming has come to purport active construction of the self that is wilfully implemented in relation to or against the confirmed standards (2011, 29–31), and has thus lost its criticality. Passive becomings work in a different way. They do not take place according to the norms, in hierarchical relation to something 'already confirmed', but emerge through material-relational singularities: the 'thisness' of each event and its varying elements. To *this* swaying fabric, to the lightness of *this* metal lath, to *this* groping, jiggling, balancing body, and to *this* itchy back.

***

To sum up this chapter: *Sappho Wants to Save You* opens up macropolitical structures of sexual identity to intensive micropolitical flows. In so doing it succeeds in undoing the boundary between the two politics: the boundary between micropolitics that functions in the realm of sensation, and macropolitics that sticks with recognisable representations (Deleuze and Guattari 1987, 213). Its imperceptible politics emerges through its immanent, formal and technical qualities in (micro)movement.

The way in which *Sappho Wants to Save You* builds its critique of politics based on recognisable identities and their visibility is gentle, yet the room where the installation was on display was not quiet. The Sapphic preachers shouted their manifesto on the screen at the back wall of the gallery. But as mentioned, the stutterings and stammerings of bodily-vocal articulation contested the noisy univocity of the lesbian manifesto. In front of the video projection, closest to the audience, six silent Sapphics sway delicately, technico-affectively, in the air, emphasising even further the impossibility of any stable identity position. Whereas loud, ironic and parodic humour has been identified as characteristically queer (Butler 1990; Roseneil 2000), *Sappho*'s humour functions on a different level: in the contesting micro-movements of the body, in the technico-affective aspects of becoming. This aligns with Deleuze's understanding of humour: 'humour is an art of pure events' (2006, 51).[119] While irony is always pre-prepared, and necessitates critical distance, humour is all about openness to the affective encounter: it queers on the level of immanence. Therefore, the subtle, relational Sapphic movement is actually more humorous than ironic or parodic. What at first looked like a parodic performance of conventional lesbian identity is now suffused with the work of technico-affective humour. This work does not prioritise language, nor does it rely on an elevated, distant point of view of a human, but is immanently conceived. In this way, the technico-affective humour of *Sappho Wants to Save You* suggests fresh questions and problems for queer politics. It does not subvert queer theory but 'perverts' it further through its attendance to that which seems too often almost imperceptible: to affective relations, to subtleties of micro-movement – the singularities of passive becoming.

9

The Screaming Mouth

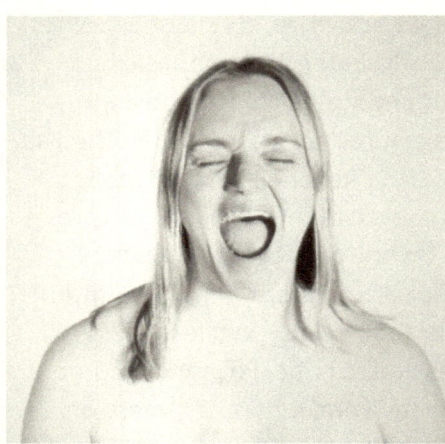

Figure 9.1. The Screaming Mouth. Helena Hietanen, *Sketches*, 1999–. Photograph by Eva Persson.

The final panel of the oral triptych stages a screaming event [Figure 9.1]. The image above is part of the series that was taken to help sculptor Helena Hietanen process and artistically elaborate on the bodily transformation she was going through due to breast cancer. At the time when the image was taken, the artist was recovering from treatment and had already had a complete mastectomy of her left breast. The series was not meant to be just still lifes; rather, Hietanen thought that she would work with the images and use them as sketches for further art-making – hence the series title, *Sketches* (1999–). Hietanen trusted this delicate job to Eva Persson, who photographed the series just before Hietanen was scheduled for TRAM flap surgery. In the operation, all of her breast tissue affected by a hereditary cell malformation, and thus posing an ongoing threat to her life, was removed. Then, new breasts were sculpted from her abdominal fat – Hietanen had purposely put on weight for the operation so that there would be enough sculpting material for the surgeon to work with.

Over fifteen years have passed, but the *Sketches* are still just sketches. Nor have they been exhibited anywhere. Falling ill again (for the second, and then for the third time) ruined Hietanen's plans for reworking the images, and then other projects, such as *Heaven Machine* (2005), enabled a different kind of bodily processing, though perhaps on a more abstract level. Hietanen notes that, in the end, she was probably too scared to work with *Sketches* because of the feelings that the process had already aroused in her and might arouse again (Hietanen, 26 August 2003). It did not help that Finnish unemployment and welfare legislation actually prohibited her from producing artworks. Hietanen had been forced to retire prematurely, because the cancer had damaged her underarm muscle tissues indispensable for art-making. As a pensioner, according to Finnish welfare legislation, any independent (or co-produced) work can put one's pension and sickness benefits in jeopardy, which is particularly challenging for self-employed individuals. For example, in the summer of 2007, Hietanen was not able to participate properly in the three art shows she was invited to because of the risk of losing her pension. Instead of displaying her installation art, Hietanen and her husband Jaakko Niemelä addressed the inequalities of the welfare system by exhibiting a simple piece of paper announcing: 'This is not a work of art' (Sederholm 2008, 82–89). In addition, Hietanen was strongly discouraged by her then gallerist, who did not approve of the *Sketches* project. The gallerist thought it was naïve, if not self-centred (Hietanen, 16 May 2002).[120] Thus, it is fair to say that *Sketches* got stuck for several reasons that span the emotional and affective as well as the institutional and societal domains. In a way, the third and final panel of the oral triptych enables *Sketches* to live on: the series emerges as an epitome of directness, intimately relating the material body, images, and cultural practices. Here, the visual medium of photography opens up to the relational events of posing and processing bodily change.

Screaming beyond sensationalism

Hietanen screams, eyes closed and mouth open [Figure 9.1]. Her mouth, however, is not a black abyss, but full of flesh – her tongue seems to fill the space. Given the bodily pain Hietanen had endured, it is tempting to suggest that she is choking on her own flesh, on the amount of suffering that her body had put her through – and this is what she says too (Hietanen, 22 May 2002). In Gilles Deleuze's analysis of Francis Bacon's 'screaming pope' paintings, the scream gains a similar function: in a scream, the mouth 'is no longer a particular organ, but a hole through which the entire body escapes, and from which the flesh descends' (2003, 26).

Drawing from Hietanen's scream and Deleuze's thinking concerning bodies, the descending flesh refers to flesh leaving the body as a closed organic system to connect with other bodies, other forces, including inorganic ones. In Deleuze–Bacon, flesh is not matter that should be turned into something else. There is no urge to textualise flesh or transcend it. The aim is not resurrection, but a conception of flesh as the source of movement and transformation. This is not the biological prison of the body–mind; rather, flesh is alive – in Braidotti's (2006a; 2006b) words, full of 'zoe'. Here, Deleuze's (2003, 26, 29) proposition, that in a scream the mouth works as an artery, is apt. In human and animal bodies arteries pulse life, get it going. According to Hietanen, she screamed out the pain her body had been through (Hietanen, 22 May 2002): escaping through the mouth, her flesh sought (self-)expression. Never is this sort of self-expression a solitary project; it feeds on forces that were once outside the body, but are now incorporated in the movement of a work of art.

For Deleuze (2003, 60–62), a scream makes invisible forces visible as they are channelled through the body, taking form, struggling in the scream. Although Bacon's paintings are unceasingly violent, the forces made visible do not push the body towards the end, to death. Instead, as mentioned, the descending flesh expresses a vitality. Crucially, these forces are the forces of the future (61). They do not belong to the sphere of the human in the sense that there is a (mastering) human behind them. They are 'natural', even cosmic forces of pressure, gravity, weight; in short, forces of vibration. In Bacon's art, something is always happening, a movement of de-formation is at work – the world is not blocked into stability, it is expressing itself. So when in Bacon's paintings 'life screams at death', there is a future involved: the scream 'is a source of extraordinary vitality' (61).

The future-oriented scream is relevant in Hietanen's case. To think about this further, let us delve in more detail into what exactly happened during the scream represented in the photograph. According to Hietanen, she could not really act out her will to scream the pain as she was embarrassed about what people in the neighbouring studios would think (Hietanen, 22 May 2002). Consequently, she burst out in laughter. In the image, then, the flesh that fills the mouth is her tongue moved by a sudden burst of laughter. What looks like a scream is actually an interrupted event of screaming redirected by an internalised cultural restriction of feeling ashamed.

What Hietanen felt was that her body, her flesh, needed an outlet for self-expression. Because of her earlier unsatisfactory experiences in linguistically expressing the transformative bodily becomings of being sick, she wanted to try to communicate the pain accurately through the visual medium of photography (Hietanen, 22 May 2002). She hoped that *Sketches*, or its re-workings, would make visible what was invisible for many: the sensations of a cancerous body. But she was insistent: 'I don't want to just show wounds and flesh' (25 August 2003).

Whilst Deleuze (2003, 38) insists that Bacon does not paint spectacles, but sensations, of violence, Bacon's paintings are, in any case, filled with torn, struggling, visibly tormented human flesh (though not only human perhaps – Bacon's figures are deformed to such an extent that they are on the verge of ceasing to be human). In Hietanen's *Sketches*, there is no blood, no bare wretched muscle tissue or clearly contorted body parts. Still, *Sketches* hosts violent sensations – only these sensations are not visibly violent, but rather calmly, quietly ruthless. Maybe, then, *Sketches* is all the *more* invested in sensation, for it does not wallow in the visible spectacle of violence. The series works through sensation without being sensationalist. There is 'no need to use images of horror or extreme cruelty', as Gustavo Chirolla Ospina (2010, 22) claims in his essay about (South American) political art that does not fall into the trap of just sensationally visualising horrifying events, but evokes politics through bodily sensations. Referring to Clemencia Echeverri's art, Chirolla Ospina claims that 'the scream is not political because it is discursive, but because it is the signature of the body, it is a speech act signed by the depths of the body' (2010, 23). In a similar manner, *Sketches* relies on the affective expression of the body, without offering a recognisable shock effect. This is not the kind of breast cancer art that celebrates victory over a torturous illness, nor the kind that splatters blood (widely present in the collection *Art. Rage. Us: Art and Writing by Women with Breast Cancer* (Tasch 1998), for example). Instead, *Sketches* carefully, delicately probes the sensations of a body sick with breast cancer.

This gentle probing and experimenting does much more than just show the body (quietly) trembling in the cosmic forces of the future – which are not only positive in terms of organic life. As

Braidotti makes clear, 'zoe can be cruel, cells split and multiply in cancer as in pregnancy' (2006b, 259). *Sketches* visualises how the cruelties of zoe as well as its joys necessarily connect to cultural powers. It is quite evident that Hietanen's scream does not emerge only from her suffering body, tortured by forces analogous to those palpable in Bacon's paintings. Cultural images such as Bacon's paintings participate in her bodily becoming in the same manner as Bacon's scream paintings extract some of their powers from Velázquez's popes and El Greco's wildly moving figures. Cultural practices and restrictions, such as that which hampered Hietanen's inclination to scream, are inseparable from the transformation of her body, and also, literally, from the future of her flesh.

New figurations: Becoming-Christ, becoming-Justice

As in Bacon's paintings of sensation, religious art is a remarkable source of inspiration for *Sketches*: there are images of Hietanen's hands and eye, of her laying prone on the floor and posing as Christ. Contesting the conventional religious context, Deleuze insists that 'Bacon is a religious painter only in butcher's shops' (2003, 24). In Bacon, there is a perplexing relation between butchering and crucifixion, explicable only in that both of these actions involve meat as their object, meat that has suffered and had to suffer for the sake of mankind. For Bacon, the meat, whether human or animal, arouses immense pity (Deleuze 2003, 23, 26). It could be said that Hietanen's body has also been butchered, and not only by cancer but also by the surgeon's knife. Yet this is not the only factor shared between them. As noted, one of the *Sketches* shows Hietanen posing as Christ: 'When the surgery approached, I related more and more to the suffering of Christ ... I wanted to photograph myself posing as Christ, in the posture of Christ' (Hietanen, 26 August 2003). In iconography, the image that depicts Christ's suffering most profoundly is that of the crucifixion.

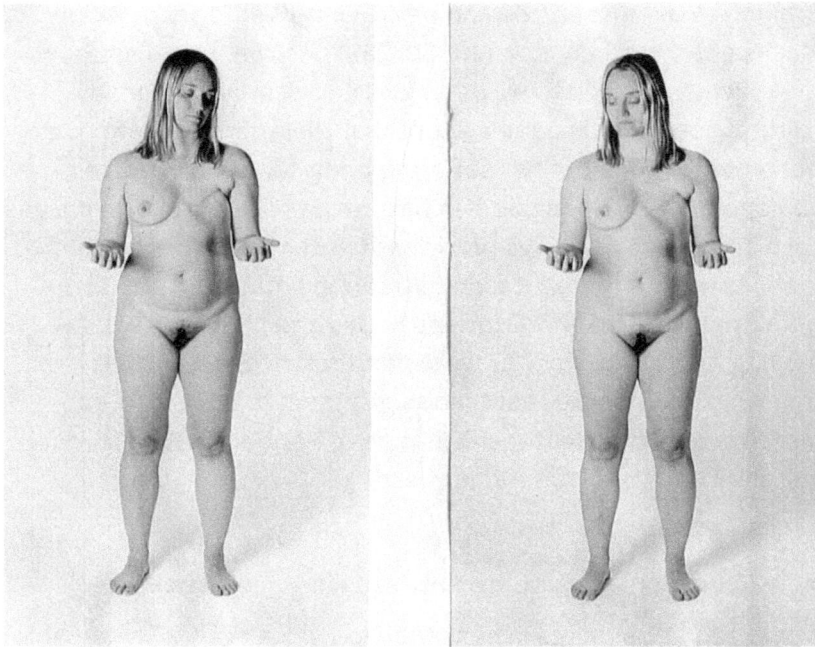

Figure 9.2. Becoming-Christ. Helena Hietanen, *Sketches, 1999–*. Photograph by Eva Persson.

By posing as Christ, Hietanen's body and the pain it had gone through find expression through other bodies, other images [Figure 9.2]. Her flesh is taking form (Manning 2009, 33) and figured anew through direct contact with cultural representations. This sort of event needs a vocabulary sensitive to its peculiar bodily nature. As was elucidated in connection with the previous panel, posing is a series of micro-movements, a continuous balancing act, and, as such, a thoroughly corporeal one. Hence, it is far from just 'pausing', freezing oneself into a chosen (cultural) pose.

The concept of 'figuration' defined by Rosi Braidotti in her book *Metamorphoses: Towards A Materialist Theory of Becoming* enables an embodied articulation of posing:

> Figurations are not figurative ways of thinking, but rather more materialistic mappings of situated, or embedded and embodied positions. A figuration renders our image in terms of a decentered and multilayered vision of a subject as a dynamic and changing entity. A figuration is a living map, a transformative account of the self – it is no metaphor. (2002, 2–3)[121]

In *Metamorphoses*, Braidotti sets herself the task of fashioning figurations that would fit in with our time of accelerating changes: 'We live in permanent processes of transition, hybridization and nomadization, and these in-between stages defy the established modes of theoretical representation' (2002, 2). In Braidotti's work, becomings do not emerge in a virtual techno-world but in and through bodies that are processes themselves. Likewise, *Sketches* is not only about representing a body with breast cancer. Nor is it simply a metaphor for bodily change and becoming. It is about what happened and what is happening to a certain material-relational composition in becoming. Equally important is Braidotti's conception that rather than fixing positions and identities, '[f]igurations deterritorialize and destabilize the certainties of the subject' (Braidotti 2006b, 90). Therefore, rather than somehow representing, depicting, the present, figurations map potentialities, bodies in transition towards something other than what they (already) are. In this respect, what might be most crucial is the act and event of figuring: a body taking shape, becoming in its relation to other bodies.

Following Braidotti, when Hietanen poses as Christ, her body is deterritorialised and re-figured through a connection to the figure of Christ. This, however, is not reducible to merely resembling Christ. To paraphrase Deleuze and Guattari (1987, 191, 301), Hietanen's posing resists the Christ-face system so precious to the European visual regime. In this system, the face renders the whole body recognisable; it identifies, facialises it. The culture of facialisation is apparent, for example, in the idiom 'being the face of' a certain cause. As explained, however, Hietanen hopes to avoid self-evident, recognisable patterns of expression, such as blood and wounds as signs of pain. Accordingly, she is also hesitant about becoming the 'face' of breast cancer. In fact, she once escaped such a simple categorisation by pulling *Sketches* out from a journal article at the very last minute. Thus, rather than belonging to the realm of facialisation, Hietanen's pose is a de-facialisation of both breast cancer and Christ; it is, instead, the re-creation of 'silhouettes and postures of corporeality' (Deleuze and Guattari 1987, 301) through a process of becoming-Christ. In becoming, there is no direct correspondence, imitation. Above all, Deleuze and Guattari remind us, 'becoming does not occur in the imagination. Becomings ... are neither dreams or phantasies. They are perfectly real' (1987, 237–38).

Patricia Cox Miller's (2009, 148–63) concept of 'image-flesh' assists us to grasp the process of becoming-Christ in the domain of the real, in and through the body. Originally, this concept contributed to the discussion about icons in late medieval Byzantine Christianity: did icons have a being of their own or were they just artistic representations? These questions were crucial to apprehending the healing power of icons. Were holy, benevolent forces really present in icons, in the images of the holy, or were these images merely representations? Whilst this debate did not find a final conclusion, Miller's concept, arising from it, provides language for fashioning direct relations between the body and image: image-flesh is 'a phenomenon in which the relation of likeness is transformed into one of immanence' (2009, 152).

Here the concept of image-flesh does not imply divine healing powers as much as it emphasises the co-emergence of images and flesh. There is no denying that, for Hietanen,

Sketches turned out to be a therapeutic process that exceeded the conscious limits of studying one's body by choosing to pose as a given figure (Hietanen, 26 August 2003). It is quite astonishing, however, that although Hietanen clearly articulated her identification with the figure of Christ (19 May 2003), the surrogate sufferer for humankind, in the canon of Western art and in Christian iconography in particular, it is not Christ but the personification of Justice who holds her hands in the same position as Hietanen does. By way of illustration, Giotto's fresco *The Allegory of Justice* (c. 1305) in the Scrovegni Chapel in Padua, Italy, reminds of Hietanen's gesture more clearly than does the *Christ in The Last Judgment* in the same chapel. Whereas Justice weighs two statues, using scales, Christ's threatening gesture and his disapproving gaze suggest that there are no concrete criteria, such as scales, on which his judgment is to be based.

These frescos from the early fourteenth century may seem distant partakers in Hietanen's bodily transformation, but the similarity between her pose and the gesture of Justice suggests a connection with this long gestural lineage. The questions elemental to justice – choosing, balancing between right and wrong – were not alien to Hietanen at the time she decided to pose as Christ. For her, the weighing up of her hands, looking towards the right one and then towards the left, was a question of life and death, and multifacetedly so (Hietanen, 22 May 2002). This gesture, and the pose, expressed her dilemma: whether to choose hormone treatment, which would start her menopause at the age of thirty-five, but which would also significantly lower the risk of falling sick again, or to have her healthy but potentially life-threatening breast removed and to go through TRAM flap surgery, that is, to have new breasts made from her own flesh (fat) in order to restore body balance, and to get rid of the painful scar.[122]

Hietanen's pose comes close to the 'open poses' that Nevado chose for *Honest Fortune Teller*, that elaborate and transform the

Catholic figure of María Madre de Misericordia (Chapters 2 and 5). For Nevado, the pose of María Madre de Misericordia was important as it did not imply the passive contemplation before God so typical for female saints, but activeness (Nevado, 16 June 2005): in many versions of the figure, the Virgin shelters people beneath her arms and her gown, whilst in others she spreads beams of divine light through the palms of her hands to the world. By the same token, weighing one's destiny, taking destiny into one's own hands, as Hietanen does when posing as Justice-Christ, can be understood as an active, affirmative act that contests the conventional passive role of a woman mourning her lost future.

The active and affirmative attitude of the Justice-Christ pose is further emphasised in Hietanen's view of surgery as a sculpting process that she was part of: 'I think of this transformation of my body as a sculptural process' (Hietanen, 22 May 2002). She was fascinated by the surgeon's careful attention to the materials: their qualities, textures and functions (Hietanen, 22 May 2002). If in her previous sculptural work Hietanen had studied the qualities of silicone and optic fibre[123] – how flexible they were, how they carried and reflected light – now it was all about blood circulation, the enhancement and placing of fat tissue, and the scarification of her skin.

Immanent transfigurations

A close-up of Hietanen's hands enacts a slight change of emphasis, from her posing as Christ or Justice to posing as part of art-making. Iconographically, this photograph relates to the healing, supporting, empowering hands that are so often associated with those of Christ[124] [Figure 9.3]. The calm, even sacred atmosphere of the hand close-up may also be seen as embodying another prevalent detail of Christian iconography: the hands of the crucified Christ. But Hietanen's hands seem to be intact: there are no wounds, no blood on them. If there were ever marks of crucifixion, they have healed. This transformation creates an interesting connection to Hietanen's argument concerning art-making as a bodily act:

> Being ill is indeed a physical experience ... [And] for me working with various materials or photographing my body in a variety of positions is likewise a physical experience, and thereby close to the experience of the body. (Hietanen, 22 May 2002)

With these words, the close-up of her (perhaps) healed hands takes on a different tone. It links to her will to process her experiences by making art. However, to work with hands does not mean diminishing photography to merely an intermediate phase before 'actual' art-making. Rather, 'the camera eye', or her other eye as she prefers to call it (Hietanen, 22 May 2002), is absorbed into *Sketches* from the very beginning. One of the photographs embodies this peculiar other eye by displaying a look that probably could hardly be more removed from a penetrating, intrusive gaze; it bears no resemblance to the objectifying, classifying medical gaze of examination rooms and laboratories, nor to that of a judging God. This look is understanding and gently approving [Figure 9.4].

The implicit relation that the gentle look creates is strictly horizontal. Hietanen is not gazing downwards, nor is her eye turned upwards.[125] Again, instead of a transcendental relation, there is an immanent one.[126] Following Hietanen, the eye, the immanent eye, relates to her feeling that there are things that she just has to go through, experience, and accept (Hietanen, 26 August 2003). There is no other way but to look at them – gracefully. So the eye and the hands are not symbols for the opposite actions of seeing optically and feeling manually. Rather, they both aim at an immanent and direct relation to what they are working with. They are mutually dependent. The immanent

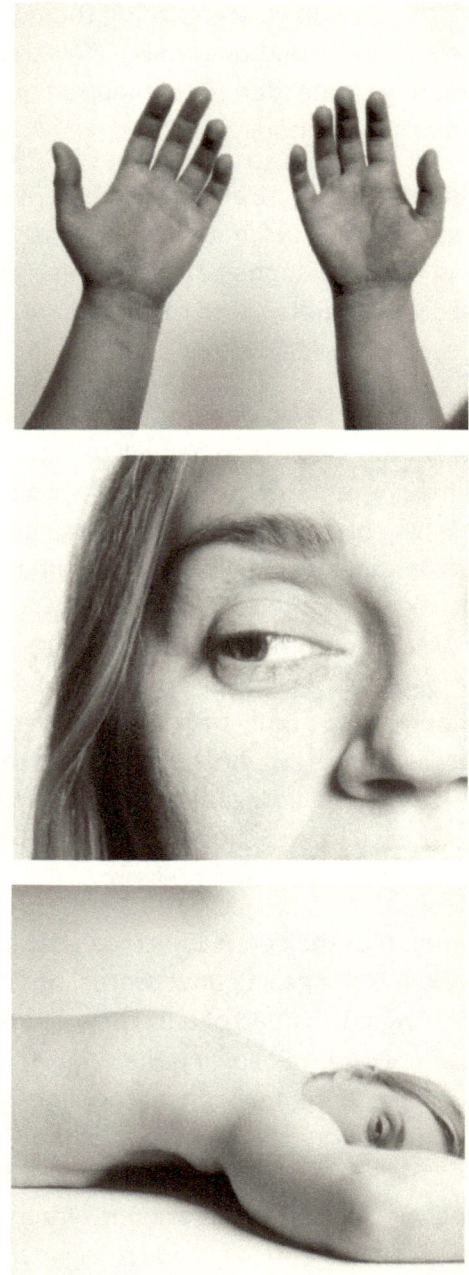

Figures 9.3, 9.4 and 9.5. Healing hands and eyes, the horizontal connection. Helena Hietanen, *Sketches, 1999–*. Photographs by Eva Persson.

eye is present in the way Hietanen moves her hands when drawing or sculpting. Similarly, cultural imagery does not reside outside the technical or physical processes of art-making; these processes are part of how hands and tools work, how they mould materials, carve lines, form new bodies.

In a way, the close-up of Hietanen's hands crystallises the entire project. *Sketches* was not meant to be a set of still lifes. Its purpose was not to freeze the moment but, rather, to further process and work on it by drawing, if not by sculpting – with hands. To work with hands is not only an intentional deed of composing an image; it is a complex event. Rosy Martin makes a similar proposition in relation to phototherapy: 'photography sessions are not about "capturing" the image, but rather seeking to make it happen, to "take place"' (1997, 154). What this performative account means is that Hietanen, by posing, does not merely converse with cultural representations, nor are they inscribed onto her body. She literally embodies, figures them, moves, and transforms, becomes with them. In other words, her body changes across and through figures: it is transfigured.

'Transfiguration', the Christian term for transformation (Miller 2009, 154), sets the ground for the final suggestions of this chapter. While the Christian conception of image-flesh and Hietanen's personal devotion are attractive paths for analysis, the fact that the Christian understanding of transfiguration involves enlightment, or irradiation even, does not quite match with the expressive dynamics of *Sketches*. Within the series, I suggest, transfiguration works, rather, as the transformative process of art-making that occurs through direct relations with bodies, images, and other materialities (see Bolt 2004a, 145–46).[127] In the realm of art-making, transfiguration is not an escape from the matters of the material world: it is a transformative process without an end; a process that reaches for the future in and through matter – both bodily and 'representational'. *Sketches* offers Hietanen's cancerous body new futures in an immanent connection to other bodies. Thus no transfiguration in the Christian sense of the term; no overcoming of the body. Just figuration in and through other figures.

In *Sketches*, although posing as Christ, Hietanen does not ascend to the heavens. Instead, she descends to the floor. Indeed, the series includes an image of Hietanen lying prone on the floor [Figure 9.5]. This image shows the hollow left behind by the cut off breast and suggests a horizontal relation to the experiences of the body instead of a vertical, transcendental one. The horizontal connection between Hietanen and the audience is accentuated by Hietanen's eye, that looks at the viewer directly, yet quietly, as if asking for a similar sort of look in response. A look that is not in control, like that of the medical or clinical gaze, but open and sensitive to her transfiguring body.

The transfiguration Hietanen enacts through her poses in *Sketches* is quite different from the transfiguration with which this book began (Chapter 1). Hietanen's light installation *Heaven Machine* seems to subscribe to a more transcendental transfiguration, as it actually involves radiating beams of light, a recognisable representation of transcendence. In *Heaven Machine*, a body connected to the rhythm of the light beams loses its organic structure, in other words, is defigured in radiance. Yet the claim that *Heaven Machine* immaterialises the body, transcends the body, is no longer really an option, given my insistence, throughout this book, on relational materialities in movement; on the immanent molecularity of all being.

A Follow-Up: Three Propositions

> We cannot help but view the world in terms of solids, as things. But [then] we leave behind something untapped of the fluidity of the world, the movements, vibrations, transformations that occur below the threshold of perception and calculation and outside the relevance of our practical concerns. [Yet] ... we have ... access to this profusion of vibration that underlies the solidity of things. (Grosz 2005, 136)

Philosopher Elizabeth Grosz's words summon what is at issue in the material turn that has recently enthralled the domain of critical theory: a newly aroused interest in subtly moving and constantly transforming materialities that are present everywhere, pointing out how the world is vibrant to begin with (see, for example, Bennett 2010b; Coole and Frost 2010b; Dolphijn and van der Tuin 2012).[128] Even in the most stable looking social structures, and in the sturdiest of materials, such as granite or marble, there is movement, a certain amount of openness, fluidity, that allows for change. It is not that structures, objects, and materials are steadfast and unchanging – we have just learned to understand them as such.

Whenever we see an image, there are always multiple material-relational processes involved, intertwined with it, co-working it – whether it is in the brushstrokes, the motion of a painter's hand, the quality of the paper or ink, a piece of software code perhaps, or movements of a poser's body before the canvas. Nor

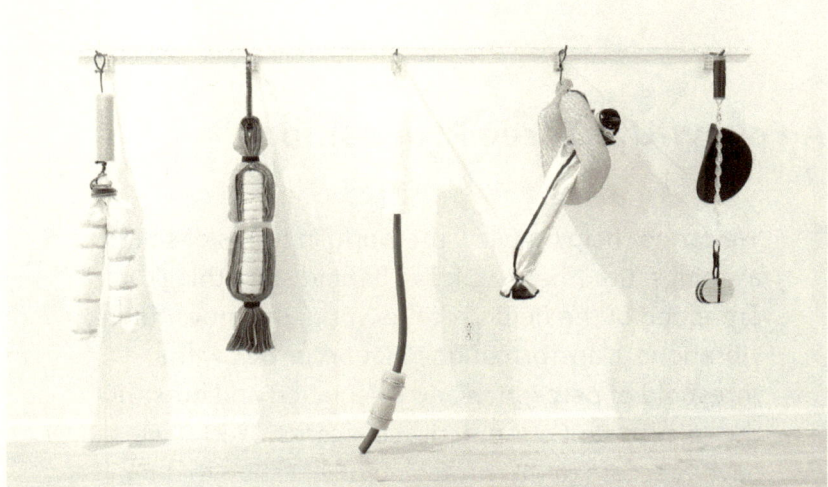

Caroline Phillips, *There's something happening here...* Installation view, Anese Projects, New York, 2017. Photograph by Alba Navarro Hierro.

do we ever encounter art by looking and thinking only; we sense textures and haptic qualities simultaneously and relationally. In these encounters, we are not confronted by stable objects. This is what Caroline Phillips's recent series (2017) of soft hard sculptures hanging from hooks insists by way of its movement and title: *'There's something happening here...'*. Recycled foam and rubber, crocheted yarn, metal parts, and layered felts hang attached to each other, in new compositions held together by gravity and traction, and they are molecularly shifting, changing, even if we cannot see that movement.

Matter is not still, concrete, but always on the move, taking shape in relation to other matters in movement, human and non-human alike. Matter, rather, is an ever-elaborating, relational difference. Materialities matter: they do things, connect, disconnect, get stuck and co-create, and therefore should not be conceived merely as a stable ground for ever-changing meanings. Complex conditions, various registers, and the numerous partakers involved in every art process always create unique events.[129] Artworks, then, cannot simply re-present what was before – there is too much heterogeneity involved in making a new constellation emerge every time. Complex events need complex concepts to attend to their specificities. The conventional vocabularies of representation, identification, and performativity popular amongst studies of contemporary art often overlook the delicate movements of art, as they tend to focus on larger cultural, social, and political structures and their re-iterations. Methods such as reading, or reading against the grain, and concepts like 'text' and 'discourse' are not equally adequate everywhere: they are not of great help when trying to deal with the moving matters of art. New concepts and methods are needed to address the radical, material-relational processuality of art, and to improve our capacity to address the world in change (Holland 2009, 148).

This kind of approach to art is often characterised by the phrase 'beyond representation', meaning that it is not sufficient to pay heed only to the representational level of art (Bolt 2004a; see also O'Sullivan 2006a; Manning 2009). Instead, the material-relational subtleties of art should be accorded equally nuanced attention as that commonly given to representations, contexts, and textual contents (Barrett and Bolt 2013; Kontturi 2014; Tiainen, Kontturi and Hongisto 2015a). If we do not pay attention to the moving materialities of contemporary art, relationally co-composing not only the object but our encounter with it, we end up with seriously restricted understandings of art's capabilities. Indeed, we might even miss its most inventive and moving offerings – how it might change our thinking-feeling.

In this follow-up, I offer three propositions that revolve around ontology, ethics, and politics, to appeal for and map the inclusion of moving matters in art encounters.[130] These propositions arise from participations with art: they are probed and provoked in attunement with art.

1) An art process is always an ontological process; it is about becoming

'Becoming' refers to process ontology, which challenges the idea of an essential(ist) being and suggests that the world is always already moving (see, for example, Tiainen, Kontturi and Hongisto 2015a; Tiainen, Kontturi and Hongisto 2015c; Massumi 2017, 7). Consequently, rather than being a somewhat coherent object that is rendered moving in the act of interpretation, art has a peculiar moving material existence of its own. Even in the case of conceptual art, say, for example, an artwork composed solely of letters, there is always the particular way in which these letters exist. What makes this material-relational existence – the colour, size, and curves of the fonts – crucial, is that it is inseparable from how the work affects us. When encountering art, we are not merely involved in a process of signification, and should therefore approach art in a manner that recognises the importance of its sensory dimension: that is, we should sense art as a material process in which meanings are immersed.

To emphasise the volatility and fluidity of material processes, Gilles Deleuze and Félix Guattari speak of 'molecularity'. Molecularity, as they define it, is an umbrella term that designates the differentiating matter of the world and thus extends well beyond the natural sciences to the realms of subjectivity, politics, and art (Deleuze and Guattari 1987). Also, and crucially, it suggests that it is at the level of the molecular that the human and the non-human meet in a most fundamental, direct manner. Molecularity comes with molarity, which signifies petrified structures such as subject–object, content–form or female–male binaries. However, molecular movements flow through any molar setting (Deleuze and Guattari 1987, 272–77).[131] To be able to sense art as a material process it is necessary to give up the comfort of positioning, the reliance on pre-conditioned knowledge and a pre-chosen political viewpoint: it entails giving up a mastering, molar attitude. Instead of being caught up in a molar position that enables critical distance, the researcher should open herself to the molecular movements of art.

Helena Hietanen and Jaakko Niemelä's *Heaven Machine* (2005), discussed in Chapter 1 'Breathing and Dancing', is an installation that calls for this kind of approach by way of its material movement. The work consists of fast-moving and colour-changing beams of light that rush through holes in a wall structure that divides the high, dark exhibition room in two. The audience is allowed to wander around the room – to be pierced by the light – but not to go beyond the wall.

According to Hietanen, *Heaven Machine* refers to her experiences of breast cancer: when she was very ill she had a vision in which a pillar of light descended from the heavens to save her (Hietanen, 27 January 2006). This information offers ample opportunity to compose a rich reading of the work determined by the binaries of lightness and darkness, sickness and salvation, in the context not only of breast cancer but also of religious art. Reading as a method, however, is rarely capable of grasping the material-relational movement of the installation, where meanings are inseparably incorporated. Neither is it able to account for how the experience of the work emerges in relation to the bodies of the audience. In short, reading attends to the signification of the work and not to its ontogenetic becoming – to the way it emerges, or becomes, in the exhibition space.

As an act, reading is quite removed from the conditions under which the audience encountered the installation: the beams of light were made visible by the pervasive haze in the space. Importantly, this haze did not only touch the faces, bodies, and clothing of the audience; its moving materiality was more intrusive. Wilfully or otherwise, every visitor inhaled the haze, its molecules of oxygen, nitrogen and hydrogen, into their body.

This connection was far more fundamental than what reading allows. Neither was it metaphorical.

Breathing offers a very concrete way of relating to material movement, to the becoming of the work. Feminist philosophers Luce Irigaray (2002, 50, 75–76) and Rosi Braidotti (2006b, 178) are incisive here. Both emphasise the fundamental value of breathing as a bodily knowledge and advocate a non-logocentric understanding of culture. Breathing serves as an alternative form of relation that necessarily extends beyond language, to sensations and perceptions, and offers a direct molecular connection to the outside, to others. Dancing, as suggested in Chapter 1, is another option, for it so profoundly necessitates corporeal-material relationality (see also Sullivan 2006a).

Participation with the molecular movement of art contests the understanding of art as an object of knowledge. Rather, art becomes 'an object of fundamental encounter' (Deleuze 1994a, 139; see also O'Sullivan 2006a, 1): that is, something that challenges one's way of being in the world by suggesting new kinds of becomings. *Heaven Machine* suggests beings well beyond the restrictive cultural understandings of what it is to be a woman ill with breast cancer. By offering an intensive sensuous experience, and a direct connection with its constantly moving matters of light and haze, *Heaven Machine* encourages a move away from a distanced representational analysis towards the practices of radical immanence.

The movement of art is not always as perceptible as in the case of constantly moving beams of light and pervasive haze. But even if a painting or a photographic installation appears to stay still, nevertheless there is movement: think of how paint cracks when it ages or is subject to changes in humidity, or how a photographic installation affects its viewer by way of its own materiality interwoven into such things as hanging. Thus, it is not that artworks do not move, it is that our capacities of thinking-feeling them as moving are restricted by the ways we understand art.

(2) Ethics is about attentiveness to the work of art

Ethics is not about evaluating the arguments art offers; rather, it is about valuing art's processes of emergence, its material-relational becoming. As the case of *Heaven Machine* exemplifies, readings of what art represents rarely pay attention to how these representations (have come to) exist (cf. Barad 2007, 53).[132] Thus, rather than asking what art means or suggests, here ethics is engaged with art's material-relational emergence – the crucial but oft-neglected element of any process of representation. Art's emergence is understood in concrete terms: it refers to the material processes in and through which art happens. To emphasise the material effort present in art processes, I call these processes *work*.

Here, the account of work values equally the efforts of human and more-than-human agent(ment)s. An artist is neither the master of the art process, nor an autonomous actor; rather, the artist is a member in a creative rhizome, a co-worker. As Gilles Deleuze puts it, an artist is a mechanic of a machine; they may start the process but cannot govern or define it (1999, 64–65). In other words, this is not about work as an individual creative effort but work as the various collaborations through which art emerges. This does not, however, suggest that the artist's work does not count: there simply would not be an artwork without an artist (or more than one), no representations to be read without her physical-mental work that possibly took days, months, even years. While working with artists and listening to what they have to say (see Deleuze 2003, 99) certainly helps in acknowledging the work that deserves attention, it is not the only way to pay respect to their work. To pay rigorous attention to the singular subtleties of art, and not only to the general structures it represents, is also to value the artist's labour.

My ethical ponderings of art's and artists' work arise from observing and participating *with* painter Susana Nevado's art-making processes. Having followed Nevado for eight months as she worked on the installation project *Honest Fortune Teller* (2004–2005) and having visited her studio dozens of times (Chapters 2, 4–5), I could not but pay attention to the copious amount of hard work that the process demanded. With regard to physical work, a little oval painting with which Nevado worked for months was especially intriguing. This painting presents a teenage mother posing as the Catholic saint María Madre de Misericordia. The underneath layers of the painting come through, although rather vaguely; these include fashion magazine covers from the 1950s or the early 1960s and a shred of black lace that had belonged to a cheap corset owned by the artist. Already, in terms of representation, this work is fascinatingly multi-layered: it brings together motherhood, girlhood, religious imagery, advertising, even pornography. But to conceptualise this work only in this frame of representation leaves out something important: there is no room for the 'work' of art.

What is particularly interesting in this process is that the painting that emerged was not just the result of the conscious and predetermined working process of the artist; it was also the product of the collaboration between the artist and the materials: how she moved the brush, layered materials – including images from magazines – and then sandpapered the layers she was not content with. But the layers also worked on their own. On a physico-chemical level, the sandpapered and hence porous material of the magazine scraps reacted with the acrylic paint, and the painting took a direction of its own. It ended up producing an image that did not emerge from the repertoire of cultural images: it created a double-navel girl that was not the intention of the artist but the result of the material layers of the work of art (Bolt, 2004a, 5).[133]

In terms of semiotics, the double navel in the middle of the painting could be termed a sign – but this sign is not reducible only to networks of signification as signs usually are; rather, it has its material-relational being. Therefore, I would rather term the double navel a 'particle-sign', where 'particle' points towards material emergence, and in which '[t]he semiotic components are inseparable from material components and are in exceptionally close contact with molecular levels' (Deleuze and Guattari 1987, 334). Crucially, the particle-sign does not dwell on the surface of an artwork as a separate, independent sign; it is an integral part of the material becoming of that work of art – the work of painting.

3) Politics is inextricable from the work of art

Sensitivity to subtle material-relational becomings and complexities does not mean ignoring the political aspects of art. What is political in art is inseparable from its affectivity – how art moves and becomes, and how we are affected by its movement. In this context, affectivity does not refer to cultural emotions, but to the capabilities of different bodies to change in their encounter, to affect and be affected. Here bodies encompass any material constellations: bodies can be paintings, books, animals, collectives, even thoughts. This conception is Spinozan (Deleuze 1988, 127). When thought of in this way, the political in art is not informed by something exterior to art, something preceding art, whether it is a researcher's standpoint in front of an artwork, or a known political agenda, event, person or group. It also entails that the viewer-participant should be able to think and feel with art beyond prescriptive ideological boundaries: to be genuinely open to what the artwork suggests, to how it moves.

Marjukka Irni's installation *Sappho Wants to Save You* (2006–2010) is a work of art that easily slips into the category of political art (Chapter 8). Yet if we do not value its material movements, but focus only on its political content, we will only have a partial perception of what it is capable of doing.

A photographic installation with a video screening – two girls reading, preaching a lesbian manifesto from the early 1970s, wearing T-shirts emblazoned with political slogans. In front of the video, six full-body portraits of women staring straight ahead, standing rather determinedly, all wearing the same T-shirts. The message is clear and strong: the shirts declare 'Sappho wants to save you', while the manifesto asserts that lesbians are 'the rage of all women condensed to the point of explosion'!

Both the words and poses point to an easily recognisable identity politics: the lesbian movement of the early 1970s is revisited with a fair amount of irony or parody. But it does not all come down to this message – to the textual content of the work. It should not be forgotten that language is not a transparent medium, nor are videos or photographs. They do things, they move and matter. So why not let them do what they do – to matter through the moving matter. Perhaps if we allowed the material matters of the installation to move and matter, the 'message' of the work might not appear so self-evident.

To feel its material-relational movement, let us revisit the installation. In *Sappho Wants to Save You*, six full-body portraits of women hang in the air, filling the exhibition space completely; making it dense and intense. But the prints do not just hang there; they oscillate in the air, moved by passers-by and also by their technical construction: the fabric of the screens is light enough to be affected by the currents of air created by the audience and the air-conditioning, the wired hanging system flexible enough to respond to the currents, and the construction not heavy enough to resist the movement.

Here lightness, flexibility, and weight should not be conceived as merely technical or formal facts indifferent to the politics of the work. Rather, they should be regarded as art's two-way bodily capacities: the capacity of being affected and the capacity to affect. This way, the affect economy of art is related to technicity as a dynamic form-force (Manning 2009; 2016; Massumi 2011, 40–41). In other words, technical form is not a fixed construction but is filled with incipient potential for movement. To highlight the often overlooked 'technicalities' of a work of art, and to perceive them in terms of movement and change, I suggest naming this ontological quality of art 'technico-affectivity'.

If perceived as representations, the stiff and static figures of the portraits appear to stand still, and, thus perceived, they confirm a conventional identity politics. However, when conceived in terms of technico-affectivity, their standing-still bodies are in constant, delicate motion. The technical construction simply affords no opportunity for fixed positions. Put differently, the rigid positions are gently challenged by the micro-movements flowing through them. This suggests a peculiar, queer micropolitics that questions the radical lesbianism based on recognisable identity positions that the artwork produces in terms of representation.

Whilst the *Sappho Wants to Save You* installation is self-evidently political, in that it addresses sexual politics, the politics of art proposed here is more inclusive. It is synonymous with the new ways of being suggested in and through art's material-relational becoming. Nevado's double navel painting and Hietanen and Niemelä's *Heaven Machine* are certainly political works. However, they are not political only because they address issues familiar to feminist body politics – respectively, girlhood and breast cancer. They are political because in their material-relational ways, they suggest new ways of thinking and being that contest our conventional views, and, in so doing, direct us towards a future.

✷✷✷

A Follow-Up: Three Propositions

These three propositions contribute to the principle of 'following the flows of process'. Instead of keeping a critical distance, following allows for sensuous proximity. It is a practice of somewhat passive, yet open participation, in which the followee and the follower are reciprocally affected. Molecularity gives following a special character. It stresses that what is followed is, by definition, in intricate movement, although this movement is often imperceptible, and at times stuck. Following does not, then, embrace well-trodden paths but strange, curvy, quirky, unexpected ones. As Deleuze and Guattari (1987, 372) underline, following is not about the reproduction of what already is from a fixed point of view but about opening oneself to what is in itself still in the making. In this way, the themes and imageries of the works of art are considered in direct relation to the molecular flows in which they emerge. They are understood as continuous actualisations of process, not pre-established ideas reproduced in artworks.

The propositions fashioned here are not intended to apply only to contemporary art. Rather, they participate in outlining how art can be made contemporaneous to us. Contemporary art, then, is not solely a chronological term (O'Sullivan 2006b, 318–20). In other words, what is at issue is attending to art as a parallel body (Chapters 7–9), being open to its offerings. Because every event is of singular kind, the propositions and the concepts involved are meant to serve as an inspiration: differentiate, find concepts and modalities that carve out something special of the processes you are co-working with.

The practice of following is dependent on the idea of art as a field of the future: there would be nothing to follow if there were no movement. The ontological conception of art as molecular becoming crystallises this future orientation. Deleuze and Guattari's (1994, 176) insistence that art was never made for contemporary subjects highlights the argument even more. Art addresses what we may become. It keeps offering new flows of process to follow and stucknesses to attend to, and therefore, also, new sensations to encounter and conceptions to create.

Notes

Introduction: ... With ...

1. In his discussion of mediators, Gilles Deleuze (1995, 121) describes being taken up in the motion of a big wave. He notes that instead of looking for points of origin, attention should be directed to mediators that enable a 'putting-into-orbit'; that facilitate the movement of concepts, sensations and matter without recourse to origins or destinations.
2. I use the term 'intercessor' instead of 'mediator' as it aligns better with Deleuze's argument, where importance is placed not on mediating between already formulated shapes or beings, but on opening beings up to movement through a third actant. For Deleuze (1995, 125), intercessors are about entering into or creating a series.
3. This book is written in minor English, meaning that there are several elements in it that contest majoritarian English: English is not my first language nor is it the first language of any of the artists involved in the making of this book. The discussions in studios and exhibition spaces, and via email, took place principally in Finnish, and sometimes partially in Spanish, as that is the first language of one of the collaborating artists. The discussions were mostly translated into English for the purposes of this book. It is my hope that minor English will affirmatively contribute to the new conceptions and vocabulary that this book offers: perhaps language that is not perfectly idiomatic might be able to carve out such peculiarities of intensive processes that perfectly idiomatic English easily ignores or almost automatically flattens out.
4. Ingold (2013, 7) calls his approach not anthropology of art, but anthropology *with* art.
5. In this book, the singular, gender-neutral pronoun 'they' is sometimes used to avoid unnecessary gender-specific pronouns that

designate gender as one. However, if the person the pronoun refers to identifies clearly with a specific gender, then the gender-specific pronoun is used.

6. Instead of the binary logic of form and matter (or that of the signifier and signified), Deleuze and Guattari speak of 'double articulation', which they draw from Danish linguist Louis Hjelmslev. Hjelmslev does not categorically separate form from content, but rather argues that content has its own substance (matter) and form, and expression has its own form and content. In this way, content and expression mutually presuppose each other – one does not pre-exist the other. (See Deleuze and Guattari 1987, 43–44, 108. See also Chapter 2, 'Forces of destratification'.)

7. Tamsin Lorraine's (2000, 179–94) article, 'Becoming-Imperceptible as a Mode of Self-Presentation: A Feminist Model Drawn from a Deleuzian Line of Flight', which focuses on how a subject and writing must become with the world, employs the verb 'follow'. Lorraine writes: 'She must follow the lines of flight that run through herself and the multiplicities of which she is a part. This entails betraying any recognizable positioning and ignoring conventional boundaries in order to follow the moving lines of this terrain' (2000, 181). She sums up: 'For Deleuze the aim of writing is to follow out, rather than stop, the lines that make multiplicities, even if this means running the risk of becoming unintelligible or unrecognizable' (2000, 188).

8. The aspirations for new materialisms are plenty and range from the metaphysical and philosophical ponderings of Marx and Bergson to Heidegger, Haraway and Deleuze–Guattari, and from poststructuralist theory (from Derrida to Kristeva) to specific fields of study (from feminist theory to art and fashion studies and neuroscience), and to the work of such artist-theorists as Jean-Luc Godard and Robert Smithson, as exemplified for instance by the 'New Materialisms' special issue of *Cultural Studies Review* (Tiainen, Kontturi and Hongisto 2015b; Tiainen, Kontturi and Hongisto 2015c). See also *New Materialism: Ontology, Agency, and Politics* by Diane Coole and Samantha Frost (2010b), *Carnal Knowledge: Towards a New Materialism Through the Arts* by Estelle Barrett and Barbara Bolt (2013) and *Art, Pedagogy, Cultural Resistance: New Materialisms* by Anna Hickey-Moody and Tara Page (2015). *New Materialisms: Interviews and Cartographies* by Rick Dolphijn and Iris van der Tuin (2012) offers a stronger emphasis on the materialist

philosophy of Deleuze and Guattari, but includes Karen Barad's (2007) work on quantum physics and Quentin Meillassoux's (2008) take on Deleuze as a metaphysical subjectivist rather than a materialist philosopher.

9. See, for example, Sara Ahmed's (2008) and Nikki Sullivan's (2012) critiques of the 'newness' of new materialisms, where they claim that new materialists have largely ignored the rich variety of 'active' materialities, especially in earlier Marxist and feminist research. However, as exemplified above, new materialisms do not celebrate a heroic break from decades of humanistic and social theory, rather the opposite. It is also crucial to acknowledge that the 'new' in new materialism refers to the following two issues and conditions, rather than aiming to highlight its newness as a practice of thinking and making. First, it refers to 'the unprecedented scale on which contemporary technologies, sciences and eco-crises produce ways of manipulating, living as and being affected by matter' (Tiainen, Kontturi and Hongisto 2015b, 5). Second, 'the "new" points to the sustained processuality – the never fully foreseeable emergence and unfolding – of any materialisations under scrutiny' (2015b, 5); to their radical processuality.

10. In our article 'Framing, Following, Middling: Towards Methodologies of Material Relationalities', we term framing, following and middling 'metamodellings' instead of tightly defined methods (Tiainen, Kontturi and Hongisto 2015a, 18): 'The "meta" in the notion of metamodelling we are summoning does not allude to constant grounding principles or criteria that would underlie and transcend their applications in research praxis. Drawn from the work of Manning and Massumi who draw on Félix Guattari, metamodelling is rather concerned with "render[ing] palpable" such lines or tendencies of formation that essentially vary. It is about acknowledging plural forces of formation "from the angle of their variations". The crux of metamodelling is thus that the models – or the propensities, ideas, potentials – that constitute a given process are never one but many. In the case of research, these models and processes comprehend both that which is explored and the ways the exploration is carried out. Moreover, each factor within the given process of formation self-differs across its respective iterations. Metamodelling cultivates this multiplicity of varying tendencies.' The concept and practice of walking, as enacted in Stephanie Springgay and Sarah Truman's (2018) *Walking Methodologies in the*

More-than-Human World: WalkingLab could be understood as a practice of metamodelling. Similarly, Norie Neumark's (2017) adaptation of wayfaring, in her book *Voicetracks: Attuning to Voice in Media and the Arts*, comes within the vicinity of following as metamodelling.

11. This is also what Marsha Meskimmon (2003, 3) argues in *Women Making Art: History, Subjectivity, Aesthetics*, in claiming that without being attentive to the details of women's art-making we might miss their specific contribution.

12. As feminist art historian Griselda Pollock (1988, 6–7) puts it: 'Ideology does not merely refer to a collection of ideas or beliefs. It is defined as a systematic ordering of a hierarchy of meanings … It refers to *material* practices embodied in *concrete* social institutions by which the social systems, their conflicts and contradictions are negotiated in terms of the struggles within the social formations between the dominant and the dominated, the exploiting and the exploited' (italics added). In her rare take on materialist art history, Gen Doy (1998), however, suggests that in fact this understanding of materiality as ideology may be Marxist, but not something that Marx himself suggested. She insists that, for Marx, paintings/painted forms have 'an ontological status of their own' (1998, 29). It is only that 'various forms of Marxist cultural history have been far happier relating content to specific historical, political and economic conjunctures, than analysing both form and content within the theoretical model' (1998, 30). See also Petra Lange-Berndt (2015, 17), who claims that 'a problem with traditional Marxist and "Material Culture" approaches is that most of the time they do not really follow the material: fibres, stones and synthetic polymers are largely thought of as dead and useless unless human agency activates them'.

13. I first met Madrid-born Nevado, who lived in Finland from 1994 to 2016, when I taught a visual studies course targeted at professional artists, in the early 2000s. Nevado was an enthusiastic student yearning for change in her habitual ways of painting, and thus open to new projects, including our collaboration. Practically all our communication took place in Finnish. Although Nevado is fluent in Finnish, sometimes the language she uses is not idiomatic. I have found this positively intriguing, for speaking non-idiomatically sometimes gave her freedom to look for alternative expressions (see also Note 3 in this introduction).

14. My article 'Eye, Agency and Bodily Becomings: Processing Breast Cancer in and through Images' (Kontturi 2009) sums up my discussions and correspondence with Hietanen, which evolved around *Sketches* in 2002. Chapter 9 of this book elaborates our discussions yet further and thus offers new futures for the project, *Sketches*.
15. The art–theory connection was present from the beginning, since we started our collaboration as part of a residency program run by the regional photography centre Peri, which in 2005 was centred around the theme of artist-researcher interaction.
16. An earlier, shorter version of this chapter, 'Double Navel as Particle-Sign: Towards the A-signifying Work of Painting', is published in the book *Carnal Knowledge: Towards A 'New Materialism' Through the Arts* (Kontturi 2013).
17. Bolt's and O'Sullivan's books insightfully introduce and delicately study a plethora of concepts and ideas at the heart of Deleuze and Guattari's philosophy of vital materialism. Although at times dense with examples, these works are mainly concerned with theory and philosophy. See also Zepke (2005).
18. Whereas the recent phenomenon of artistic research (see, for example, Barrett and Bolt 2007) has turned the focus to processes of making, the social history of art has a much longer commitment to it, albeit from the organisational viewpoint of the patronage systems and art education. Moreover, as Doy writes, even the social history of art has tended to privilege 'consumption over production' (1998, 87).
19. See also Anne Wagner's (1996) *Three Artists (Three Women): Modernism and the Art of Hesse, Krasner, and O'Keeffe*, and *Mother Stone: The Vitality of Modern British Sculpture* (2005); Briony Fer's (2009) *Eva Hesse: Studiowork* and especially her earlier essay concerning Hesse's art-making, titled 'Sculpture as Sample' (2006). In addition, the collection *Reclaiming Female Agency* by Norma Broude and Mary Garrard (2005), with its more expanded focus on the representations of female agency in art is an important book on this theme. A research project that focused mainly on modern Finnish women artists and designers, led by professor Eeva Maija Viljo at the Department of Art History at the University of Turku, needs to be mentioned too (see Palin 2004a). In addition, the work of Kirsi Saarikangas (1993; 1997; Saarikangas and Johansson 2009),

focusing on gendered lived spaces, has been important in its references to women's agency and the materiality of experience.

20. Discussions within visual culture studies about the presence and agency of art has encouraged this approach too. Keith Moxey (2008, 142) terms this development an 'iconic turn' that joins 'the dimension of presence to our understanding of the image, calling for analyses of media and form that add richness and texture to established forms of interpretation' and where visual objects demand new methods and understandings as 'they refuse to be contained by the interpretations placed on them' (2008, 143). See also W. J. T. Mitchell (2005), who asks, 'What do pictures want?' (rather than, 'What do we want from pictures?'). While *Ways of Following* is sympathetic to the interest in visual agencies (see also Alfred Gell 1998), it resists anthropomorphising visual-material doings and resists also direct applications of human emotional 'dramas', such as are implied in the title of Mitchell's book *What Do Pictures Want? The Lives and Loves of Images*.

1. Breathing and Dancing

21. It is important to acknowledge that the way Hietanen explained her work, its contexts and inspiration are discursive, and strongly connected to the space and situation in which she delivered her talk, the public event in a prestigious art museum. In more private circumstances, at her studio for example, her focus has been different, revolving mainly around the practical processes of making art, as well as her personal feelings of the process (see Chapter 9).

22. Of course, artist's talk events are not representational happenings per se. Their structures and practices are not sealed, unchangeable – yet they are guided by prevalent (museum)pedagogical understandings. As my colleague Margaret Mayhew once suggested, a less hierarchical, less artist/context-focused event would probably have taken my research along different routes.

23. It is because of these biological aspects of their thinking that John Marks (2006, 81–97) calls Deleuze and Guattari's thinking a 'biophilosophy'. Marks focuses on two quasi-scientific publications on molecular biology that target the general audience, and that are not only frequently cited in *Anti-Oedipus* and *A Thousand Plateaus* but were also immensely popular in France in the late sixties and

early seventies. Deleuze and Guattari elaborated the molecular sort of neo-Darwinism that François Jacob's *The Logic of Living Systems* ([1970] 1974) and Jacques Monod's *Chance and Necessity* ([1970] 1972) pursue in connection with Henri Bergson's earlier book *Creative Evolution* ([1911] 2009). Elizabeth Grosz (2004; 2005; 2008; 2011), for her part, claims that Charles Darwin's work notably affected Deleuze and Guattari's thinking. An interesting detail is that Guattari had a professional connection to molecular biology because of his early studies in pharmacy, and this might have influenced his and Deleuze's work, both together and independently (Genosko 2009, 26–27).

24. Spinoza and Bergson are the two great predecessors of Deleuze and Guattari's molecular materialism. See especially Bergson's concept Élan vital ([1911] 2009). According to Jane Bennett, Élan vital is an agent 'in the sense of engaging in actions that are more than reflexes, instincts, or prefigured responses to stimuli' and has a 'generative power to produce, organise, and enliven matter' (Bennett 2010b, 80). Deleuze and Guattari's 'molecular' is an elaboration of Baruch Spinoza's seventeenth-century monism: the univocal substance matter of the world, Nature, that endlessly differentiates and individuates in Spinoza ([1677] 1996), finds its contemporary expression in Deleuze and Guattari as molecularity. This materialist tradition of Spinoza is crucial for such philosophers as Nietzsche, Bergson and Simondon, all of whom are of central importance to Deleuze and Guattari.

25. On the dynamics at the heart of the machinic, see Deleuze and Guattari's Spinozist definition of a body: 'We know nothing about a body until we know what it can do, in other words what are its affects, how they can or cannot enter into composition with other affects, with affects of another body' (1987, 257).

26. Jane Bennett compares an assemblage to a thing: whereas an assemblage refers to an 'interactive interference of many bodies and forces' (Bennett 2010b, 21), a 'thing' usually implicates a more coherent, even individual actant – thingness evokes an image of stability and coherence. To be more precise, '[a] figure of "thing" lends itself to an atomistic rather than congregational understanding of agency. While the smallest or simplest body or bit may indeed express a vital impetus, conatus or clinamen an actant never really acts alone' (Bennett 2010b, 20–21).

27. Simon O'Sullivan (2006a, 22) embraces this approach when he points out that art is not only about art-machines, but also about subject-machines, and their coupling.

28. To read more on how Deleuze's sensation relates to Kantian sensation see Edward Willatt (2010) *Kant, Deleuze and Architectonics*. See also Deleuze's (2003) book *Francis Bacon: The Logic of Sensation*, that works mostly in the realm of painting. I will discuss this book in Chapters 5 and 9 as well as in the introduction to the third part, *Sensations*. Before Grosz, Brian Massumi, in his book *Parables for the Virtual: Movement, Affect, Sensation* (2002b), reintroduced sensation as a key concept in the study of cultural research from Superbowl Sunday to Sinatra, and synesthetics of aesthetic experience.

29. Grosz (2008, 76) specifies: 'Sensations are ... midway between subject and object, their subjects and objects, the point at which this one can convert into the other'.

30. Irigaray's inspiration for this book comes from her practice of yoga and the breathing methods intrinsic to it. Whilst phenomenology (and especially Heidegger) is an important source of interest for Irigaray, Jay Johnston (2008, 221–31) connects Irigaray's argument also to Hegel, claiming that breathing and 'pneumatology' are the forgotten aspects of his thinking. See also Lone Bertelsen's (2013) essay in which she approaches air and becoming-woman in Francesca Woodman's photography.

31. In Irigaray's writing (2002, 85) breathing is something that fundamentally separates the two sexes: whereas man makes use of his breath to build and organise the world outside him, thus harnessing air for his own uses, woman is in greater harmony with the cosmos, and inhales and exhales more naturally, both sharing air and keeping enough vital air inside her. However, Irigaray also thinks that in sexual difference 'the split between human and divine identities can be overcome, thanks to a cultivation of energy, in particular a cultivation of breathing' (2002, 90). These are intriguingly interesting points, especially as Irigaray connects breathing with both Western and Eastern spirituality (see, for example, Johnston 2008).

32. Rituality is something that often occurs in the analysis of techno dance. In Portanova's analysis techno dance is not directly connected to 'primitive rituality', but such 'primitive' dances as the

Tarantella are tackled alongside it. Saldanha (2007, 70–74) discusses 'techno-shamanism' enacted by trance DJs of Goa, India. He tells about a DJ who claims that trance rituals are 'unlike the hierarchical, patriarchal, traditional Christian ritual which is dominated by a priest', as they are 'free for all' and 'created by a group of equals'. Saldanha, however, is very critical of how the 'Christian' hierarchies are really overcome in a trance ritual: '[T]echno-shamanism and hallucinogenic mysticism belong to a series of white amateur intellectualisms, more often than not concealing rather narcissistic, masculinist feelings of being different, a new stage in human evolution' (Saldanha 2007, 74). Whilst the 'ritual' that *Heaven Machine* offers is obviously neither guided by any person nor directly comparable to the techno or dance scenes, the theme of corporeal rituality is certainly something to think about.

33. This expression comes from Friedrich Nietzsche. For an elaborate analysis of 'dance' in his philosophy, see Kimerer LaMothe (2006), who begins her book *Nietzsche's Dancers* evocatively: 'On the pages of Nietzsche's texts, multitudes dance. Dionysian revellers, satyrs of tragic chorus, and Dionysus himself, medieval Christians, free spirits, inspiring muses, and Zarathustra; god and goddesses, young girls, women, and higher men – all dance. So too do thoughts, words, pens, stars and sometimes even philosophers' (LaMothe 2006, 1).

34. In techno-raves, connectedness with the world is often enhanced by drugs, which have acquired much-telling names such as Speed and Ecstasy. In their rigorous analysis, Deleuze and Guattari do not give all molecular 'escapes' an all-praising welcome; instead, they are open about the negative usages of molecularity: fine segmentations can be as harmful as more rigid ones; molecularity, in itself, does not make anything self-evidently better (Deleuze and Guattari 1987, 160–61, 166, 214–15). For example, citing historian Daniel Guérin, they claim: 'If Hitler took the power, rather than taking over the German State administration, it was because from the beginning he had at his disposal micro organisations giving him "an unequaled, irreplaceable ability to penetrate every cell of society", in other words, a molecular and supple segmentarity, flows capable of suffusing every kind of cell.' In fact, Deleuze and Guattari (1987, 217–31) use the last pages of their ninth plateau to sum up the dangers of drawing molecular lines and lines of flight, giving a wide array of examples. Using drugs is one of these.

However, in the end it does not matter that 'risks are ever-present', for 'it is always possible to have the good fortune of avoiding them' (Deleuze and Guattari 1987, 250). See also Saldanha (2007) who discusses drug use and techno dance in the political context of whiteness and race.

35. Deleuze and Guattari borrow this concept from Antonin Artaud's play *To Have Done with the Judgment of God* (1947); see Deleuze and Guattari (1987, 150, 158–60, 163–64, 531n1).

36. Importantly, '[d]ismantling the organism has never meant killing yourself but rather opening the body to the connections that presuppose an entire assemblage, circuits, conjunctions, levels and thresholds, passages and distributions of intensity, and territories and deterritorializations measured with the craft of a surveyor' (Deleuze and Guattari 1987, 160).

37. See, in particular, *What Is Philosophy?* (1994), the last book co-authored by Deleuze and Guattari. There are also some important sections regarding music in *A Thousand Plateaus* (Deleuze and Guattari 1987, 310–50). Here, the contradiction with the modernist understanding that celebrates music as the highest and most spiritual of the arts must be brought up. Whilst the modernist ethos emphasises a spiritual, non-material understanding of music, Deleuze and Guattari stress the corporeal and deterritorialising qualities of music: 'Sound invades us, impels us, drags us, transpierces us. ... Colors do not move people. Flags can do nothing without trumpets. [Even] [l]asers are modulating on sound' (1987, 348). For evocative analyses of sound and music prompted by Deleuze and Guattari, see, for example, *Musical Encounters with Deleuze and Guattari* (2017), edited by Pirkko Moisala, Taru Leppänen, Hanna Väätäinen and Milla Tiainen; see also Tiainen (2007; 2009; 2018; forthcoming).

38. Darwin can be seen as a source of inspiration for Deleuze and Guattari via molecularity. Although there are references to Darwin in their work (see, for example, Deleuze and Guattari 1987, 46–49; Deleuze 1994a, 248–49), today Darwin is rarely regarded as their predecessor in the same way as are Nietzsche and Bergson (who were both strongly influenced by Darwin's thought). It is Grosz's suggestion (2005, 14) that Darwin's impact on cultural studies and feminist readings should be recognised as being as important as that of, for example, Marx, Freud or Hegel.

39. Neo-Darwinists and sociobiologists, however, are a whole different lot, and their sexist views, such as their assigning a biological and evolutionary basis to rape (Grosz 2005, 43), obviously harm and violate any sort of feminist politics.
40. Grosz (in Kontturi and Tiainen 2007, 249), in fact, claims that Darwin was the first theorist of becoming and the first major theorist of differentiation: 'Darwin is perhaps richer and more interesting than almost all of his commentators. Darwin's work is incredibly rich and open-ended. And feminists have, I think, somewhat foolishly neglected this work because the concept of nature or biology has been so alarming. What Darwin offers us is a notion of life as not only open-ended, but as directed to forces in the future, which we cannot predict in the present'.
41. This might remind the reader of the notion of the sublime. Barbara Bolt (2007, 43n3) has described the sort of 'flow of sensation producing a collapse in subjective boundaries' that *Heaven Machine* evokes as 'techno-sublime'. Although Bolt does not take the subject any further, she points out that the techno-sublime can be seen to operate in, among other things, 'particular forms of immersive art' (2007, 43n3). Historically, experiences of the sublime have been connected to natural events such as great storms, experiences of awe before waterfalls, or images of such events – think of Friedrich's famous 'Wanderer above the Sea Fog' or Turner's trembling, bolting skies! 'Techno-sublime', however, emphasises the blurring of distinction between natural and unnatural.
42. Deleuze and Guattari have also been critical of their conceptual creation of 'line of flight': 'Perhaps … the words 'line' and 'segment' should be reserved for the molar organisation, and other, more suitable, words should be sought for molecular composition' (Deleuze and Guattari 1987, 217).
43. Note, again, the positive use of the indefinite article. See Deleuze and Guattari (1987, 164–65).
44. Cf. what Zepke (2005, 130–31) writes about the power of Byzantine mosaics, while elaborating on Deleuze (2003, 128–29): 'to ascend into this divine light means transcending our organic form, and the church in this sense was a machine through which we could achieve … transfiguration' – a true heaven machine, then, one could argue. Interestingly, if mosaics, and especially those constructed on the ceiling, provide the viewer with an experience of vertical

heavenly light, then light shifting through multi-coloured stained glass windows might be experienced as horizontal heavenly light. For a version of 'horizontal' transfiguration, see Chapter 9.

45. Deleuze and Guattari (1987, 227–28) warn against associating molecularity with the clarity of a microscopic gaze. Molecularity is not about seeing more clearly, about detecting smaller details. Molecularity is not a method that calls for the use of technical devices such as microscopes or infra-red light. In fact, these kinds of devices are often used when the origin and hence value of an artwork are in question – that is, they are used in making molar judgments in the name of the art trade.

46. 'Philosophy of life' refers to the materialist-vitalist branch of thinking of such figures as Spinoza, Darwin, Nietzsche and Bergson. Vitalism, in Deleuze's and Guattari's thinking, is a highly disputed subject; for its proponents, see, for example, Braidotti (1994; 2002; 2006b; 2008a; 2008b); Grosz (2004; 2005; 2008); Zepke (2005); O'Sullivan (2006a; 2006b) and Bennett (2010a; 2010b); and for its critical opponents, see, for example, Hallward (2006).

2. Work of Painting

47. Holy cards usually depict a holy person on the front and bear an instructive note, often quoted from the Bible, on the back. The imagery of these popular collectible items can perhaps be best described as religious kitsch. The materiality or 'thingness' of the holy card, its everyday use and its nature as a commodity, was one of the issues Nevado was fascinated with. She was also going to produce a whole new set of cards: the images on these were to be reproductions of her paintings in the same installation, texts she would find from her collection of newspaper scraps. The holy cards would extend the installation beyond the confines of the exhibition space, as the audience could take them home at no cost.

48. For Bolt (2004a, 87–122), the work-being of a work of art is a concept that refers all the way back to Martin Heidegger's essay 'The Origin of the Work of Art' (1935). See also Bolt's book *Heidegger Reframed* (2010a). However, Bolt (2010b, 268–69) also connects work of art to the plane of composition at the heart of Deleuze and Guattari's understanding of art.

49. Erin Manning often stresses the work of art – for example, by asking, 'What makes a work work?' (Manning 2013, 10). For Manning, this question connects to Deleuze and Guattari's (1994, 164–65) question, 'What makes a work stand on its own?'. In their respective ways both Stephen Zepke and Simon O'Sullivan take up the question of work and art in relation to Deleuze and Guattari. Zepke (2005, 9) claims that in the first place 'Deleuze and Guattari offer a philosophy of art-*work*'. O'Sullivan (2006a, 111) utilises a slightly different conceptualisation as he claims to study the workings of art that Deleuze and Guattari evoke. See also Jussi Parikka's (2010) article 'Ethologies of Software Art: What Can a Digital Body of Code Do?', that addresses how art works, rather than what it represents.

50. Geology appears here as an especially interesting association for at least three reasons. First, because the double navel truly is a work of layers, and, as such, probably comes closer to the slow process of shaping the bedrock of the earth than to a process of creation understood as a sudden flash of genius. A second (and perhaps more far-fetched) explanation is that geology and painting share the basic elements of water and rock. As Elkins (2000) shows, painting is fundamentally a series of negotiations between the very elements of water and stone: the paint is usually made by mixing certain proportions of fluids (containing water) and powdered stone (pigment). Third, if we add Barbara Bolt's (2004a, 149–86) concept of 'working hot', meaning that it is in the heat of the working process that creation, the emergence of the new, takes place, then a link to geology seems almost too perfect. For is it not in the great heat of the Earth, in the pressure of the molten mass, that new stone is born?

51. Whilst Tamsin Lorraine (1999, 114) is interested in the potentials of Deleuze and Guattari's transdisciplinary conceptual creations, she also notes that when used unethically they might lead to 'dangerous abstractions' harmful to (feminist) analyses of power relations. But she is willing to take the risk in the name of the potentials that these concepts open up in terms of being.

52. For example, the physico-chemical strata are about how different materials react to each other, how they transform each other and form new constellations. It cannot be stressed enough how strata are formed of processes and forces, and not of already complete objects or particles, which then move and mingle.

53. Stratoanalysis is an alternative or parallel to the practices more often exercised under the labels of rhizomatics, schizoanalysis, nomadology, and micro-politics (Deleuze and Guattari 1987, 43), which have become indicative of an approach that focuses on singularities in terms of movement and positive difference.
54. I will come back to this shred of lace more specifically in Chapter 5 'Manual Labour', when discussing Nevado's modes of art-making in the section titled 'Getting physical'.
55. Interestingly, these are images that second wave feminists have accused of propagating submissive gender roles, but which have also made a critical comeback as popular feminist accessories, as magnets and postcards with slogans that challenge those very roles. A whole range of these critical products, 'visual wise-cracks', can be viewed at http://www.ephemera-inc.com/ (accessed 9 January 2010).
56. For example, American artists such as Barbara Kruger illustrate well this deconstructive tradition, which critically recycles oppressive imagery. In the early 1980s the deconstructive strategy was introduced as a counterforce to 'subjective and essentialist body art' (see, for example, Barry and Flitterman-Lewis 1987). For a more contemporary account of feminist art that runs more parallel to Nevado's material practice see Rosemary Betterton's (2004b) edited collection *Unframed: Practices and Politics of Women's Contemporary Painting*, which also includes Barbara Bolt's (2004b) essay 'Painting is not a Representational Practice'.
57. Deleuze and Guattari borrow the concept of 'double articulation' from the Danish linguist Hjelmslev – as usual, their adaptation of the term is a twisted one, that is, not entirely faithful to its origin but rather a bastard take on it.
58. Powers of a-signifying semiotics are, however, more than anything else affective. This is why a-signifying signs affect us, our bodies, for better and for worse, without the involvement of conscious interpretation. This has made it very profitable for capitalism. For a range of examples on a-signifying signs varying from the pin codes of all sorts of plastic transaction cards to contemporary cinema, see Genosko (2009).
59. This concept will be deployed in more detail in Chapter 4 'Autonomy of Process'.

60. Brian Massumi's (1992, 11–12) description of the sign and meaning-process might aid understanding as to what these concepts signify to Deleuze and Guattari: 'Meaning is the encounter of lines of forces, each of which is actually a complex of other forces'. Sign, for its part, is 'an envelopment of difference, of a multiplicity of actions, materials, and levels'.
61. It is not by coincidence, then, that I address the figure in the double navel painting as a *girl* and not as a young mother, for example. For a study of the figure of a girl, not as a representation but as an event, see Elfving (2009, 44–130), where she discusses the girl in and through Eija-Liisa Ahtila's video-installations. See also a special issue of *Rhizomes* titled 'Becoming-Girl' (Preston 2011).

3. Impersonal Connections

62. See Deleuze: '[A] theatre of multiplicities opposed in every respect to the theatre of representation, which leaves intact neither the identity of the thing represented, nor author, nor spectator, nor character, nor representation which, through the vicissitudes of the play, can become the object of production of knowledge or final recognition. Instead a theatre of problems and always open questions which draws the spectator, setting and characters into the real movement of apprenticeship of the entire unconscious, the final elements of which remain the problems themselves' (1994a, 192). For Deleuze, through theatre 'we experience pure forces, dynamic lines in space which act without an intermediary upon the spirit and which link it directly with nature and history, with the language that speaks before words, with gestures which develop before organized bodies, with masks before faces, with spectres and phantoms before characters' (1994a, 10). See also Boundas and Olkowski (1994); Toscano (2006); and Bolt's (2004a, 50–51) conceptualisation of the theatre of practice that materialises in the work of art.
63. For example, Nevado's mother got very anxious and angry when she first saw a painting her daughter was making in relation to the holy card tradition (see Chapter 2). Her mother came to the studio and yelled: 'What are you doing?! You can't do that!!' Nevado explained: 'My mum is not a believer, but she comes from a very religious family'. Nevado then asked her mother: 'Can you really say what's wrong with them?' Her mother answered: 'You know well

that you cannot paint the Virgin Mary like that'. Nevado responded: 'Well, it is not the Virgin Mary'. Her mother exclaimed: 'Don't you ever bring those paintings to me!' Nevado answered: 'These are not meant for you; they're meant for an exhibition'. Something similar also happened with the Caisa exhibition (Chapters 5 and 6), when Nevado's mother first declined any contact with the artworks but later changed her mind (Nevado, 5 December 2004).

64. There is, of course, a long history of men (and sometimes also women) working together in artistic groups. Rozsika Parker (1987), however, argues that these groups often had strong, sometimes even despotic leaders and that this is what feminist groups tried to avoid, although they did not always succeed.

65. Connecting by identifying is not a feminist cliché in itself; rather, it is a poststructuralist common sense understanding that somewhat ambivalently personalises and subjectifies connections that are, after all, far more blurred, and impersonal.

66. One could argue that in explaining her reactions to the works, rather than describing them as works by certain individuals, Nevado wanted to keep authorship to herself, to claim an active role. But the manner in which she describes her part in the creative process is, in fact, modest in terms of authorship. As we will see in Chapter 4, she speaks of the creative process in the passive rather than the active voice.

67. Artist and theorist Bracha Ettinger, whose work will be discussed more in the following chapter, calls her impersonal co-workers, that are present only in terms of what the painting does, 'friends'. For example, it is not Monet who is a friend, it is Monet's greening: 'Greening is the force that extends beyond Monet, into a perceptual tendency – a violeting, perhaps – as it enters Ettinger's work' (Manning and Massumi 2014, 68).

68. The difference that Julia Kristeva (1984, 21–106) draws between the symbolic and the semiotic is elucidating here. Whereas the symbolic refers to a sign system that operates through laws and codes, and is a shared and established system, the semiotic refers to material and corporeal processes/rhythms, as well as instinctual drives that disrupt and multiply meanings. Importantly, Kristeva writes: 'The subject is always both semiotic and symbolic, no signifying system [s]he produces can be either "exclusively" semiotic or "exclusively" symbolic, and is necessarily marked by indebtedness

to both' (1984, 24). See also Estelle Barrett (2010, 21) who claims that Kristeva's account of the semiotic helps us understand that the logic of artistic practice does not function according to the logic of rational thought. Yet, as Kristeva claims, semiotic functioning is not separate from the symbolic: as in poetry, the semiotic introduces itself through the symbolic, moves through it and threatens it. In other words: 'Art – semiotization of the symbolic – thus represents the flow of jouissance' (Kristeva 1984, 81) that cracks the socio-symbolic order. Put in Kristeva's terms, this is what characterises Nevado's intensive connection to Tàpies.

69. Massumi's thinking draws on Félix Guattari's notion of the collective as presented in Guattari's (1995) book *Chaosmosis: An Ethico-Aesthetic Paradigm*: 'The term "collective" should be understood in the sense of a multiplicity that deploys itself as much beyond the individual, on the other side of the socius, as before the person, on the side of preverbal intensities, indicating a logic of affects rather than a logic of delimited sets' (1995, 7). Importantly, then, 'collective is not here synonymous with group; it is a description which subsumes on one hand elements of human intersubjectivity, and on the other pre-personal, sensitive and cognitive modules, microsocial processes and elements of the social imaginary. It operates in the same way on non-human subjective formations (machinic, technical and economic). It is therefore a term which is equivalent to heterogeneous multiplicity' (Guattari 1995, 70).

70. For an impeccable example of this kind of impersonal collectivity, see Braidotti (2008b), where she focuses on Virginia Woolf's and Vita Sacksville's connection in terms of letter-writing. The article is an extended and reorganised version of the chapter 'Desire, or the Art of Living Intensively', from Braidotti's book *Transpositions: On Nomadic Ethics* (2006b).

71. According to Daniel W. Smith (2005, 182) the initial idea behind Deleuze's essays in *Critical and Clinical* was to explore how the names of two writers, literary figures, the Marquis de Sade and Leopold von Sacher-Masoch, were constantly used as labels for the perversions of 'sadism' and 'masochism', respectively. For Deleuze, it was not enough to label; it was necessary to look for an explanation behind the labelling – to make actual (and virtual) connections.

4. Autonomy of Process

72. It might be tempting to deconstruct Nevado's rather open and obscure account of the creative process by claiming that she was trapped in the 'games' of romanticism and modernism, describing her art-making in sort of mystic, if not transcendent, terms in the wake of 'great masters'. For she so clearly leaves open what the work will become. In this scenario, Nevado's role would be that of a mere mediator, of a midwife even, as some romantics put it (see Battersby 1989). I would, however, continue to explore her practice rather than be satisfied with this discursive explanation.

73. For a discussion of Deleuze's fascination with Alois Riegl, and also with Heinrich Wölfflin and Wilhelm Worringer, see Ionescu (2011, 52–62); see also Deleuze and Guattari (1987, 415, 492–93, 495–99) and Deleuze (2003).

74. For another example that prioritises the haptic-visual over the representational-textual see Nevado's description of the making of the installation consisting of old books, displayed at the WAM exhibition: 'In the trash bin, I found more of these books, the Bible, New Testament and stuff. I've made some of these myself, but many of these are just books [as such]. The point is that you can't read the contents' (Nevado, n.d. August 2003). The artist had made a similar point at her solo exhibition at the Gallery Sirkka-Liisa Topelius. When an exhibition visitor explained the work by saying that in the painting in question there is not only an image that has a meaning but also a text, a quotation that has its own significance, Nevado intervened and corrected quickly. 'You don't necessarily have to understand the text. It is also visual', she explained (Nevado, 27 May 2003). So not even a text has a solely textual meaning; in the process of painting, it becomes a field of visually charged particles.

75. Another example:
    > I'm sure the unconscious is involved in this, the unconscious ... It is difficult [to explain], for it's a kind of a whole many kinds of things have their influence on the fact that I happened to choose this way. Sometimes it is based on colour, sometimes ... the painting doesn't have too many events, also the colours are even, then you suddenly need something to catch attention. In my opinion, painting has many things in one; one is a surprising factor, another is the balance and there are many kinds of balances, then there are colours and forms, and

then the texture. How does the eye move there, you lie to the eyes, to the brain, you confuse eyes, wallpaper – what is it for real? What's in the front, what's behind? Has it been torn, or something? It is quite difficult ... I can't explain it any better. (Nevado, 23 March 2005)

76. See also Deleuze and Guattari (1987, 4): 'There is no difference between what a book talks about and how it is made'.
77. See also Nevado's description of process in relation to her private exhibition *Family Album* at the Ama Gallery, Turku: 'A Process ... it's rather exciting. Occasionally you don't know what you are doing and where you are going. It will emerge little by little, in one way or another. And sometimes it goes wrong, and sometimes you feel better – but never perfect! [laughing]' (Nevado, n.d. December 2003).

5. Manual Labour

78. Deleuze and Guattari connect facialisation to the Christian image tradition, and to Christ: 'The face is Christ' (1987, 176–78), and stress that faciality is part of European racism (in most Christian imagery Christ's face is white).
79. There is, of course, the history of futurist and cubist painterly expression and sculpture emphasising movement and multiple perspectives, and their predecessors in late nineteenth-century photography which captured facial movements on film both on purpose and by accident. See, for example, Manning's work on the art of Umberto Boccioni, Etienne-Jules Marey and Eadweard Muybridge (2009, 83–111, 127–31).
80. In Nevado's usage, the verb 'to struggle' connects with the Marxist class struggle: she has a working-class background and a politically aware family who regularly took part in demonstrations against Franco during her childhood. In addition, 'struggling' refers to more general political and institutional 'everyday' critique: 'It's probably about being Spanish, but it's about my family too. My dad has always been very political in the sense that you have to struggle for ... I find it difficult just to adjust quietly ... You don't have to shout out loud, but you don't have to be satisfied with everything there is, with everything other people kind of give you either. Oh yes,

I've been battling a lot with art museums. Everywhere. In Madrid, Barcelona, Bilbao' (Nevado, 21 January 2005).

81. In addition, Nevado stresses that sometimes when she leaves her studio she is 'like a workman ... dusty and all' (Nevado, 22 May 2004), thus highlighting the fact that doing art is not a clean job – physicality has its consequences. This coincides with Arlene Raven's (1994, 50–51) discussion about building and creating 'Womanhouse' (1971–1972), a crucial part of one of the first feminist art programs ever taught. Raven claims that by making students build and renovate their environment for art-making, the students were meant to learn that 'hard work' is not separated from creation, any more than is conceptual thinking: 'for Feminist Art Program workers, skills such as carpentry and window glazing became part of the creative process' (Raven 1994, 50).

82. This evocative quotation of 'hand-to-hand combat of energies' goes back to Proust via Deleuze and Guattari (1987, 321). See also Bolt (2004a, 83–84).

83. Although Massumi does not refer to Gilbert Simondon but only to Deleuze and Guattari, it is Simondon (see, for example, 2005, 40–60) who discusses the complex relations of the woodworker and his tools at great length. Compare with Deleuze and Guattari (1987, 408–409); Deleuze (2004, 4). In addition, see the examples of metallurgy in Deleuze and Guattari (1987, 410–15) and Guattari (1995, 40–41).

84. Massumi's word choice, as a translator, stresses this as he does not use the noun 'carpenter', but 'woodworker', also known as a joiner and a connector! Gilbert Simondon (2005), however, from whom the discussion is derived, writes simply about 'artisans'.

85. Barbara Bolt uses the term 'athleticism' to describe 'the confrontation with the forces in painting'. To emphasise the hard work involved, she adds: 'Figured this way ... painting is not for the faint hearted' (2010b, 280). The term itself comes from Deleuze, who uses it not so much to describe Francis Bacon's painting processes as the dynamics of bodies in his paintings (2003, 12–19, 23, 33, 45).

86. For feminist criticism of mourning (and melancholia) see, for example, Colebrook (2001, 22–24); Braidotti (2002, 52–58).

87. Observing the opening of the Ama exhibition in February 2004, I noticed that almost every time Nevado's artist colleagues

commented on the works, a question of the layering technique was raised. They all seemed to be thrilled about the way in which Nevado had brought together old family photographs, food recipes, et cetera, in book shaped plaster and paraffin casts and how these materials seemed to be inseparable. Her fellow artists were not satisfied with learning that Nevado had used a gel medium called 'Medium' to transfer and connect images to the various materials, but required a precise explanation of the procedure. In a telling contrast to this focus of interest, the newspaper review of the exhibition (by an art historian and museum employee) focused on the family album theme of the exhibition and referred extensively to the exhibition release (Turun Sanomat, 22 February 2004, 'Kaikilla on tarina' ['Everybody has a story']). The critic was disappointed about the theme, as it was so common and overused, and connected Nevado's application of private photos with the trend that had become popular in recent years. The critic only briefly mentioned that the exhibition was interesting in terms of 'handicraft' and 'aesthetics', and most of the review handled the theme of family albums, disconnecting it from the processes of making, from 'handicraft and aesthetics', and thus separating form and content.

6. Zigzagging Art and Life

88. For a summarising discussion of zigzagging, lightning, the lightning's strike and its various references in Deleuze and Deleuze-Guattari, see Stivale (2006, 25–33). See also Väliaho's concept of the lightning-image (2010, 149–56).

Prelude: An Oral Triptych

89. In ingestion, bodies – the body that eats and the body that is eaten – come together and are transformed corporeally. What was ingested will not stay the same; in contact with the fluids and tissues of the digestive system it starts to transform immediately after its entrance into the body. This process is as direct as it is reciprocal, it changes the eating body too – you are what you eat (Bennett 2010a, 40–43).

90. In *Chaosmosis: Towards an Ethico-Aesthetic Paradigm,* Félix Guattari (1995, 46–48) brings up the animist West-African tradition of Legba to promote the heterogeneous registers of object-processes

considered, commonsensically, as only social. He writes that in West Africa, Legba – a blobbing sort of ritual sculpture formed of muck and often placed at the entrance of a village or of a house, has, at the same time, social and symbolic value and its own ontological existence. Guattari gives Legba as an example of how in archaic, primitive societies 'things' were thought to dwell in various registers simultaneously: affective, symbolic, godly, earthly. What Guattari does not say is that a crucial element of Legba is its monstrous mouth, into which offerings are often poured in order to communicate with it. Again, it is the open mouth that serves as a passage for entering into a direct, affective relation.

91. See for, example, chapter 7 in *What Is Philosophy?* (Deleuze and Guattari 1994, 163–200), where Deleuze and Guattari claim that 'we paint, sculpt, compose and write with sensations' (166); see also Bogue's (2003) *Deleuze on Music, Painting and the Arts* with its all-inclusive title; Grosz's (2008) *Chaos, Territory, Art: Deleuze and the Framing of the Earth* that discusses architecture and music as well as painting; Guattari's *Chaosmosis* (1995, 49–50, 90–93), which considers sensation as elemental to the arts from performance to Gregorian chant, and from the poetics of Manet and Mallarmé to blues, hip hop and all the 'underground' arts.

92. Deleuze is not the only one to point out that there is a special bond between religiosity/spirituality and sensation in the field of art. When contemporary scholars of art and philosophy tackle art's ability to produce sensations, their examples are often drawn from religious or spiritual art: icons, relics, totems, and Aboriginal paintings are the kinds of art objects that have been seen to come equipped with affective powers, if not an agency of their own (Gell 1998; Mitchell 2005; Bolt 2004a, 2006; Didi-Huberman 2006; Manning 2009). See also Zepke, who discusses religious art at length, especially his consideration of Byzantine mosaics and Venetian painting (2005, 128–39).

93. The concept of *zoe* comes to Braidotti (2006b, 36–42) via the Spinozism of Deleuze and Guattari and their references to the thought of Simondon, and also via Irigaray.

94. This continental interpretation of Foucault is supported by Deleuze. However, many widely-read Anglo-American commentators of Foucault have paid much less attention to the affirmative side of his philosophy, and consequently Foucault is better known

for his work on disciplined bodies. According to Rosi Braidotti, Judith Butler's influential understanding of the body falls into this category: 'Butler emphasizes performances, but chooses to play the compulsion to repeat back onto the refrain of negativity and bad consciences' (2002, 52). Thus, in the end, hers is 'a rather static understanding of the materiality of the embodied subject: matter has neither memory nor a dynamic force of its own, certainly none outside a symbolic [realm] that is ruled by lack and negativity' (2002, 56).

7. The Grimacing Mouth

95. It might be possible to interpret the expression of translating and ingesting life into art as a romantic idea of sublimation. However, whereas sublimation entails transcendence, an act of ingestion does not try to go beyond anything, and least of all beyond the material and bodily processes of everyday life. Rather, transformation occurs in terms of immanence and at the plane of immanence where bodies meet and transform each other. Then, processes of everyday life are not destroyed in the name of art; rather, they are channelled into a different affective form that is neither private nor subjective.

96. Created in Finland, Nevado's country of residence for over two decades, the installation was exhibited in trans-cultural surroundings at the Instituto Iberoamericano de Finlandia in Nevado's childhood home city of Madrid. This probably not only allowed, but also called for, consideration of cross-cultural aspects.

97. Originally the installation comprised fifteen painting-assemblages, but at the time of my writing this, there were only ten pieces left for me to work with – in Nevado's practice of transformative recycling the others had been made into something else; layered, covered, if not destroyed. In February 2010, Nevado was not quite sure what had happened to those five works that she could not find in her storage space. She could trace one of the 'boxes' to the ARS exhibition – it was exhibited there, densely covered with copies of holy cards. The destiny of four others remained a mystery: all Nevado was able to say was, 'I must have been dissatisfied with them, and re-used them for something else. Since that is what I usually do when I am not happy with what I have done' (Nevado, n.d. February 2010). However, once I had finished with this chapter, she called,

saying that she would like to come for a visit – she had something she needed to bring me. When she came, she brought the missing painting-assemblages that she had found at her grandmother's place in Spain.

98. See Chapter 2 (the case of the little oval painting) and Chapters 5 and 6 (the redecorated second-hand plates) for corresponding layering techniques enabled by the use of 'Medium'.

99. To write 're-member' with a hyphen is to emphasise the bodily quality of remembering, as the word 'member' has its origin in the physicality of the body, referring to a limb.

100. To be exact, Deleuze and Guattari (1994, 164–65) claim that *artists* create affects and that their biggest effort is directed towards making these works of art stand on their own. However, as was suggested in Chapter 6, they emphasise that the artist is only a component in the makings of a painting, or in more general terms, an 'expression machine' (Deleuze and Guattari 1986, 28–29).

101. Cf. Hongisto's (2015) *Soul of the Documentary: Framing, Expression, Ethics,* a new materialist re-conceptualisation of documentary film beyond the task of merely documenting the actual.

102. A timely example of this is the holy card containing as a relic a tiny piece of cloth from the doctor's gown of the quite recently (1987) canonised St. Giuseppe Moscati (1880–1927). Giuseppe Moscati was a medical doctor whose 'cult' is still active today: the marble statue set up at his grave in the church of Gesú Nuovo in Naples, Italy, is visited daily by hundreds of people seeking cure, healing, and blessing. Thanks to Professor Altti Kuusamo for sharing this example with me.

103. See also Felicity Colman's (2007) essay 'Affective Intensity: Art as Sensorial Form' that visits the Capuchin Crypt in Rome filled with bones of Capuchin friars.

104. Compared to this, and according to the anti-relic views of Protestantism (Michalski 1993, 34), it is no surprise that in Finland the fallen-out milk teeth are most likely to be thrown away immediately or stored for some time and then thrown away, usually in a couple of years time. There are exceptions on both sides, of course. Whilst explanations for these ritual habits are necessarily manifold, the fact that in Catholic countries tooth relics, and relics more generally, are part of everyday visual culture and not just

primitive curiosities, provides one likely answer. It might be claimed that molecular remembering is also making a kind of comeback. Currently several websites are offering custom-made jewellery, rings and pendants in which milk teeth are used instead of stones. See, for example, toothgems.co.uk (accessed 1 November 2011). The owners of Toothgems acknowledge that they are well aware of the disgust that their products may induce: 'Whilst the concept of this jewellery sounds *slightly creepy*, it is probably true to say that *this jewellery is much more subtle* than the other tooth jewellery we have looked at. A simple necklace is much less noticeable and much more wearable than a diamond encrusted solid gold dental grill; even if the idea of the necklace does sound *a hundred times stranger*. You can have your chosen piece of jewellery covered in precious metal or encrusted with precious stones and gems making it as precious as can be; needless to say, though, that it will most likely be your child's little golden tooth hanging from the piece that makes it truly priceless' (italics added).

105. Milk teeth's replacement by permanent teeth also suggests an alimentary transformation, although this has lost its relevance during the long history of evolution. However, the belief that meat is needed for intellectual growth was long held, and milk teeth were not seen as strong enough to tear meat. Relating to this, in Renaissance times teeth were used as pendants to prompt the growth of the child's own teeth (Musacchio 2005, 154) – for when the child developed teeth, and was able to eat the same kind of food as adults, there was no need for wet-nurses, so less economic expense also.

106. Whilst the text extracts signal the first steps into the world of written language (note, first cookbooks for children are targeted precisely at this age group), the recipe also connects Paula to her maternal family history – it was her great grandmother on her mother's side who wrote the original recipe transferred to the painting-assemblage.

107. Grosz refers to Deleuze and Guattari's (1994, 78, 178) discussion of Vincent van Gogh's paintings, with their rich, deeply warm and vital yellow giving an expressive, even autonomic quality in the manner of Giotto's blue, discussed in Julia Kristeva's (1980) essay 'Giotto's Joy'. In this essay, Kristeva addresses the triple register of the physical, the psychic, and the social, and sees 'jouissance' escaping and disrupting the laws and codes of the ideological visual narrative of

the Christian iconography of the thirteenth and early fourteenth centuries (see Barrett 2010, 16). In Kristeva (1980, 231), Giotto's experimentations with this specific blue contest any possibility for realism. Barbara Bolt (2011, 65–66) has made an intriguing further suggestion: maybe what Kristeva is proposing could be termed 'new material realism', that by means of material sensation disturbs realism but does not deny it altogether.

8. The Preaching Mouth

108. The song 'Kenen joukoissa seisot' [Whom do you stand for] (1968) was composed by Kaj Chydenius and the lyrics were written by Aulikki Oksanen, who also performed the song. The English translation is mine. See http://www.youtube.com/watch?v=TvrLV2Glvwo (accessed 30 November 2011).
109. These are, importantly, also questions and claims with which political art and cultural theory of the following decades was to work hard and persistently. See, for example, Phelan (1989); Butler (1990); hooks (1992); and Hall and Gay (1996).
110. Both of these examples – the parallel bodies – were introduced in Shannon Roszell's (2009) unpublished paper 'The Female Protesting Body', presented at Inter-auto-prese-turbance-docu-formativity Symposium at Theatre Academy in Helsinki, 4 June 2009.
111. For more information about the Greenham women, see the well-maintained web archive including statements, pictures, videos and a songbook, at http://www.guardian.co.uk/yourgreenham (accessed 20 November 2011).
112. In addition to their passive bodily actions, the Greenham women went to the civil court in the US. Their case was known as 'Greenham women against Ronald Reagan'. Despite their non-violent tactics, several of the women were arrested and some were even imprisoned because of illegal acts, such as the passive-blockades. See the video at http://www.guardian.co.uk/yourgreenham/video/page/0,,2075900,00.html (accessed 20 November 2011).
113. According to Radicalesbians (1970): 'Those sex roles dehumanise women by defining us as a supportive/serving caste in relation to the master caste of men, and emotionally cripple men by demanding that they be alienated from their own bodies and emotions

in order to perform their economic/political/military functions effectively'.

114. For this and other personal statements by the Greenham women, see the video *A Day in A Life* at http://www.guardian.co.uk/yourgreenham/video/page/0,,2071833,00.html (accessed 20 November 2011).

115. For Bergson's influence on Deleuze's thinking on time, see O'Sullivan (2009, 251): 'We might also understand these moments or rupturing events in Bergsonian terms as opening further the gap between stimulus and response that define us as human ... This is to identify a certain slowness, even stillness, which might work against the incessant speed of contemporary life ... It is through this gap that we become creative rather than reactive creatures'. See also Bergson ([1896] 1991, 101–102).

116. For a concept and practice that relates to passive time see 'Dreamtime', central to the art and culture of Indigenous Australian people. Both Bolt's (2006, 57–63) essay 'Rhythm and the Performative Power of the Index' and Manning's (2009, 157–61, 165–68, 181–83) article 'Relationscapes: How Contemporary Aboriginal Art Moves beyond the Map' present Dreamtime as a challenge for Western art theories of representation.

117. Similarly, the room in which the installation was set up should not be taken as a form framing the content of the work: in the beginning of this chapter I suggested that the portraits filled the exhibition room at Ars Nova museum completely, creating a dense atmosphere. However, the narrowness of the room should not be understood as a determining factor in the creation of that dense atmosphere. In a way, it was the *moving* body of the installation that made the room narrow. This is to say that both contributed to the felt narrowness. For the complex relations of the body and the room, see Manning (2009, 15–18): 'The room becomes configuring as the body recomposes. ... The body-room stratum is therefore neither object nor form, but an infinite potential for recombination. ... In a space-time of continuous orientation, not only bodies metamorphose, but so does the space created by the incessant re-orientation of the malleable co-ordinates of the stagecraft. Space and body are in continuous shifting dialogue'.

118. See also Lone Bertelsen's (2013, 17–18) essay on 'Francesca Woodman: becoming-woman, becoming-imperceptible,

becoming-a-subject-in-wonder', where she addresses becomings in relation to photography and makes a claim for open-endedness of becoming: 'On this plane, becomings are not put into fixed structures or transcendent forms, as they are, for example, within the optic.'

119. See also Deleuze's (2004, 153–60) 'Nineteenth Series of Humor' in *The Logic of Sense*; and Garnett (2010).

9. The Screaming Mouth

120. I have tackled this aspect in earlier versions of this chapter delivered as papers at the Visual Cultures – Finnish National Summer School in Art History (2002) and at the Flesh Made Text conference in Thessaloniki (2003), a revised version of which was published as 'Eye, Agency and Bodily Becomings: Processing Breast Cancer in and through Images' (2009).

121. Whilst Braidotti is a committed Deleuzian philosopher, her conceptual work is happily unruly and differs at times from that of Deleuze. In Deleuze (2003, xiv–xv), figuration equals representation and the concepts of the Figure and the figural are freed from the laws of representation. Braidotti, for her part, makes it clear that figuration is not a representational concept.

122. See also Marilyn Yalom's (1998, 205–40) proposition that breasts can be viewed in terms of life and death. In medical history, she argues, they are seen both as life-givers and life-destroyers, in reference to lactation and breast cancer. The hollow that the cutaway breast has left behind could then be understood as a constant reminder of death, not just because it is marked by disease, but because it cannot fulfil its task as a provider of life. Gender roles are at play in the assumption that women, specifically, are to be the providers of life.

123. Hietanen's breakthrough as an artist owes much to her first light installation *Techno Lace* (1996), in which she 'crocheted' optic fibre following a traditional pattern (see Sederholm 2008, 82–84); for feminist analyses of *Techno Lace*, see Kontturi (2015, 39–40, 114–16, 155–58).

124. Although the hands of God or Christ appear repeatedly in Christian art throughout the centuries, they do so principally as part of compositions, not as autonomous entities. In contemporary visual

culture, Christian kitsch represents the hands again and again in the form of plastic figurines, and, for example, in posters inspired by the famous ceiling fresco of the Sistine chapel in Rome by Michelangelo Buonarroti. Perhaps even more globally, the Nokia mobile phone opening visuals play on the same theme. [Author's note: the popularity of Nokia phones has since declined, and these visuals have been replaced by the less biblical visual of an apple.]

125. In fact, it could be described as a benevolent and healing eye – a definition given by Jo Spence (1995, 181) to the caring eye of a photo therapist.

126. The same quietly approving gaze can be found in the photograph where Hietanen lies on the floor. The connection between Hietanen and the viewer is accentuated by the viewing eye that is almost on the same level with the female body, instead of looking down at it in a controlling manner. This composition is comparable to a picture in Spence's analysis, where a woman in a prone position undergoes alternative Chinese medical treatment (Spence 1995, 117). Both Spence (1995, 97, 116–21, 98–110) – who curated the exhibition in which the photo was displayed – and Jackie Stacey (1997, 207–10) have suggested that this particular non-hierarchical setting challenges the medical expert gaze. The conflict between the gaze and the body emerges only when the gaze is separated from the body, when the gaze looks down on the body. The gaze as a part of the bodily dynamic, directly involved in the experiences of breast cancer, solves the conflict. In Hietanen's *Sketches*, the camera is not an extension of the body; it is interwoven with the experiences of the body. It is the transformative gaze – or, rather, the immanent eye that partakes in the transformation of the body.

127. In this claim, one of Bolt's sources of inspiration is Heidegger's essay 'The Question Concerning Technology'. However, contra Heidegger's idea of transfiguration as a process of illumination or immaterialisation, Bolt (2004a, 145–46) argues that transfiguration occurs through direct relation with matter; in other words, matter is productive.

A Follow-Up: Three Propositions

128. Although Jane Bennett's (2010a) *Vibrant Matter: A Political Ecology of Things* is listed here as the first example of the material turn, there

are, of course, plenty of writers who have addressed the issue before her, such as philosophers Elizabeth Grosz, Rosi Braidotti, and Manuel de Landa. The idea of the non-human or inhuman is what brings these thinkers together: humans are not the only agents in the world; non-human activities are present everywhere on the nature–culture continuum. However, Bennett's book is among the first to put the material turn into practice, in showing how non-human matter works all around and through us in such everyday procedures as eating. While Erin Manning and Brian Massumi (for example, 2014) do not associate themselves with the material turn, their work – which opens materiality to (affective) relations, and all sorts of subtle movements – has been simply indispensable to the material turn as I understand it.

129. See, for example, Massumi (2011, 149–50): 'The event precisely expresses the coming-together of its parts, not the parts themselves or their structure. … An event of lived abstraction is strictly speaking uncaused. Its taking-effect is spontaneous: experiential self-combustion. It is uncaused but highly conditioned: wholly dependent on the coming-together of its ingredient factors, just so. The conditioning always includes pragmatics of change. There is always the odd detail that might unexpectedly assert itself and destroy the effect. Or positively inflect it. … The necessary incoming of chance toward the outcome of the experiential event gives newness to every event. It makes every occurrence the appearance of novelty. Every event a creative event'.

130. As Erin Manning writes, 'propositions are thoughts in motion. A proposition is a lure for concept formation, an alliance that forces the relational taking-form of a work in progress' (2008, 17).

131. To speak of materiality as molecularity is also to separate it from earlier materialist and material histories of art that tend to understand materiality in more solid terms: as persistent socio-political structures (see, for example, Pollock 1988), as technicalities and forms, and as materials that have an internal logic and essence and which are also hierarchically arranged and judged according to monetary value in the art trade, for example.

132. Barad (2007, 53) says: 'Representationalism marks a failure to take account of the practices through which representations are produced. Images or representations are not snapshots or depictions

of what awaits us but rather condensations or traces of multiple practices of engagement'.

133. To grasp the work that art does, artist and art theorist Barbara Bolt's concept of 'work' of art is crucial. This concept emphasises the material activity of an art process. Bolt contrasts the concept of work of art to that of artwork. She claims that whereas artwork is clearly a noun, work of art is, by contrast, a verb, an action. In her account, artwork refers to an art object that must be scrutinised, categorised and interpreted, and 'work' of art to a creative process that is surprising by nature (Bolt 2004a, 5).

Acknowledgements

Writing is a practice that necessarily co-emerges with multiple more-than-human companions, and so I want to begin by acknowledging the climates, computers, desks, and even the fabric of the dresses I have worn during this book's composition. With each and all having played a part in enabling my, our, writing and thinking, it seems fitting that I express my gratitude here for the soothing humidity of West Africa (which kept me company when tackling the task of transcribing hours of studio discussions), and for the vibrant, caressing emerald silk cloth that helped my argument to flow on one exhausting mid-summer afternoon. From weather patterns to felt textures, and everything in-between (including the cockroach that poignantly left its mark on my conceptual fashioning of the particle-sign), these co-emergences have been indispensable to this book's coming-to-being.

The first drafts for Chapter 1 were written on the stormy shores of the Pacific in Bronte, Sydney, more than a decade ago. Much later, it was in the midst of a snowy-slushy Montreal winter that I received Erin Manning's most encouraging, generous and attentive reading of my manuscript – so vital to my revisions to come. After returning to Bronte, everything came full circle, geographically and seasonally, and the book was completed where it was begun, in the heat of the Southern summer.

The intellectual meadow that nourished this book, particularly in its earliest stages, was one full with the brightest of minds and the wildest of dances. For their caring friendship and collegiality, and for their unconditional belief in my work, Milla Tiainen, Matleena Kalajoki, Ilona Hongisto, Jussi Parikka, Pasi Väliaho, Kaisa Kurikka, and Jukka Sihvonen deserve my most earnest thanks.

I am very grateful to the artists Helena Hietanen, Marjukka Irni and Susana Nevado for sharing with me their *work* of art. Their generosity in this respect has been invaluable to the emergence of this book. My gratitude and thanks are extended also to Maria Miranda, Amie Anderson, and Caroline Phillips in Melbourne, with whose works of art this book opens and closes.

My humble thanks go collectively to my desks, and to my peers, teachers, supervisors, and students in the School of History, Culture and Arts Studies at the University of Turku and the Victorian College of the Arts at the University of Melbourne; to Senselabbers in Montreal, Melbourne and Sydney; and to those who work between and beyond these institutions – especially Barb Bolt, Lone Bertelsen, Kim Donaldson, Marja-Liisa Honkasalo, Kate Just, Taru Leppänen, Margaret Mayhew, Andrew Murphie, Tutta Palin, Celine Pereira, Indira Shanahan, Mattie Sempert, and Alanna Thain.

In its different stages, this book has benefitted from the feedback and expertise of a number of reviewers and examiners. My thanks go to Norie Neumark, Kirsi Saarikangas and Stephanie Springgay, and also to my anonymous referees. For their indispensable and thoughtful copy editing services, I thank Sophia Dacy-Cole, Jason Grice, Otto Lehtonen, Camille Nurka, Rhubarb Academic Editing, Victoria Reeve, and Päivi Valotie.

My heartfelt and warmest thanks go to my family, for their loving care, conversations, dinners, laughter and trampoline jumps. I especially want to express my affectionate gratitude to Milla for being the most trusted and treasured, sharpest and funniest companion in enthusiasm for all things material (from food to weather, feminism, fashion, art, and theory) – this book simply would not exist without you; and Matleena, for your sustaining, sympathetic support, and intuition, and for sharing the joy in the beauty of detail.

The happiest person to see this book published must be Ilona, so I dedicate *Ways of Following* to her. Thank you for your love, patience and impatience, for your insistence, and for the wisdom of letting go; thank you for travelling with me, and following *this*nesses wherever we go.

✳✳✳

I also thank the Emil Aaltonen Foundation, Kone Foundation, Villa Karo Foundation, Turku University Foundation, and the McKenzie Postdoctoral Scheme at the University of Melbourne for funding my research in Australia, Benin, California and Finland. The work has also significantly benefitted from the EU mobility project 'New Materialism: Networking European Scholarship on "How Matter Comes to Matter"' (COST action IS1307, 2014–2018), chaired by Iris van der Tuin and Felicity Colman. This book was completed when working for the Academy of Finland funded project 'Localizing Feminist New Materialisms' (2017–2021) directed by Taru Leppänen.

✳✳✳

I wish to acknowledge the following previous publications through which I have been able to develop my thinking and writing, and also the work of editors involved:

Chapter 2, *Work of Painting*, contains revised sections from the article, 'From Double Navel to Particle-Sign: Towards the A-signifying Work of Painting', that appeared in *Carnal Knowledge: Towards 'A New Materialism' Through the Arts*, eds Estelle Barrett and Barbara Bolt, London and New York: I.B. Tauris (2013), 17–27.

Chapter 8, *The Preaching Mouth*, is a revised version of the article that first appeared in Finnish as 'Sappho wants to save you: Identiteettipolitiikasta taiteen mikroliikkeisiin' [From Identity Politics to Micromovements] in *Sukupuolentutkimus – Genus Forskning* [Gender Studies] 24:4 (2011), 6–18.

Chapters 2 and 8 also contain revised sections from the article that appeared in Finnish as 'Taideprosessi liikkuvana, luovana sommittumana: kaksi kohtaamistapahtumaa' [Art Process as Moving, Creative Assemblage: Two Encounter-Events] in *Kuinka tehdä taidehistoriaa?* [How to Do Art History?], eds Minna Ijäs et al., Turku: Utukirjat (2010), 179–209.

Chapter 9, *The Screaming Mouth*, contains revised sections from the article that appeared in Finnish as 'Rintasyöpä, taide ja uusi ruumis: katseen teknologioista poseerauksen teknisyyteen' [Breast Cancer, Art and A New Body: From Technologies of Gaze to Technicity of Posing]. *Tahiti Journal of Art History* 4 (2013) (dossier). http://tahiti.fi/04-2013/dossier/rintasyopa-taide-ja-uusi-ruumis-katseen-teknologioista-poseerauksen-teknisyyteen/.

A Follow-Up is a revised, expanded version of the article that was previously published as 'Moving Matters of Contemporary Art: Three New Materialist Propositions'. *A+M: Journal of Art and Media Studies* 5 (2014): 42–54.

References

Adamson, Glenn and Julia Bryan-Wilson. 2016. *Art in the Making: Artists and their Materials from the Studio to Crowdsourcing.* London: Thames and Hudson.

Ahmed, Sara. 2008. 'Imaginary Prohibitions: Some Preliminary Remarks on the Founding Gestures of "New Materialism"'. *European Journal of Women's Studies* 15(1): 23–39.

Arlander, Annette. 2016. 'Artistic Research and/as Interdisciplinarity'. *Artistic Research Does* series, edited by Catarina Almeìda and Andre Alvez. Oporto: i2ADS Research Group in Artistic Education/Research Institute in Art, Design and Society, Faculty of Fine Arts, University of Porto.

Bal, Mieke. 1991. *Reading 'Rembrandt': Beyond the Word–Image Opposition.* Cambridge: Cambridge University Press.

Bal, Mieke. 1996. 'Reading Art?' In *Generations and Geographies of the Visual Arts: Feminist Readings*, edited by Griselda Pollock, 25–41. New York: Routledge.

Bal, Mieke. 2007. 'Working with Concepts'. In *Conceptual Odysseys*, edited by Griselda Pollock, 1–10. London and New York: I.B. Tauris.

Barad, Karen. 2007. *Meeting the Universe Halfway: Quantum Physics and the Entanglement of Matter and Meaning.* Durham: Duke University Press.

Barrett, Estelle. 2010. *Reframing Kristeva.* London and New York: I.B. Tauris.

Barrett, Estelle and Barbara Bolt, eds. 2007. *Practice as Research: Approaches to Creative Arts Inquiry.* London and New York: I.B. Tauris.

Barrett, Estelle and Barbara Bolt, eds. 2013. *Carnal Knowledge: Towards a 'New Materialism' Through the Arts*. London and New York: I.B. Tauris.

Barrett, Estelle and Barbara Bolt, eds. 2014. *Material Inventions: Applying Creative Arts Research*. London and New York: I.B. Tauris.

Barrett, Estelle, Barbara Bolt and Katve-Kaisa Kontturi. 2017. 'Editorial'. *Studies in Material Thinking* 16 (Transversal Practices: Matter, Ecology, Relationality). https://www.materialthinking.org/sites/default/files/papers/199_SMT_Volume16_Editorial_FA.pdf

Barry, Judith and Sandy Flitterman-Lewis. 1987. 'Textual Strategies: The Politics of Art Making'. In *Framing Feminism: Art and The Women's Movement 1970-1985*, edited by Rozsika Parker and Griselda Pollock, 313-21. London: Pandora Press.

Battersby, Christine. 1989. *Gender and Genius: Towards A Feminist Aesthetics*. London: Women's Press.

Belting, Hans. 1994. *Likeness and Presence: A History of the Image before the Era of Art*. Translated by Edmund Jephcott. Chicago: University of Chicago Press.

Bennett, Jane. 2001. *The Enchantment of Modern Life: Attachments, Crossings, and Ethics*. Princeton and Oxford: Princeton University Press.

Bennett, Jane. 2010a. 'A Vitalist Stopover on the Way to a New Materialism'. In *New Materialisms: Ontology, Agency, and Politics*, edited by Diana Coole and Samantha Frost, 47-69. Durham: Duke University Press.

Bennett, Jane. 2010b. *Vibrant Matter: A Political Ecology of Things*. Durham and London: Duke University Press.

Berger, John. 1972. *Ways of Seeing*. London: Penguin Books.

Bergson, Henri. [1896] 1991. *Matter and Memory*. Translated by N. M. Paul and W. S. Palmer. New York: Zone Books.

Bergson, Henri. [1911] 2009. *Creative Evolution*. Portland: The Floating Press.

Bertelsen, Lone. 2013. 'Francesca Woodman: becoming-woman, becoming-imperceptible, becoming-a-subject-in-wonder'. *Performance Paradigm: A Journal of Perfromance and Contemporary Culture* 9. http://www.performanceparadigm.net/index.php/journal/article/view/132.

Betterton, Rosemary. 2004a. 'Susan Hiller's Painted Work: Bodies, Aesthetics and Feminism'. In *Unframed: Practices and Politics of Women's Contemporary Painting*, edited by Rosemary Betterton, 77–95. London and New York: I.B. Tauris.

Betterton, Rosemary, ed. 2004b. *Unframed: Practices and Politics of Women's Contemporary Painting*. London and New York: I.B. Tauris.

Bishop, Claire. 2005. *Installation Art: A Critical History*. London: Tate Publishing.

Bishop, Claire. 2012. *Artificial Hells: Participatory Art and the Politics of Spectatorship*. London: Verso.

Bogue, Ronald. 2003. *Deleuze on Music, Painting and the Arts*. London and New York: Routledge

Bolt, Barbara. 2004a. *Art Beyond Representation: The Performative Power of the Image*. London and New York: I.B. Tauris.

Bolt, Barbara. 2004b. 'Painting Is Not a Representational Practice'. In *Unframed: Practices and Politics of Women's Contemporary Painting*, edited by Rosemary Betterton, 41–61. London and New York: I.B. Tauris.

Bolt, Barbara. 2006. 'Rhythm and the Performative Power of the Index: Lessons from Kathleen Petyarre's Paintings'. *Cultural Studies Review* 12(1): 57–64.

Bolt, Barbara. 2007. 'The Techno-Sublime: Towards a Post-Aesthetic'. In *Sensorium: Aesthetics, Art, Life*, edited by Barbara Bolt et al., 43–51. Newcastle: Cambridge Scholars Publishing.

Bolt, Barbara. 2010a. *Heidegger Reframed*. London and New York: I.B. Tauris.

Bolt, Barbara. 2010b. 'Unimaginable Happenings in the Plane of Composition'. In *Deleuze and Contemporary Art*, edited by Simon O'Sullivan and Stephen Zepke, 266–85. Edinburgh: Edinburgh University Press.

Bolt, Barbara. 2011. 'Whose Joy? Giotto, Yves Klein and Neon Blue'. *International Journal of the Image* 1(1): 57–67.

Bolt, Barbara. 2014. 'Beyond Solipsism in Artistic Research: The Artwork and the Work of Art'. In *Material Inventions: Applying Creative Arts Research*, edited by Estelle Barrett and Barbara Bolt, 22–37. London: I.B. Tauris.

Botting, Fred. 1999. *Sex, Machines and Navels: Fiction, Fantasy and History in the Future Present*. Manchester: Manchester University Press.

Boundas, Constantin V. and Dorothea Olkowski, eds. 1994. *Gilles Deleuze and the Theatre of Philosophy*. London and New York: Routledge.

Braidotti, Rosi. 1994. *Nomadic Subjects: Embodiment and Sexual Difference in Contemporary Feminist Theory*. New York: Columbia University Press.

Braidotti, Rosi. 2002. *Metamorphoses: Towards A Materialist Theory of Becoming*. Cambridge: Polity Press.

Braidotti, Rosi. 2006a. 'Posthuman, All Too Human: Towards a New Process Ontology'. *Theory, Culture and Society* 23(7–8): 197–208.

Braidotti, Rosi. 2006b. *Transpositions: On Nomadic Ethics*. Cambridge: Polity Press.

Braidotti, Rosi. 2008a. 'In Spite of the Times: The Postsecular Turn in Feminism'. *Theory, Culture and Society* 26(6): 1–24.

Braidotti, Rosi. 2008b. 'Intensive Genre and the Demise of Gender'. *Angelaki* 13(2): 45–57.

Bronfen, Elisabeth. 1998. *The Knotted Subject: Hysteria and Its Discontents*. Princeton: Princeton University Press.

Broude, Norma and Mary Garrard, eds. 2005. *Reclaiming Female Agency: Feminist Art History After Postmodernism*. Berkeley and Los Angeles: University of California Press.

Brunner, Christoph. 2015. 'Affective Politics of Sensation: Anonymity and Transtemporal Activism in Argentina'. *Conjunctions: Transdisciplinary Journal of Cultural Participation* 2(1). http://dx.doi.org/10.7146/tjcp.v2i1.22276.

Butler, Judith. 1990. *Gender Trouble: Feminism and the Subversion of Identity*. London and New York: Routledge.

Carter, Paul. 2004. *Material Thinking: The Theory and Practice of Artistic Research*. Carlton: Melbourne University Publishing.

Chare, Nicholas. 2006. 'Passages to Paint: Francis Bacon's Studio Practice'. *Parallax* 12(4): 83–98.

Chirolla Ospina, Gustavo. 2010. 'The Politics of the Scream in a Threnody'. In *Deleuze and Contemporary Art*, edited by Simon O'Sullivan and Stephen Zepke, 15–33. Edinburgh: Edinburgh University Press.

Chydenius, Kaj and Aulikki Oksanen. 1968. 'Kenen joukoissa seisot' [Whom do you stand for]. Composed by Kaj Chydenius, lyrics and performance by Aulikki Oksanen. http://www.youtube.com/watch?v=TvrLV2Glvwo (accessed 30 November 2011).

Colebrook, Claire. 2001. 'Passive Synthesis and Life'. *Parallax* 7(4): 9–28.

Colebrook, Claire. 2002. *Irony in the Work of Philosophy*. Lincoln: University of Nebraska Press.

Colebrook, Claire. 2005. 'How Can We Tell the Dancer from the Dance?: The Subject of Dance and the Subject of Philosophy'. *Topoi* 24(1): 5–14.

Colebrook, Claire. 2011. 'Queer Aesthetics'. In *Queer Times, Queer Becomings*, edited by E. L. McCallum and Mikko Tuhkanen, 25–46. Albany: SUNY Press.

Colman, Felicity. 2007. 'Affective Intensity: Art as Sensorial Form.' In *Sensorium: Aesthetics, Art, Life*, edited by Barbara Bolt et al., 64–83. Newcastle: Cambridge Scholars Publishing.

Coleman, Simon. 1996. 'The Words as Things: Language, Aesthetics and the Objectification of Protestant Evangelicalism'. *Journal of Material Culture* 1(1): 107–28.

Coole, Diana and Samantha Frost. 2010a. 'Introducing New Materialisms'. *New Materialisms: Ontology, Agency, and Politics*, edited by Diana Coole and Samantha Frost, 1–43. Durham and London: Duke University Press.

Coole, Diana and Samantha Frost, eds. 2010b. *New Materialisms: Ontology, Agency, and Politics*. Durham and London: Duke University Press.

Deleuze, Gilles. 1988. *Spinoza: A Practical Philosophy*. Translated by Robert Hurley. San Francisco: City Lights Press.

Deleuze, Gilles. 1994a. *Difference and Repetition*. Translated by Paul Patton. New York: Columbia University Press.

Deleuze, Gilles. 1994b. 'He Stuttered'. In *Gilles Deleuze and the Theatre of Philosophy*, edited by Dorothea Olkowski and Constantin V. Boundas, 23–29. Translated by Constantin V. Boundas. London and New York: Routledge.

Deleuze, Gilles. 1995. *Negotiations, 1972–1990*. Translated by Martin Joughin. New York: Columbia University Press.

Deleuze, Gilles. 1999. 'Le froid et la chaud'. In *Gérard Fromanger: La Peinture Photogénique*. Revisions 2 series, edited by Sarah Wilson, 61–80. London: Black Dog Publishing.

Deleuze, Gilles. 2001. *Pure Immanence: Essays on A Life*. Translated by Anne Boyman. New York: Urzone.

Deleuze, Gilles. 2003. *Francis Bacon: The Logic of Sensation*. Translated by Daniel W. Smith. London and New York: Continuum.

Deleuze, Gilles. 2004. *The Logic of Sense*. Translated by Mark Lester and Charles Stivale. London: Continuum.

Deleuze, Gilles [1977] 2006. 'On the Superiority of Anglo-American Literature'. In *Dialogues II*, by Gilles Deleuze and Claire Parnet, 36–76. Translated by Hugh Tomlinson, Barbara Habberjam and Eliot Ross Albert. London: Continuum.

Deleuze, Gilles. 2007a. 'Eight Years Later: 1980 Interview'. In *Gilles Deleuze: Two Regimes of Madness: Text and Interviews 1975–1995*, edited by David Lapoujade, 175–81. Translated by Ames Hodges and Mike Taormina. Los Angeles and New York: Semiotext(e).

Deleuze, Gilles. 2007b. 'What is the Creative Act?'. In *Gilles Deleuze: Two Regimes of Madness: Text and Interviews 1975–1995*, edited by David Lapoujade, 317–29. Translated by Ames Hodges and Mike Taormina. Los Angeles and New York: Semiotext(e).

Deleuze, Gilles and Félix Guattari. 1983. *Anti-Oedipus: Capitalism and Schizophrenia*. Translated by Robert Hurley, Mark Seem and Helen R. Lane. Minneapolis: University of Minnesota Press.

Deleuze, Gilles and Félix Guattari. 1986. *Kafka: Toward a Minor Literature*. Translated by Dana Polan. Minneapolis and London: University of Minnesota Press.

Deleuze, Gilles and Félix Guattari. 1987. *A Thousand Plateaus: Capitalism and Schizophrenia*. Translated by Brian Massumi. Minneapolis: University of Minnesota Press.

Deleuze, Gilles and Félix Guattari. 1994. *What Is Philosophy?* Translated by Hugh Tomlinson and Graham Burchell. New York: Columbia University Press.

Deleuze, Gilles and Claire Parnet. 2002. *Dialogues II*. Translated by Hugh Tomlinson, Barbara Habberjam and Eliot Ross Albert. London: Continuum.

Didi-Huberman, Georges. 2006. *Ex-voto: Image, Organe, Temps*. Paris: Bayard.

Dolphijn, Rick and Iris van der Tuin. 2012. *New Materialisms: Interviews and Cartographies*. Ann Arbor: Open Humanities Press.

Doy, Gen. 1998. *Materializing Art History*. Oxford and New York: Berg Publishers.

Elfving, Taru. 2009. *Thinking Aloud: On the Address of the Viewer*. PhD diss., Goldsmiths College, University of London.

Elkins, James. 2000. *What Painting Is? How to Think about Oil Painting Using the Language of Alchemy*. London and New York: Routledge.

Ettinger, Bracha. 2006. *The Matrixial Borderspace*. Theory Out of Bounds series, edited by Brian Massumi. Minneapolis: University of Minnesota Press.

Fer, Briony. 2006. 'Sculpture as Sample'. In *Eva Hesse Drawing: Exhibition,* edited by Catherine de Zegher, 273–306. New York and New Haven: Drawing Center/Yale University Press.

Fer, Briony. 2009. *Eva Hesse: Studiowork*. Edinburgh: Fruitmarket Gallery.

Firestone, Shulamith. 1970. *The Dialect of Sex: The Case for Feminist Revolution*. London: Women's Press.

Freud, Sigmund. [1899] 2006. *The Interpretation of Dreams*. London: Penguin Books.

Garnett, Robert. 2010. 'Abstract Humour, Humorous Abstraction'. In *Deleuze and Contemporary Art*, edited by Stephen Zepke and Simon O'Sullivan, 176–88. Edinburgh: Edinburgh University Press.

Gell, Alfred. 1998. *Art and Agency: An Anthropological Theory*. Oxford: Clarendon Press.

Genosko, Gary. 2009. *Félix Guattari: A Critical Introduction*. London: Pluto Press.

Goodchild, Philip. 1996. *Deleuze and Guattari: An Introduction to the Politics of Desire*. London: Sage.

Gouma-Peterson, Thalia. 1997. 'Miriam Schapiro: The Art of Becoming'. *Art in America* 11(1): 11–45.

Grosz, Elizabeth. 1993. 'A Thousand Tiny Sexes: Feminism and Rhizomatics'. *Topoi* 12(2): 167–79.

Grosz, Elizabeth. 1994. *Volatile Bodies: Towards a Corporeal Feminism*. Bloomington and Indianapolis: Indiana University Press.

Grosz, Elizabeth. 2004. *The Nick of Time: Politics, Evolution and the Untimely*. Sydney: Allen and Unwin.

Grosz, Elizabeth. 2005. *Time Travels: Feminism, Nature, Power*. Sydney: Allen and Unwin.

Grosz, Elizabeth. 2006. 'Vibration, Deleuze and the Music of the Cosmos'. In Proceedings for *New Constellations: Art, Science and Society* held in Sydney 17–19 March 2006. Sydney: Museum of Contemporary Art.

Grosz, Elizabeth. 2008. *Chaos, Territory, Art: Deleuze and the Framing of the Earth*. New York: Columbia University Press.

Grosz, Elizabeth. 2010. 'Feminism, Materialism, Freedom'. In *New Materialisms: Ontology, Agency, and Politics,* edited by Diana Coole and Samantha Frost, 70–91. Durham and London: Duke University Press.

Grosz, Elizabeth. 2011. *Becoming Undone: Darwinian Reflections on Life, Politics, and Art*. Durham: Duke University Press.

Guattari, Félix. 1995. *Chaosmosis: An Ethico-Aesthetic Paradigm*. Translated by Paul Bains and Julian Pefanis. Bloomington: Indiana University Press.

Hall, Stuart and Paul du Gay, eds. 1996. *Questions of Cultural Identity*. London: Sage.

Hallward, Peter. 2006. *Out of This World: Deleuze and the Philosophy of Creation*. London: Verso.

Hickey-Moody, Anna and Tara Page, eds. 2015. *Art, Pedagogy, Cultural Resistance: New Materialisms*. London: Rowman and Littlefield.

Holland, Eugene. 2009. 'Karl Marx'. In *Deleuze's Philosophical Lineage*, edited by Graham Jones and Jon Roffe, 147–66. Edinburgh: Edinburgh University Press.

Hongisto, Ilona. 2015. *Soul of the Documentary: Framing, Expression, Ethics*. Amsterdam: Amsterdam University Press. http://www.oapen.org/search?identifier=579464.

hooks, bell. 1992. *Black Looks: Race and Representation*. Boston: South End Press.

Ingold, Tim. 2013. *Making: Anthropology, Archaeology, Art and Architecture*. London and New York: Routledge.

Ionescu, Vlad. 2011. 'Deleuze's Tensive Notion of Painting in the Light of Riegl, Wölfflin and Worringer'. *Deleuze Studies* 5(1): 52–62.

Irigaray, Luce. 2002. *Between East and West: From Singularity to Community*. Translated by Stephen Pluháček. New York: Columbia University Press.

Jacob, François. [1970] 1974. *The Logic of Living Systems: A History of Heredity*. Translated by Betty E. Spillmann. London: Allen Lane.

James, William. 1912. *Essays in Radical Empiricism*. New York: Longmans.

Johnston, Jay. 2008. *Angels of Desire: Esoteric Bodies, Aesthetics and Ethics*. London and Oakville: Equinox.

Jones, Amelia. 2005. 'The "Sexual Politics" of *The Dinner Party*'. In *Reclaiming Female Agency: Feminist Art History after Postmodernism*, edited by Norma Broude and Mary D. Garrard, 409–34. Berkeley: University of California Press.

Jones, Caroline A. 1996. *Machine in the Studio: Constructing the Postwar American Artist*. Chicago and London: University of Chicago Press.

Kontturi, Katve-Kaisa. [2006] 2015. *Feminismien ristiaallokossa. Keskusteluja taiteen ja teorian kytkennöistä* [In the Cross-Swell of Feminisms: Conversations on the Connections of Art and Theory]. Turku: Eetos. https://eetos.org/2012/10/02/eetos-3/.

Kontturi, Katve-Kaisa. 2009. 'Eye, Agency and Bodily Becomings: Processing Breast Cancer in and through Images'. In *The Future of Flesh: A Cultural Survey of the Body*, edited by Zoe Detsi-Diamanti, Katerina Kitsi-Mitakou and Effie Yiannopoulou, 115–31. London and New York: Palgrave Macmillan.

Kontturi, Katve-Kaisa. 2013. 'Double Navel as Particle-Sign: Towards the A-signifying Work of Painting.' In *Carnal Knowledge: Towards A 'New Materialism' Through the Arts*, edited by Estelle Barrett and Barbara Bolt, 17–27. London and New York: I.B. Tauris.

Kontturi, Katve-Kaisa. 2014. 'Moving Matters of Contemporary Art: Three New Materialist Propositions'. *A+M: Journal of Art and Media Studies* 5: 42–54. https://fmkjournals.fmk.edu.rs/index.php/AM/article/view/60.

Kontturi, Katve-Kaisa and Milla Tiainen. 2007. 'Feminism, Art, Deleuze and Darwin: An Interview with Elizabeth Grosz'. *NORA – Nordic Journal of Women Studies* 15(4): 246–56.

Kristeva, Julia. 1980. 'Giotto's Joy'. In *Desire in Language: A Semiotic Approach to Literature and Art*, edited by Leon S. Roudiez, 210–36. Oxford: Blackwell.

Kristeva, Julia. 1984. *Revolution in Poetic Language*. Translated by Margaret Waller. New York: Columbia University Press.

Lambert, Gregg. 2007. *Who's Afraid of Deleuze and Guattari?* London: Continuum.

LaMothe, Kimerer L. 2006. *Nietzsche's Dancers: Isadora Duncan, Martha Graham, and the Revaluation of Christian Values.* Gordonsville: Palgrave Macmillan.

Lange-Berndt, Petra. 2015. 'Introduction: How to Be Complicit with Materials'. In *Materiality,* edited by Petra Lange-Berndt, 12–23. Documents in Contemporary Art. London: Whitechapel Art Gallery; and Cambridge, MA: MIT Press.

Lorraine, Tamsin. 1999. *Irigaray and Deleuze: Experiments in Visceral Philosophy.* Ithaca: Cornell University Press.

Lorraine, Tamsin. 2000. 'Becoming-Imperceptible as a Mode of Self-Presentation: A Feminist Model Drawn from a Deleuzian Line of Flight'. In *Resistance, Flight, Creation: Feminist Enactments with French Philosophy,* edited by Dorothea Olkowski, 179–94. Ithaca: Cornell University Press.

Lovelace, Carey. 2008. 'Together, Again. Women's Collaborative Art and Community'. http://www.careylovelace.com/bxmuseum/MAKING-IT-TOGETHER-ESSAY.pdf (accessed 7 November 2010).

Mahler, Julia. 2008. *Lived Temporalities: Exploring Duration in Guatemala. Empirical and Theoretical Studies.* New Brunswick and London: Transaction.

Manning, Erin. 2007. *Politics of Touch: Sense, Movement, Sovereignty.* Minneapolis: Minnesota University Press.

Manning, Erin. 2008. 'Creative Propositions for Thought in Motion'. *Inflexions: A Journal for Research-Creation* 1. http://www.inflexions.org/n1_manninghtml.html.

Manning, Erin. 2009. *Relationscapes: Movement, Art, Philosophy.* Cambridge, MA and London: MIT Press.

Manning, Erin. 2013. *Always More Than One: Individuation's Dance.* Durham: Duke University Press.

Manning, Erin. 2016. *The Minor Gesture*. Durham and London: Duke University Press.

Manning, Erin et al. Forthcoming. *Immediations: Art, Media, Event*. London: Open Humanities Press.

Manning, Erin and Brian Massumi. 2014. *Thought in the Act: Passages in the Ecology of Experience*. Minneapolis: Minnesota University Press.

Marks, John. 2006. 'Molecular Biology in the Work of Deleuze and Guattari'. *Paragraph* 29(2): 81–97.

Martin, Rosy. 1997. 'Looking and Reflecting: Returning the Gaze, Re-enacting Memories and Imagining the Future through Phototherapy'. In *Feminist Approaches to Art Therapy*, edited by Susan Hogan, 150–76. London and New York: Routledge.

Massumi, Brian. 1992. *A User's Guide to Capitalism and Schizophrenia: Deviations from Deleuze and Guattari*. Cambridge, MA and London: MIT Press.

Massumi, Brian. 2002a. 'Introduction: Like a Thought'. In *A Shock to Thought: Expression after Deleuze and Guattari*, edited by Brian Massumi, xiii–xxxix. London and New York: Routledge.

Massumi, Brian. 2002b. *Parables for the Virtual: Movement, Affect, Sensation*. Durham: Duke University Press.

Massumi, Brian. 2006. 'Afterword: Painting the Voice of the Grain'. In Ettinger, Bracha, *The Matrixial Borderspace*, edited by Brian Massumi, 201–14. Minneapolis: University of Minnesota Press.

Massumi, Brian. 2009a. 'Of Microperception and Micropolitics: An Interview with Brian Massumi, 15 August 2008'. *Inflexions: A Journal for Research-Creation* 3. http://www.senselab.ca/inflexions/volume_3/node_i3/massumi_en_inflexions_vol03.html.

Massumi, Brian. 2009b. 'Technical Mentality Revisited: Brian Massumi on Gilbert Simondon', with Arne De Boever, Alex Murray and Jon Roffe. *Parrhesia* 7: 36–45. https://www.parrhesiajournal.org/parrhesia07/parrhesia07_massumi.pdf.

Massumi, Brian. 2011. *Event and Semblance: Activist Philosophy and the Occurent Arts*. Cambridge, MA and London: MIT Press.

Massumi, Brian. 2015. *The Power at the End of Economy*. Durham: Duke University Press.

Massumi, Brian. 2017. *The Principle of Unrest: Activist Philosophy in the Expanded Field*. London: Open Humanities Press.

Meillassoux, Quentin. 2008. *After Finitude: An Essay on the Necessity of Contingency*. London: Continuum.

Meskimmon, Marsha. 2003. *Women Making Art: History, Subjectivity, Aesthetics*. Abingdon and New York: Routledge.

Meskimmon, Marsha and Phil Sawdon. 2016. *Drawing Difference*. London and New York: I.B. Tauris.

Michalski, Sergiusz. 1993. *Reformation and the Visual Arts: The Protestant Image Question in Western and Eastern Europe*. London: Routledge.

Miller, Patricia Cox. 2009. *The Corporeal Imagination: Signifying the Holy in Late Ancient Christianity*. Philadelphia: University of Pennsylvania Press.

Mitchell, W. J. T. 2005. *What Do Pictures Want? The Lives and Loves of Images*. Chicago and London: University of Chicago Press.

Moisala, Pirkko, Taru Leppänen, Milla Tiainen and Hanna Väätäinen, eds. 2017. *Musical Encounters with Deleuze and Guattari*. London: Bloomsbury.

Monod, Jacques. 1972. *Chance and Necessity: Essay on the Natural Philosophy of Modern Biology*. Translated by A. Wainhouse. New York: Harper Collins.

Morgan, David. 2007. *The Lure of Images: A History of Religion and Visual Media in America*. London and New York: Routledge.

Moxey, Keith. 2008. 'Visual Studies and the Iconic Turn'. *Journal of Visual Culture* 7(2): 131–46.

Mules, Warwick. 2006. 'Creativity, Singularity and Techné: The Making and Unmaking of Visual Objects in Modernity'. *Angelaki* 11(1): 75–87.

Musacchio, Jacqueline Marie. 2005. 'Lambs, Coral, Teeth, and the Intimate Intersection of Religion and Magic in Renaissance Tuscany'. In *Images, Relics, and Devotional Practices in Medieval and Renaissance Italy*, edited by Sally J. Cornelison and Scott B. Montgomery, 139–56. Phoenix: Arizona State University.

Neumark, Norie. 2017. *Voicetracks: Attuning to Voice in Media and the Arts*. Cambridge, MA: MIT Press.

Neimanis, Astrida. 2012. 'On Collaboration (For Barbara Godard)'. *NORA: Nordic Journal of Feminist and Gender Research* 20(3): 215–21.

Nissi, Marjukka. 2007. Unpublished handout about the *Sappho Wants to Save You* project. Marjukka Irni's personal collections.

Nochlin, Linda. 1971. 'Why Have There Been No Great Women Artists?' *ARTnews* 69(9): 22–39.

O'Sullivan, Simon. 2006a. *Art Encounters Deleuze and Guattari: Thinking Beyond Representation*. London: Palgrave Macmillan.

O'Sullivan, Simon. 2006b. 'Pragmatics for the Production of Subjectivity: Time for Probe-Heads'. *Journal for Cultural Research* 10(4): 309–22.

O'Sullivan, Simon. 2009. 'From Stuttering and Stammering to the Diagram: Deleuze, Bacon and Contemporary Art Practice'. *Deleuze Studies* 3(2): 244–58.

Olkowski, Dorothea. 1999. *Gilles Deleuze and the Ruin of Representation*. Berkeley: University of California Press.

Palin, Tutta, ed. 2004a. *Modernia on moneksi. Kuvataiteen, taideteollisuuden ja arkkitehtuurin piirteitä maailmansotien välisen ajan Suomessa* [Many Kinds of Modern]. Taidehistoriallisia tutkimuksia – Konsthistoriska Studier 29. Helsinki: The Society for Art History in Finland.

Palin, Tutta. 2004b. *Oireileva miljöömuotokuva. Yksityiskohdat sukupuoli- ja säätyhierarkian haastajina* [The Symptomatics of the Milieu Portrait: Detail in the Service of the Challenging of Gender and Class Hierarchies]. Helsinki: Taide.

Parikka, Jussi. 2010. 'Ethologies of Software Art: What Can a Digital Body of Code Do?' In *Deleuze and Contemporary Art*, edited by Simon O'Sullivan and Stephen Zepke, 116–32. Edinburgh: Edinburgh University Press.

Park, Katharine. 1994. 'The Criminal and Saintly Body: Autopsy and Dissection in Renaissance Italy'. *Renaissance Quarterly* 47(1): 1–33.

Parker, Rozsika. 1987. 'The Story of Art Groups'. In *Framing Feminism: Art and the Women's Movement 1970–1985*, edited by Rozsika Parker and Griselda Pollock, 181–83. London: Pandora Press.

Peirce, C. S. 1955. *Philosophical Writings of Peirce.* Selected and edited with an introduction by Justus Buchler. New York: Dover Publications.

Phelan, Shane. 1989. *Identity Politics: Lesbian Feminism and the Limits of Community.* Philadelphia: Temple University Press.

Pollock, Griselda. 1988. *Vision and Difference: Feminism, Femininity and the Histories of Art*. London and New York: Routledge.

Portanova, Stamatia. 2005. 'Rhythmic Parasites: A Virological Analysis of Sound and Dance'. *Fibreculture Journal* 4. http://journal.fibreculture.org/issue4/issue4_portanova.html.

Preston, Leandra, ed. 2011. 'Becoming-Girl: A Special Issue'. *Rhizomes* 2. http://www.rhizomes.net/issue22/index.html.

Probyn, Elspeth. 2000. *Carnal Appetites: FoodSexIdentities.* London and New York: Routledge.

Purdom, Judy. 2000. 'Nancy Spero and Woman in Performance'. In *Differential Aesthetics: Art Practices, Philosophy and Feminist Understandings*, edited by Penny Florence and Nicola Foster, 161–74. Aldershot: Ashgate.

Radicalesbians. 1970. *The Woman-Identified Woman*. http://library.duke.edu/rubenstein/scriptorium/wlm/womid/.

Rajchman, John. 2000. *The Deleuze Connections*. Cambridge, MA and London: MIT Press.

Raven, Arlene. 1994, 'Womanhouse'. In *The Power of Feminist Art: The American Movement of the 1970s, History and Impact*, edited by Norma Broude and Mary Garrard, 48–65. New York: Henry N. Abrams.

Rogoff, Irit. 2001. '"Without": A Conversation'. *Art Journal* 60(3): 34–41.

Roseneil, Sasha. 1995. *Disarming Patriarchy: Feminism and Political Action at Greenham*. London: Open University Press.

Roseneil, Sasha. 2000. *Common Women, Uncommon Practices: The Queer Feminism of Greenham*. London: Open University Press.

Roszell, Shannon. 2009. 'The Female Protesting Body'. Paper presented at the *Inter-auto-prese-turbance-docu-formativity* symposium, Theatre Academy, Helsinki, 4 June 2009.

Saarikangas, Kirsi. 1993. *Model Houses for Model Families: The Type-Planned Houses of the 1940s in Finland*. Helsinki: Societas Historica Fennica.

Saarikangas, Kirsi. 1997. 'Äitiyden esittäminen ja Post-Partum Document'. In *Ruumiin kuvia. Subjektin ja sukupuolen muunnelmia* [Body Images: Modifications of Subjectivity and Sex], edited by Sara Heinämaa, Martina Reuter and Kirsi Saarikangas, 102–26. Helsinki: Gaudeamus.

Saarikangas, Kirsi and Hanna Johansson. 2009. *Homes in Transformation: Dwelling, Moving, Belonging*. Helsinki: Suomalaisen Kirjallisuuden Seura.

Saldanha, Arun. 2007. *Psychedelic White: Goa Trance and the Viscosity of Race*. Minneapolis: Minnesota University Press.

Sederholm, Helena. 2008. 'Bright Noise – From Light Sculpture to Political Activism'. *Framework: The Finnish Art Review* 8: 82–89.

Simondon, Gilbert. 2005. *L'individuation à la lumière de notion de forme et d'information*. Grenoble: Editions Jérome Millon.

Smith, Daniel W. 2005. 'The Clinical and the Critical'. In *Gilles Deleuze: Key Concepts*, edited by Charles J. Stivale, 182–93. London: Acumen.

Spence, Jo. 1995. *Cultural Sniping: The Art of Transgression*. London and New York: Routledge.

Spinoza, Baruch. [1677] 1996. *Ethics*. Translated by Edwin Curley. London: Penguin Books.

Springgay, Stephanie and Sarah Truman. 2018. *Walking Methodologies in the More-than-Human World: WalkingLab*. London and New York: Routledge.

Stacey, Jackie. 1997. *Teratologies: A Cultural Study of Cancer*. London and New York: Routledge.

Stein, Judith. 1994. 'Collaboration'. In *The Power of Feminist Art: The American Movement of the 1970s, History and Impact*, edited by Norma Broude and Mary D. Garrard, 226–45. New York: Harry N. Abrams.

Stivale, Charles J. 2006. 'From Zigzag to Affect, and Back'. *Angelaki* 11(1): 25–33.

Sullivan, Nikki. 2012. 'The Somatechnics of Perception and the Matter of the Non/Human: A Critical Response to the New Materialism'. *European Journal of Women's Studies* 19(3): 299–313.

Tasch, Jacqueline A., ed. 1998. *Art. Rage. Us: Art and Writing by Women with Breast Cancer*. San Francisco: Chronicle Books.

Tiainen, Milla. 2007. 'Corporeal Voices, Sexual Differentiations: New Materialist Perspectives on Music, Singing and Subjectivity'. *Thamyris/Intersecting* 18: 147–68.

Tiainen, Milla. 2009. 'Towards Intensive Audiovisual Encounters: Interactions of Opera and Cinema'. In *Sonic Mediations: Body, Sound, Technology*, edited by Carolyn Birdsall and Anthony Enns, 211–26. Newcastle upon Tyne: Cambridge Scholars Publishing.

Tiainen, Milla. 2018. 'Sonic Techno-Ecology: Voice and Non-anthropocentric Survival in the Algae Opera. *Australian Feminist Studies* 32(94): 359–76.

Tiainen, Milla. Forthcoming. *Becoming-Singer: A Cartography of Singing, Music-Making and Opera*. Minneapolis: Minnesota University Press.

Tiainen, Milla, Katve-Kaisa Kontturi and Ilona Hongisto. 2015a. 'Framing, Following, Middling: Towards Methodologies of Material Relationalities'. *Cultural Studies Review* 21(2): 14–46. http://dx.doi.org/10.5130/csr.v21i2.4407.

Tiainen, Milla, Katve-Kaisa Kontturi and Ilona Hongisto, eds. 2015b. 'New Materialisms'. Special issue, *Cultural Studies Review* 21(2). http://epress.lib.uts.edu.au/journals/index.php/csrj/issue/view/334.

Tiainen, Milla, Katve-Kaisa Kontturi and Ilona Hongisto. 2015c. 'Preface: Movement, Aesthetics, Ontology'. *Cultural Studies Review* 21(2): 4–13. http://dx.doi.org/10.5130/csr.v21i2.4737.

Toscano, Alberto. 2006. *The Theatre of Production: Philosophy and Individuation between Kant and Deleuze*. Basingstoke: Palgrave Macmillan.

Väliaho, Pasi. 2010. *Mapping the Moving-Image: Gesture, Thought and Cinema circa 1900*. Amsterdam: Amsterdam University Press.

Walker, Caroline Bynum. 2011. *Christian Materiality: An Essay on Religion in the Late Medieval Europe*. New York: Zone Books.

Wagner, Anne. 1996. *Three Artists (Three Women): Modernism and the Art of Hesse, Krasner, and O'Keeffe*. Berkeley and Los Angeles: University of California Press.

Wagner, Anne. 2005. *Mother Stone: The Vitality of Modern British Sculpture*. New Haven and London: Yale University Press.

Watson, Janell. 2008. 'Schizoanalysis as Metamodeling'. *Fibreculture Journal* 12. http://twelve.fibreculturejournal.org/fcj-077-schizoanalysis-as-metamodeling/.

Willatt, Edward. 2010. *Kant, Deleuze and Architectonics*. London and New York: Continuum.

Williams, James. 2003. *Gilles Deleuze's Difference and Repetition: A Critical Guide*. Edinburgh: Edinburgh University Press.

Yalom, Marilyn. 1998. *History of the Breast*. New York: Ballantine Books.

Zepke, Stephen. 2005. *Art as Abstract Machine: Ontology and Aesthetics in Deleuze and Guattari*. London and New York: Routledge.

Interviews and Correspondence

Anonymous march participant. 20 November 2009, discussion, Turku.

Berber, Diana. 19 June 2009, discussion, on the train from Helsinki to Turku.

Hietanen, Helena. 16 May 2002, audio recording, Hietanen's studio, Helsinki.

———. 22 May 2002, email interview.

———. 26 August 2003, email correspondence.

———. 27 January 2006, audio recording, Wäinö Aaltonen Museum, Turku.

Nevado, Susana. 7 March 2003, audio recording, Nevado's studio, Turku.

———. 27 May 2003, private exhibition opening at the Gallery Sirkka-Liisa Topelius, Helsinki.

———. n.d. August 2003, audio recording, Nevado's studio, Turku.

———. n.d. December 2003, audio recording, Nevado's studio, Turku.

———. 21 January 2004, audio recording, Nevado's studio, Turku.

———. 11 April 2004, audio recording, Nevado's studio, Turku.

———. 18 April 2004, audio recording, Nevado's studio, Turku.

———. 22 May 2004, audio recording, Nevado's studio, Turku.

———. 6 June 2004, audio recording, Nevado's studio, Turku.

———. 3 August 2004, audio recording, Nevado's studio, Turku.

———. 24 October 2004, audio recording, Nevado's studio, Turku.

———. 5 December 2004, audio recording, Nevado's studio, Turku.

———. 19 December 2004, audio recording, Nevado's studio, Turku.

———. 21 January 2005, audio recording, Nevado's studio, Turku.

———. 23 January 2005, audio recording and Kontturi's field notes following a meeting at Nevado's studio, Turku.

———. 6 March 2005, audio recording, Nevado's studio, Turku.

———. 20 March 2005, audio recording, Nevado's studio, Turku.

———. 23 March 2005, audio recording, Nevado's studio, Turku.

———. 16 June 2005, audio recording, Nevado's studio, Turku.

———. n.d. February 2010, discussion, Nevado's studio, Turku.

Index

Affirmation 42, 44, 112–16, 128, 135, 155, 164, 186, 172–73.

Affect 10, 15, 23, 26, 63, 106, 111, 120–21, 131–37, 139–45, 149, 152, 157–61, 165–70, 173–75, 199–202, 209n25, 216n58, 219n69, 224n90, 225n95, 226n100, 232n128.

Agency 14, 20, 45, 64, 68, 85, 113, 134, 142, 206n12, 207–8nn19–20, 209n26, 224n92.

Agencement 33, 45–46, 68, 89.

Artistic research 11, 207n18.

Assemblage 32–33, 62–64, 85, 106, 112, 118, 120–22, 124, 137, 144, 209n26, 212n36.

Autonomy 61, 64, 85, 94–96.
    Autonomy of art 23, 94–95.
    Autonomy of process 83–85, 93–95.

Bacon, Francis 23, 58, 82, 104, 133, 178–81, 210n28, 222n85.

Barad, Karen 20, 197, 204–5n8, 232–33n132.

Becoming 14–21, 24, 33, 35, 37, 40–42, 50, 54–56, 63, 65–67, 91–92, 113–14, 119–21, 128, 131, 133–34, 155–59, 165–66, 173–75, 179–84, 194–201, 210n30, 213n40.
    Becoming-Christ 181–86.
    Becoming-Girl 67, 217n61.
    Becoming-Justice 185–86.
    Becoming-Imperceptible 37, 172–75, 204n7, 229–30n118.

Bennett, Jane 14, 21, 160, 191, 209n24, 214n46, 223n89, 231–32n128.

Bergson, Henri 29, 204n8, 208–9n23, 214n46, 212n38.

Betterton, Rosemary 23, 113, 216n56.

Bolt, Barbara 10, 20, 22, 28, 42, 50–52, 80, 106, 110, 189, 193, 207nn17–18, 213n41, 214n48, 215n50, 216n56, 217n62, 222n85, 224n92, 228n107, 229n116, 231n127, 233n133.

Braidotti, Rosi 24, 35, 42, 67, 134–35, 140, 142, 144–45, 152–53, 178, 181–83, 196, 214n46, 219n70, 222n86, 224–25nn93–94, 230n121, 232n128.

Breast cancer 19, 24, 26, 131, 133–34, 176, 180, 183–84, 195–96, 201, 207n14, 230n122, 231n126.

Breathing 34–35, 38, 40, 46, 196, 210.

Butler, Judith 156, 175, 225n94, 228n109.

Cancer 19, 24, 26, 28, 41, 131, 133–34, 176–77, 180–81, 183–84, 189–90, 195–96, 201, 207n14, 230n120, 231n126.

Catholic Religion 19, 23, 47–48, 72, 86–87, 89, 103, 132, 137, 145–46, 149–50, 185–86, 198, 226–27n104.

Colebrook, Claire 37, 157, 174, 222n86.

Collaboration 7, 13, 18–23, 27, 68, 71–81, 89, 95, 104–6, 110–12, 125–27, 197–98, 206n13, 207n15.

Collaboration Series (Miriam Schapiro)73–74, 76–77.

Contrast 58–59, 86–89, 90fig.4.2–4.3, 91, 95, 124, 128, 140.

Complexity 68, 75, 132, 135, 137.

D2I (Susana Nevado) 23, 130fig.1, 137, 138fig.7.1–7.2, 137–140, 141fig.7.3–7.4, 143fig.7.5–7.6, 144–46, 147fig.7.7–7.8, 148fig.7.9–7.10, 149–50, 152.

Dancing 10, 15, 35–39, 45–46,99, 164, 196, 210–212nn32–34.

Darwin, Charles 33, 40, 113, 208–9n23, 212n38, 213nn39–40, 214n46.

Deleuze, Gilles 8, 23, 28, 37, 44, 54–55, 58, 65, 80, 82, 84, 92, 96, 99–100, 104, 110–11, 113, 115, 119, 124, 126–27, 133, 135, 162, 165, 169, 175, 178–81, 196–97, 203n1–2, 204n7, 205n8, 210n28, 217n62, 219n71, 220n73, 222n83.

Deleuze, Gilles and Félix Guattari 12–14, 24, 29, 31–33, 37, 39, 41–45, 56–57, 61–64, 74–75, 86, 120–22, 127, 135, 142, 152, 173–74, 183–84, 194, 199, 202, 204n6, 205n8, 207n17, 208n23, 209n23–25, 211n34, 212n34–38, 213n42–43, 214n45–47, 215n49, 215n51, 216n53, 216n57, 217n60, 220n73, 221n76, 221n78, 222n82–83, 223n88, 224n91–92, 224–25nn93–94, 226n100, 227n107, 229n115, 230n119, 230n121.

Demonstration 155–57, 162–68, 221–22n80.

Deterritorialisation 33–35, 38, 41–42, 56, 103, 183, 212n37.

Difference 40–41, 50, 65, 80, 112, 173, 192, 210n32, 216n53, 217n60.

Encounter 15, 19, 21–23, 26–38, 43–46, 54–55, 57, 65, 75–78, 80, 108, 126, 131–32, 134, 140, 152–53, 175, 192–96, 199, 217n60.
    Object of fundamental encounter 54–55, 196.

Ettinger, Bracha 91–92, 95, 218n67.

Ethics 12, 24, 153, 193, 197.

Event 7–12, 16, 21, 29–30, 33, 37, 46, 76, 89, 91, 94, 106, 112–13, 121, 126, 128, 131–33, 157–66, 169–70, 174–76, 178–83, 189, 193, 199, 202, 208n22, 213n41, 217n61, 229n61, 232n129.
    Event-time 166.

Experiment 10, 14, 18, 39, 41–42, 115–16, 180, 228n107.

Faciality 103, 221n78.
    Facialisation 184, 221n78.
    De-facialisation 103, 184.

Feminism 23, 37, 40, 59, 66–67, 72–74, 77, 111, 119, 150, 162, 164, 167, 172–73, 201, 204n7, 205n9, 206n12, 212n38, 213n39–40, 215n51, 216n55, 218n64–65, 222n81, 230n123.

Feminist philosophy 24, 40, 113, 156–57, 196, 212n38.

Figuration 14, 133, 153, 182–83, 190, 230n121.

Following 7–15, 18–21, 23, 44, 76, 83, 202, 205–6n10.
    as writing 10–13.

Follower 7–9, 12–13, 202.

Followee 8–9, 15, 202.

Following Amie: The Artist at Work (Maria Miranda and Amie Anderson) 7–9, 8fig.0.1, 15.

Force 13–14, 29, 33–35, 39–40, 42, 54–55, 57, 66, 78, 81, 106, 108, 111, 119, 121, 124, 133–34, 142, 153, 160, 172–74, 178–81, 184, 201, 205n10, 209n26, 213n40, 215n52, 217n60, 218n67, 222n85, 225n94.
    Force fields 78, 108.

Future 13–14, 24, 40–41, 108, 113, 115, 134, 157, 165–66, 170, 179–81, 189–90, 201–2, 207n14, 213n40.

Greenham Women's Peace Camp 162–68, 228–29nn112–14.

Grosz, Elizabeth 13, 22, 24, 33–34, 39–41, 46, 81, 113, 121, 128, 152, 172–73, 191, 208–9n23, 210nn28–29, 212n38, 213nn39–40, 214n46, 224n91, 227–28n107, 231–32n128.

Guattari, Félix 32, 50, 55, 61, 63–64, 95, 209n23, 219n69, 223–24n90.

Hapticity 86–87, 65, 101, 111–12, 192, 220n74.
    Haptic eye 75, 111.

Heaven Machine (Helena Hietanen and Jaakko Niemelä) 19, 22, 26–30, 27fig.1.1, 31fig1.2–1.3, 33–35, 36fig1.4–1.5, 37–41, 44–46, 130, 177, 190, 195–97, 201, 210–11n32, 213n41.

Hietanen, Helena 19, 24, 26–46, 130–34, 176–90, 195, 201, 207n14, 208n21, 230n123, 231n126.

Holy card 47–48, 49fig.2.2, 59, 100–101, 103, 105fig.5.4–5.6, 146–49, 214, 217–18, 225–26.

Honest Fortune Teller (Susana Nevado) 19, 47, 49fig.2.1, 53fig.2.3–2.5, 60fig.2.6–2.7, 77, 84fig.4.1, 86, 90fig.4.2–4.3, 97–99, 125, 185–86, 198.

Hongisto, Ilona 14, 21, 193–94, 204–6nn8–10, 226n101.

Iconography 44, 181, 185–86, 227–28n107.

Idea 14, 51, 63, 85, 87–89, 91–96, 111, 121, 124, 126, 202, 206n12.
    Painterly idea 87–89.

Image-flesh 184, 189.

Immanence 44, 95–96, 135, 164, 175, 184, 225n95.
    Radical immanence 66, 134–35, 196.

Imperceptible 24, 29, 37, 172–75, 202.

Impersonal 37, 44, 56, 71, 74, 77, 79–81, 119–20, 128, 134, 173, 218n65, 218n67, 219n70.

Indefinite article 41, 213n43.

Influences 23, 76–81, 220–21n75.

Ingestion 43, 130, 136–37, 153, 223n89, 225n95.

Ingold, Tim 12, 17, 22, 203n4.

Installation 9, 14–15, 19–20, 22–23, 26–46, 27fig.1.1, 31fig.1.2–1.3, 36fig.1.4–1.5, 47–48, 76–77, 97–98, 101, 125–26, 139–40, 144–45, 149–55, 161, 168–71, 175, 176fig.8.3, 190, 195–96, 198–201, 214n47, 217n61, 220n74, 225–26nn96–97, 229n117.

Intensity 10, 38–41, 78, 89, 108–9, 128, 165, 212n36.

Intention 21–22, 48, 55, 95–96, 108, 110, 189, 198.

Invisible Spirit [Espíritu Invisible] (Susana Nevado) 100–102, 102fig.5.2–5.3, 117–25, 118fig.6.1–6.2, 123fig6.3.

Irigaray, Luce 34–35, 196, 210nn30–31, 224n93.

Irni, Marjukka 19–20, 23–24, 130–34, 154–75, 199.

Kelly, Mary 150–52.

Layering 79, 103–4, 115, 127–28, 222–23n87, 226n98.

Layers 13–14, 51–52, 54, 56–58, 61–62, 64, 67, 85, 89, 93, 96, 98–100, 103–4, 112, 114–15, 127, 137, 145, 198, 215n50.

Life 7,–8, 28–29, 33, 35, 39–40, 44–46, 57–58, 66–67, 92, 99, 111–13, 115, 118–28, 133–37, 142, 153, 165–67, 176–80, 185, 213n40, 214n46, 225n95, 230n122.
    A Life 44, 119.
    Art and life 26–29, 33, 41, 44–46, 57, 112, 117–28, 136, 149–50, 176–81, 184–90.

Light 26–45, 75, 186, 189–90, 195–96.

Line of flight 43, 65, 67, 126, 204n7, 213n42.

Lorraine, Tamsin 37, 39, 56, 204n7, 215n51.

Machine 30–33, 63, 67, 91, 124–28, 197, 210n27, 226n100.
    Painting-machine 124–25, 127–28.
    Machinic assemblage 32, 124–25.

Madres de Plaza de Mayo 163, 167–68.

Abuelas de Plaza de Mayo 167.

Mahler, Julia 165–67.

Manning, Erin 10–12, 14–18, 20–21, 24, 33, 38, 63, 91, 159, 166, 169–70, 172, 182, 193, 201, 205–6n10, 215n49, 218n67, 221n79, 224n92, 229nn116–17, 231–32n128.

Manual 99, 101–4, 109–12, 187.
    Manual Labour 97–116.

María Madre de la Misericordia 19, 48, 49fig.2.1-2.2, 52, 54, 66, 72, 83, 98, 103, 105fig.5.4–5.6, 186, 198.

Massumi, Brian 11–12, 16–17, 24, 30, 34, 63, 78–79, 91–92, 94, 106, 108, 110, 119, 159, 161, 194, 201, 205–6n10, 210n28, 217n60, 218n67, 219n69, 222nn83–84, 231–32nn128–29.

Material agency (see agency, work of art) 14, 45, 64, 68, 85.

Material-relational 15–16, 18, 20–24, 29–30, 32, 45–46, 54–56, 66–68, 75–78, 87, 91, 95, 127, 155, 157, 160, 174, 183, 193–97, 199–201.

Materialism 14, 24, 33, 146, 204–5nn8–9, 207n17, 209n24.
    New Materialisms 14–15, 204–5nn8–9, 226n101.
    Marxist Materialism 17–18, 59, 205n9, 206n12.
    Vital Materialism 13–15, 18–19, 29, 207n17, 214n46.

Materiality. 11, 13, 15, 19, 26, 28, 34, 47–48, 54, 61, 78–79, 85, 91, 95, 128, 140, 170, 195–96, 206n12, 214n47, 224–25n94, 232n128.

Meskimmon, Marsha 12, 23, 206n11.

Micromovement 175.

Modelling 9–10, 19, 48, 66–67, 71, 103, 172.

Molar 13–14, 29, 42–43, 45, 57, 62, 67, 121, 140–42, 144, 194–95, 213n42, 241n45.

Molecular 13–14, 26, 29–30, 34, 37–40, 42–43, 45, 57, 62, 67, 91, 121, 142, 169, 190, 192, 194–96, 199, 202, 208–9nn23–24, 211–12n34, 212n38, 213n42, 214n45, 226–27n104, 232n131.
    Molecular memory 141–42, 226–27n104.

Monument 121–22, 152, 167.

More-than-human 18–19, 21, 38, 121–22, 158, 197, 205–6n10.

Navel 17, 22, 47–52, 53fig.2.3–2.5, 54–59, 60fig.2.6–2.7, 64–67, 70, 86, 110, 112, 198–99, 215n50, 217n61.

Nevado, Susana 19, 22–23, 47–68, 70–128, 132–34, 136–53, 185–86, 198, 201, 206n13, 214n47, 216n56, 217–18n63, 219n68, 220n72, 220n74, 221n75–77, 221–22nn80–81, 223n87, 225n96–97.

New Materialisms (see Materialism).

Nietzsche, Friedrich 29, 209n24, 211n33, 212n38, 214n46.

Nochlin, Linda 73.

Ontology 32, 35, 50, 65, 100, 128, 169, 193–97, 201–2, 204–5n8, 206n12.
    Ontology of Becoming 50, 194.

Ontogenetics 24, 100, 195.

O'Sullivan, Simon 22, 32, 38, 54–55, 135, 139, 196, 202, 207n17, 210n27, 214n46, 215n49, 229n115.

Painting 47–68, 70–128, 136–53, 197–99.
    Painting-assemblage 137, 145, 149, 151, 153, 225–26n97, 227n106.

Parallel-body 135, 145, 153, 202, 228n110.

Participation 21, 24, 35, 37–38, 161, 193, 196, 202.

Particle-sign 64–68, 199.

Passive 42, 45, 106, 158, 162–64, 166–68, 186, 202, 218n66, 228n112.
    Passive becoming 174–75.
    Passive time 165–68, 229n116.
    Passive synthesis 165.

Patriarchy 154–55, 164–65, 210–11n32.

Performance 94, 155, 157–58, 161–62, 175, 224n91, 224–25n94.

Plane of Composition 80–81, 96, 214n48.

Plane of Immanence 225n95.

Politics 24, 29, 67, 156, 172–75, 180, 194, 199–201, 213n39.
    Identity politics 155–57, 162, 172, 200–2001.
    Micropolitics 168, 174, 201, 216n53.
    Minoritarian politics 173–74.

Posing 66, 82–83, 135, 154–55, 172, 177–78, 181–83, 186, 189–90, 198.

Positionality 20, 24, 30, 32.

Preaching 23–24, 130–34, 154–62, 164, 168, 175, 200.

Recognition 42, 54, 57, 61, 100–103, 127, 172–73, 217n62.
    Un-recognition 99–100, 102fig.5.2–5.3, 103–4, 105fig.5.4–5.6, 127.

Radicalesbians 154–55, 164, 228–29n113.

Relics 23, 132, 134–35, 141fig.7.4, 145–46, 149–50, 153, 224n92, 226n102, 226–27n104.

Representation 10, 28–30, 34–35, 37–39, 45–46, 51, 59, 64–66, 78, 80, 85–87, 91, 95, 111–12, 170, 182–84, 189–90, 193, 197–98, 201, 207–8n19, 217n61, 229n116, 230n121, 232–33n132.
    Representationalism 28, 232–33n132.

Research-creation 11.

Resemblance 28, 119–20, 187.

Rhythm 9, 33–35, 37–41, 58, 67, 79, 82, 95, 104–6, 108–10, 114–15, 119, 122, 133, 137, 158, 165–67, 190, 218–19n68, 229n116.

Roseneil, Sasha 163–66, 168, 175.

Rubbing 61–62, 137, 151.

Saarikangas, Kirsi 152, 207–8n19.

Sappho Wants to Save You (Marjukka Irni) 20, 23–24, 130fig.2, 130–32, 134–35, 154–58, 159fig.8.1, 160–62, 163fig.8.2, 164–69, 171fig.8.3–8.4, 172–75, 199–201.

Sappho 155–56, 167.
    Sapphics 133, 156, 164–67, 169–70, 172–73, 175.

Schapiro, Miriam 73–74, 76–77.

Sensation 14, 23–24, 29, 32–35, 63, 67, 77–78, 80, 124, 133–35, 140, 142, 152, 157, 174, 179–81, 196, 202, 203n1, 210nn28–29, 213n41, 224nn91–92, 227–28n107.

Signification 10, 33, 57, 63, 85, 95, 194–96, 199.

Signifiance 61, 103.

Simondon, Gilbert 29, 78, 209n24, 222nn83–84, 224n93.

Singularity 9, 15, 55, 83–84, 101, 115–16, 152, 158, 162.

Sketches (Helena Hietanen) 19, 24, 130fig.3, 132, 176–77, 176fig.9.1, 179–81, 182fig.9.2, 183–85, 187, 188fig.9.3–9.5, 189–90, 207n14, 231n126.

Spinoza, Baruch 29, 113, 209n24, 214n46.

Spinozan 199.

Strata 56–59, 61–62, 65–66, 95, 120, 127, 215n52.

Stratification 57, 59, 111.
    Destratification 65–66, 111.

Stuckness 16, 24, 65–66, 106, 202.

Sustainable 131–32, 134–35, 152–53.

Tàpies, Antoni 75, 77–81, 218–19n68.

Technicity 169–70, 201.

Technico-affective 170, 175.

Technico-intensive 78, 81.

Territorialisation 33.

Texture 55, 86, 88–89, 91, 94, 101, 106, 117, 122, 161, 186, 192, 220–21n75.

Tiainen, Milla 14, 21, 41, 113, 193–94, 204–6nn8–10, 212n37, 213n40.

Transfiguration 24, 134, 186–90, 213–14n44, 231n127.

Transformation 39, 66, 79, 99, 113–15, 121, 124, 130–31, 133, 137, 139, 144, 149, 151–52, 176, 178, 181, 185–87, 189, 191, 225n95, 227n105, 231n126.

Triptych 131–34, 176–77.

Vibration 35, 37–41, 44, 155, 159, 179, 191.

Vitalism 13, 42, 214n46.

Virtual 17, 85, 89, 121, 183, 219n71.

Way 9–11, 13, 16–18, 20–22, 24, 29, 35, 40, 42–4, 61, 65–66, 68, 71, 75–76, 79–80, 83, 87–88, 91–92, 96, 115, 117, 121, 124, 126–28, 130, 132–33, 136, 158–59, 162–65, 168, 175, 189, 195–97, 201, 206n10, 222–23n87.

Woodworker 13, 106, 107fig.5.7, 110, 222nn83–84.

Work of art 9, 10, 12, 15–16, 24, 50–52, 54–5, 57, 61, 64–66, 78, 80, 85–86, 89, 108–9, 112, 114, 119, 122, 124, 127, 145, 152–53, 157, 169, 173, 179, 198–99, 201, 214–15nn48–49, 217n62, 233n133.

Work of painting 22, 52–54, 64–65, 68, 80, 85, 92, 94, 99, 112, 124, 199, 207n16.

Writing-with 11–12, 45.

Zigzagging 119, 126, 223n88.

Zoe 134, 178, 181, 224n93.

www.ingramcontent.com/pod-product-compliance
Lightning Source LLC
Chambersburg PA
CBHW031612210526
45464CB00004B/1546